Intrapersonal Communication: Different Voices, Different Minds

LEA'S COMMUNICATION SERIES
Jennings Bryant/Dolf Zillmann, General Editors

Selected titles in General Theory & Methodology (Jennings Bryant, Advisory Editor) include:

Casmir • Building Communication Theories: A Socio/Cultural Approach

Heath/Bryant • Human Communication Theory and Research: Concepts, Contexts, and Challenges

Perloff • The Dynamics of Persuasion

Sloan • Perspectives on Mass Communication History

For a complete list of other titles in LEA's Communication Series, please contact Lawrence Erlbaum Associates, Publishers.

INTRAPERSONAL COMMUNICATION: DIFFERENT VOICES, DIFFERENT MINDS

Edited by
DONNA R. VOCATE
University of Colorado at Boulder

LAWRENCE ERLBAUM ASSOCIATES, PUBLISHERS
1994   Hillsdale, New Jersey   Hove, UK

Lawrence Erlbaum Associates, Inc., Publishers
365 Broadway
Hillsdale, New Jersey 07642

Cover design by Kate Dusza

Library of Congress Cataloging-in-Publication Data

Intrapersonal communication : different voices, different minds / [edited by] Donna R. Vocate.
        p.   cm.
    Includes bibliographical references and indexes.
    ISBN 0-8058-1128-1 (alk. paper)
    1. Self-talk.   2. Psycholinguistics.   I. Vocate, Donna R.
    BF697.5.S47I58   1994
    153.6—dc20   94-237
                                                                                            CIP

Books published by Lawrence Erlbaum Associates are printed on acid-free paper,
and their bindings are chosen for strength and durability.

Printed in the United States of America
10 9 8 7 6 5 4 3 2 1

Contents

Contributors

Michael Cole, Laboratory of Comparative Human Cognition, University of California, San Diego, 9500 Gilman Drive, La Jolla CA 92093-0092

Frank E. X. Dance, School of Communication, University of Denver, University Park, Denver, CO 80208

John R. Johnson, Department of Communication, University of Wisconsin-Milwaukee, Milwaukee, WI 53201

Gail Ramsberger, Department of Communication Disorders and Speech Science, University of Colorado at Boulder, Campus Box 409, Boulder, CO 80309-0409

Samuel C. Riccillo, Department of Communication, University of Texas at El Paso, El Paso, TX 79968-0550

Don W. Stacks, School of Communication, University of Miami, PO Box 248127, Coral Gables, FL 33124-2030

Daniel E. Sellers, Department of Speech Pathology and Audiology, College of Allied Health, University of South Alabama, Mobile, AL 36688

Donna R. Vocate, Young Scholars, Honors Department, University of Colorado at Boulder, Campus Box 73, Boulder, CO 80309-0073

Julia T. Wood, Department of Speech Communication, University of North Carolina at Chapel Hill, Campus Box 3285, Chapel Hill, NC 27599-3285

Julie Yingling, Department of Speech Communication, Humbolt State University, Arcata, CA 95532-4957

Preface

Donna R. Vocate

Communication is ubiquitous. If our boss ignores our innovative ideas, the popular press suggests it is because we failed to communicate those ideas effectively. If our spouse leaves us, the reason, according to Donohue's guest expert, is a breakdown in marital communication. If our dog fails obedience school, the dog trainer indicates it is because we did not successfully communicate our expectations to the dog. In short, communication constitutes a buzz word in the current popular culture. Whether the topic is discussed in the media or in more private forums, widespread agreement exists that communication in any context is an important phenomenon that merits our attention and analysis. In contrast, no comparable consensus exists among the specialists in academe with respect to what characterizes communication or what is the most viable theoretical perspective from which to examine it.

One consequence of this is that prominent scholars such as Wood (1992) are reduced to labeling *speech communication* "an interdisciplinary field" when attempting to account for its disjunctive explanations. This presumed fragmentation in the discipline could be ameliorated by an increase in logically consistent general theory by communication theorists cognizant of their own metatheoretical assumptions (e.g., Dance's [1982] speech theory; Cronen, Pearce, & Harris' [1982] coordinated management of meaning). General theory, of course, accounts for a phenomenon across contexts (family, organization, classroom, etc.) and levels (intrapersonal, interpersonal, or public).

In addition to the minimal presence of general theory, other factors have added to the ostensible disparity in communication studies. The expansion of communication scholarship during recent decades to include a social science perspective as well as a humanistic one has contributed to speech communication's diversity, and lack of the singular focus that characterizes and unifies the idealized academic discipline. Another factor contributing to communication's heterogenous character is the failure of some communication scholars to consider the compatibility of exogamous or extrinsic metatheoretical assumptions before borrowing concepts from other academic fields (Vocate, 1991). Such indiscriminate borrowing could be attributed to an inadequate review of metatheory in some graduate programs, or again to the shortage of general theory in the field to guide research efforts on various communication topics.

One annoying outcome of communication's diversity is an on-going indentity crisis about what "correct" academic focus would integrate the discipline, accompanied by periodic attempts to change the major professional association's name in order to secure better public relations in the academic community. I am tempted to suggest that we follow the example set by the Linguistic Society of Paris when it resolved the heated controversy over the origins of language in 1866 by simply forbidding any further discussion. The "appropriate" focus, of course, depends on the scientific or humanistic perspective from which one defines communication; and the merit of a name (and the concept to which it refers) depends on the quality of scholarship supporting it.

Diversity need not lead to fragmentation, and it is not inherently bad. A multiplicity of epistemic perspectives within a theoretically sophisticated and mature discipline can provide an enrichment of knowledge. Numerous general, thematic, and contextual theories within a field can enhance substantive research. However, similar metatheoretical variety is not desirable within one's effort to establish a theory. An integrated theoretical framework of some sort is essential to set guidelines from which to examine a specific topic or context in a coherent fashion. Otherwise, the conceptual divergence of unexamined metatheoretical assumptions about a particular phenomenon, such as intrapersonal communication, may yield logical inconsistencies and invalidate any progress in theory construction. Rhetoric has been around for centuries and has a developed theoretical foundation, but intrapersonal communication is a relatively new phenomenon for speech communication study and still lacks the grounding of a sound theoretical base. The recency of our attention combined with the near absence of any pertinent general theory to guide us explains why little, if any, organized intrapersonal theory has been developed to date. This book is intended to provide a base of knowledge and integrated theory to which intrapersonal communication scholars can respond in their attempts at further explanatory theory.

In 1986, Charles Roberts presented a petition to the national Speech Communication Association's (SCA) Legislative Council asking it to create a Commission on Intrapersonal Communication Processes, thereby recognizing intrapersonal as a topic of substantial study within SCA. As a member of the council that year, I remember the discussion about whether or not SCA should endorse such a focus. One older council member harrumphed and dismissed intrapersonal communication as "just thinking," inferring it really was not appropriate for communication scholars to think about thinking! The council decided, however, that if our colleagues wished to think about thinking, listening, or any other communicative process within the individual, then SCA should facilitate their efforts. Establishing the Intrapersonal Commission demonstrated the interest of many scholars in the topic; however, it did not follow that a consensus existed on how to investigate or even on how to define intrapersonal communication.

The following chapters are an attempt to present interaction, thinking, and talking on the level of the individual in a theoretically integrated way using a view derived from George Herbert Mead and L. S. Vygotsky. This sociogenetic perspective mandates an emphasis on *social interaction*; the *developmental nature of mind*;

and the *crucial role of speech* in creating a self, a culture, and a mind that then interact in human intrapersonal communication. Taking a theoretical perspective derived from Mead and Vygotsky, therefore, can render intrapersonal communication study compatible with other scholarly efforts concerned with social, cognitive, or performance aspects of communication phenomena.

Authors in this text typically emphasize talk or spoken language as the most viable focus for understanding intrapersonal communication, and many draw upon the spoken language theory of Frank Dance. It is a common sense observation that human voices influence human behavior, but numerous explanations have been advanced to account for the process. For example, Jaynes (1976) spoke of voices embodied in human brains—gods made manifest through their voices to lead and direct human behavior. This book is also concerned with the voices that shape human behavior, but its voices are not of divine origin. Rather, the voices of intrapersonal communication arise from the dialectic of brain and culture that produces a synthesis of mind unique to each individual. This synthesis is, metaphorically speaking, expressed through the voice that characterizes and reveals each mind, yet it is derived from the literal voices that historically created the culture, and that currently constitute each child's social milieu and frame its future.

To have a voice, to express one's mind, is to be human. To be voiceless in that sense is to have no being, no personality. On the physical level, one may be unable to produce articulate speech, but still possess a metaphoric voice as an expression of individuality. Current studies of the gestural communication of the deaf illustrate that voice as the expression of self is not constrained by mode.

Anyone with a voice, physical or metaphoric, engages in talk. Talk is dynamic. It is process and interaction, the object of which may be a crowd, an individual, or the self. It is an understanding of the latter, of self-talk, that is the focus of this volume although the chapters of necessity also deal with speech (the normal physical manifestation of talk) as well as talk with others to increase our understanding of human communication on the intrapersonal level.

I have divided the book into two main sections—one emphasizing theory and the other concerned with application. The first section focuses on establishing a base of knowledge and theoretical understanding. The initial chapter provides a theoretical overview of intrapersonal communication and its relationship to inner speech delineated under the influence of sociogenetic theorists, George Herbert Mead and L. S. Vygotsky. Building on their tenets together with those of A. R. Luria, I emphasize the role of speech and society in establishing the metaphoric voice of mind, and identify uniquely human intrapersonal communication as consisting of self-talk and inner speech. I maintain that inner speech is the competence behind all human communication; hence its understanding is vital to advancing our knowledge in other areas such as interpersonal, persuasion, organizational, and public speaking. However, my central thesis is that an increased emphasis on the dialogic (self-talk) and coding (inner speech) processes of human intrapersonal would coordinate and enlighten future theory construction and research for intrapersonal communication scholars.

Riccillo's chapter on phylogenesis argues the dependence of the metaphoric voice on the biological organism, and outlines how the phylogenetic development of the physical voice allowed the metaphoric voice to occur. The chapter on physical bases of intrapersonal by Ramsberger explicates the physical structure of the brain and how its pathological functioning may distort both mind and voice. Culture, the other crucial component of mind, is considered in Cole's chapter. He focuses on how cultural mediation structures human thought and activity. Cole's insightful analysis of schema, script, and context makes it clear that no intrapersonal theorist should consider culture an independent variable.

The second section examines manifestations of the theory in individual reality. What we do not know about intrapersonal talk far exceeds what is known at present; but Stacks and Sellers provide an examination of intrapersonal studies in communication to date and the methods by which present knowledge has been secured and future acquisitions might be obtained. Yingling presents the developmental progression of speech and voice in children. Wood, on the other hand, examines the role of self-talk in the establishment and maintenance of gender identities. Interpersonal competence and the role of inner speech in influencing it are discussed in Johnson's chapter.

The final chapter/section by Dance presents internal spoken language and higher mental processes as two competencies made manifest in one performance—external spoken language. In addition, Dance provides some very practical pedagogical resonances on how to positively influence both competency and performance. The chapter serves as a capstone for the text by commenting on the current state of intrapersonal study and its future prospects.

No book, especially one about how talk establishes mind, is written without many conversations with self and others. I would like to express my appreciation to Frank Dance for the ongoing influence of his scholarship and his voice on myself, and many of the other authors, as well as for his review of this book during its preparation. My gratitude also to my fellow authors for enriching my self-talk with their insights, and to Anneke-Jan Boden and to Tobi Siffert for their editorial assistance.

REFERENCES

Cronen, V. E., Pearce, W. B., & Harris, L. M. (1982). The coordinated management of meaning: A theory of communication. In F.E.X. Dance (Ed.), *Human communication theory: Comparative essays* (pp. 61–89). New York: Harper & Row.

Dance, F.E.X. (1982). A speech theory of human communication. In F.E.X. Dance (Ed), *Human communication theory: Comparative essays* (pp. 120–146). New York: Harper & Row.

Jaynes, J. (1976). *The origin of consciousness in the breakdown of the bicameral mind.* Boston: Houghton Mifflin.

Vocate, D. R. (1991). Consciousness and linguistic competency. *Issues in Integrative Studies, 9,* 35–48.

Wood, J. T. (1992). *Spinning the symbolic web: Human communication and symbolic interaction.* Norwood, NJ: Ablex.

. . . the human being who is alone retains the functions of interaction.
—L. S. Vygotsky

Born in external speech and further developed in egocentric speech, inner speech preserves all the functions of social interaction.
—A. R. Luria

Thinking is a process of conversation with one's self when the individual takes the attitude of the other . . . . The mechanism that we use for this process is words, vocal gestures. And we need, of course, only a very few of these as compared with those we need when talking to others. A single symbol is enough . . . . But it is just as real a conversation in terms of the significant symbols as if the whole process were expressed.
—G. H. Mead

I THEORETICAL FOUNDATIONS

The complexity of intrapersonal communication precludes the data-to-theory approach theorists might use with more discrete and easily observed phenomena. Instead, the intrapersonal theorist needs an *a priori* theory to guide him or her in selecting a research path through the maze of physiological, neurological, cultural, psychological, linguistic, social, and other possible data available for study. This section provides the guidance of such a general theory together with background information on: (a) the history of those biological structures that underlie intrapersonal processing; (b) the neurological structure and functioning of the human brain; and (c) the cultural mediation which expands the intrapersonal world to include the abstract as well as the physical. These theoretical foundations provide a base from which the intrapersonal theorist may construct his or her own perspective and express it in subsequent theory.

Chapter 1.   The attributes of intrapersonal communication or any other phenomenon are dependent on the subjective, metatheoretical decisions of the theorist. Rhetoric has come close to a consensual definition because its attributes have been a topic of scholarship for approximately 2,000 years. In contrast, confusion and ambiguity still prevail over what constitutes intrapersonal communication because it is a new area of study for speech communication.

In chapter 1, Vocate seeks precision by delimiting intrapersonal communication to uniquely human activities—self-talk and inner speech. These processes are identified using the tenets of Vygotsky and Mead—that any human activity is dynamic, developmental, and emerges from the interaction of biological and social forces in the individual, with speech playing a major role in creating a mindful self.

Chapter 2.   The dual influences of nature and nurture are problematic for any theorist attempting to explain human behavior. The biology–mind conundrum is exacerbated for intrapersonal theorists because inner speech and self-talk are relatively inaccessible to observation. In this chapter, Riccillo presents the phylogenetic heritage of the biological structures necessary for intrapersonal communication to occur; and resolves the mind–body dualism problem facing theorists by endorsing Pribram's neural monism—a position that mind and body exist in the same relationship as matter and energy (i.e., one entity can transform into the other so neither is dominant).

The importance of a biological perspective to a comprehensive understanding of intrapersonal communication is emphasized throughout chapter 2, and illustrated by Watterson and Riccillo's research with newborn infants.

Chapter 3.   The previous chapter considered biological influences on the development of intrapersonal communication in the human race. In this chapter, Ramsberger explains how the individual's neurological functioning either makes talk possible or impedes it.

No realistic prediction/understanding with respect to the coding or dialogic processes of inner speech can occur until the theorist comprehends the hard-wiring that underlies its functioning. Ramsberger's consideration of the pathologies of talk clarifies the effects of disconnects in its neurological base. The relationship between intrapersonal communication and brain functioning, however, is still far from being completely clear. Her report on the inner speech experience of a recovered aphasic raises some intriguing questions for the intrapersonal theorist with respect to the neurological bases of inner speech's coding and dialogue processes.

Chapter 4.   Understanding culture and its role in intrapersonal communication is crucial to developing a viable intrapersonal theory. In chapter 4, Cole maintains that the traditional conceptualizations of culture in cognitive psychology are inadequate for the task. Accepting the view of cultural-historical theorists that artifacts mediate between humans and direct experience, Cole emphasizes that the dual nature of artifacts (natural and cultural) expands human consciousness to include the concrete and the abstract simultaneously.

The units of culture that inhere in human thought are identified as cultural schemas. These schemas provide some structuration to one's interpretation and action, but because they are always incomplete, they cannot determine thought in a causal fashion. Similarly, context is presented as the dynamic here-and-now activity of people engaged in constituting a particular context. The result of these views is that neither culture nor context are independent environments in which humans function, but rather exist as intrinsic components of humanness. We are, in short, so permeated by culture that any person's thought/action exemplifies the weaving together of individual biology and societal culture into a unique occurrence in a given moment. This means that the intrapersonal theorist is always a participant-observer in his or her consideration of cultural influences rather than an independent experimenter manipulating extrinsic variables.

1
Self-Talk and Inner Speech: Understanding the Uniquely Human Aspects of Intrapersonal Communication

Donna R. Vocate
University of Colorado at Boulder

Talk creates, sustains, and governs the human world. It is talk that breathes life into language and gives it voice. Talk transmits the culture and embodies it in each of us. The voices of parents, grandparents, and significant others in our lives talked us into being and continue to speak to us. Our own voices are raised in an exultation of life beginning at birth. Upon gaining control of our voices, we attempt to influence others and to guide ourselves through the symbolic world we inhabit as humans. We hear the voices of others comforting, chastising, and attempting to persuade us from infancy onward; it is talk that shapes and defines human lives from beginning to end.

The talk created by voice enables us to perceive both self and other, and to conceive of subjective and objective experience. Talk has such power because the spoken word allows us to experience the contrast between internal and external feeling, between speaking the word and hearing it spoken. This is the sensation that Langer (1972) so eruditely argued gives rise to consciousness, and that Dance (1979) envisioned as the rudimentary beginning of human conceptualization. The mechanism permitting the perception of this significant contrast and all future ones, the human brain, is uniquely wired both to produce and to comprehend the spoken word (Luria, 1973). Yet, the sensation and the wiring are not sufficient for a mindful self. The catalyst of symbolic interaction is also necessary. It is talk that permits the dialectic between individual and society that gives a unique mind to each of us. As Langer noted, "It is in society, and more particularly in the verbal intercourse called conversation, that men have acquired what the most intelligent other animals have never developed—intellect" (1972, p. 355).

This essay, in presenting a theoretical paradigm for intrapersonal communication, explores a particular type of talk—self-talk, that is commonly referred to as *intrapersonal communication*. It is engendered by symbolic interaction and arises from a mental foundation of inner speech. The concepts of intrapersonal communication and inner speech are frequently confused and not easily distinguished, so a consideration of both is mandated to clarify an understanding of either. A succinct way of previewing their basic distinction is to note that intrapersonal is *one* level or context of speech communication performance and that inner speech is the competence that makes possible *all* levels of performance although it occurs at the intrapersonal level.

This theoretical perspective on self-talk and inner speech draws heavily on the symbolic interactionist theory of George Herbert Mead as well as the sociocultural theory articulated by L. S. Vygotsky and A. R. Luria. These geographically divergent theories share the view that society and speech have important roles in individual development. Though Mead and Vygotsky evidently were not familiar with each other's work, they did share an intellectual heritage grounded in the sociogenetic tradition originated by Baldwin and Royce in the late 1800s. Thus, both Mead and Vygotsky emphasized "the *dynamic,* dialectical nature of the self in its social context" (Valsiner & Van der Veer, 1988, p. 130). The sociogenetic perspective had two basic tenets: that human cognition is inherently social; and that human cognition develops as external social interactions are internalized.

Valsiner and Van der Veer (1988) adduced that Royce had a direct influence on Mead and that his "I" and "Me" were a version of Royce's social opposition of "Ego" and "non-Ego." Similarly, Baldwin's ideas about imitation, feedback, and internalization shaped the thought of Pierre Janet, a major resource for Vygotsky (Van der Veer & Valsiner, 1988). In addition, many of the commonalties in the theories of Mead and Vygotsky can be traced to their intense study of the writings of Hegel. For example, Hegel's "view that without interpersonal interaction there would be no self and no self-consciousness" (Van Der Veer, 1987a, p. 91) became a common axiom for both. Pragmatism's influence on Mead, and Marxism's influence on Vygotsky also served to intensify the effect of the German philosopher through indirect means (Van Der Veer, 1987a). The combination of principles derived from Hegel and the sociogenetic theorists thus made the theories of Mead and Vygotsky compatible despite their mutual ignorance of each other's work. Language differences accounted for their lack of knowledge in part, but time and distance were also factors—Mead had been an active scholar for some three decades in Chicago before Vygotsky even emerged on Moscow's psychological scene in the early 1920s (Valsiner & Van der Veer, 1988).

My discussion commences with a consideration of intrapersonal as a level of speech communication and as a phenomenon; and then moves to the phenomenon of self-talk—its definition, development, purposes, and functions. That is followed by a discussion of inner speech that operationally embodies internal self-talk as well as the coding process that creates and sustains all human talk. The essay concludes with the argument that a focus on these processes would coordinate future intrapersonal theory construction and research as well as inform other areas of the field such as interpersonal competency. The conclusion also provides a summary of the salient differences between the intrapersonal level spoken language processes of dialogue (self-talk) and coding (inner speech).

DEFINITION
OF INTRAPERSONAL COMMUNICATION

Communication can be considered a ubiquitous process. If it is viewed as the transmission of stimuli and a response or action upon the same, then literally everything alive communicates—earthworms, elm trees, mold spores, squirrels, and so forth. The often quoted axiom from Watzlawick, Beavin, and Jackson (1967) that "one cannot *not* communicate" (p. 51) illustrates the inclusiveness of that definition. Such a view, however, extends our scope to absurd proportions and provides no insight into *human* communication. It is my position that human communication is unique for two reasons: (a) human speech and (b) the symbolic process made possible by language. These two phenomena are united in the concept of spoken language, which Dance (1990) defined as "the fusion of genetically determined speech with culturally determined language" (p. 2). This fusion, to which I have referred by the more colloquial label "talk," delineates the unique means by which humans act upon information and thus differentiates specifically human communication from communication processes that we share with other life forms.

Intrapersonal as a Level

Our academic consideration of human communication typically portrays it as occurring on three levels categorized by the number of communicators involved—intrapersonal, interpersonal, and public communication. The research and focus of communication scholars to date, however, have been almost exclusively on the latter two. Frequently, a consequence of this has been that intrapersonal communication is equated with the intrapersonal level and identified simply as communication involving a single communicator, with no further explanation offered. These levels identify contexts but provide no substantive information about the nature of the communication that occurs in each tier. Thus, the intrapersonal level definition refers to a setting in which the communicator is both sender and receiver, but it fails to differentiate between human communication in this context and the communication of a single elm tree biologically responding to an insect invasion.

Intrapersonal as a Phenomenon

In reviewing the various published definitions of intrapersonal, Cunningham (1989) declared it critical to stop and take stock of our treatment of the phenomenon because we had failed thus far to clearly define it. Roberts, Edwards, and Barker (1987) pushed for specificity by defining intrapersonal as "all of the physiological and psychological processing of messages that happens within individuals at conscious and nonconscious levels as they attempt to understand themselves and their environment" (p. 2). This was a beginning, yet it excluded *overt* self-talk, which, given current definitions, cannot be assigned to another level of processing. It also set up too broad a domain because it conflated all internal processing into an amorphous mass of organismic and human functioning, making any systematic examination problematic, if not impossible, and building a dualism of the ideal and the material into the phenomenon of intrapersonal communication.

As noted previously, some of the confusion results from using the same term, intrapersonal, to refer to a level of processing as well as to the process itself. As a *level* of human communication, intrapersonal merely identifies a context, one in which a single human communicator is both the source and the object of interaction. Thus, a reflexive utterance such as "ouch," and an intentional, syntactically complete sentence such as "How could I be so stupid?" could both be assigned to intrapersonal although their differences have precipitated some convoluted discussions of "mindful" and "mindless" communication (Chautauqua, 1992). Organismic communication, of course, also occurs on the intrapersonal level, such as when proprioceptive nerve cells transmit the information to the brain that one's stomach is filled. Such data, however, do not become symbolic components in human communication until the interpretive process has attached meaning to them.

It is my interpretation that defining the phenomenon of intrapersonal communication as the transmission of stimuli and action upon the same in a single human organism may be taxonomically correct in a very general sense (Dance, 1990), but it places speech communication scholars who wish to study intrapersonal in the unfortunate position of either examining cellular transmissions or maintaining that our theoretical focus includes attributes and processes that we are unprepared to examine because we are not biologists. Therefore, as theorists, we must necessarily be more precise in identifying the intrapersonal phenomena being considered by us as central to speech communication. Consequently, I have excluded organismic functioning from my consideration of self-talk and inner speech; although in later chapters Riccillo and Ramsberger make it clear that the abstract process of human symbolizing and the resultant human dialogue exist only because of the functioning of relevant physiological underpinnings.

Self-Talk as a Phenomenon

Earlier, I equated the terms *talk* and *spoken language* using Dance's definition of the latter as "the fusion of genetically determined speech with culturally determined language" (1990, p. 2). I now wish to differentiate between the two because differences, albeit relatively minor ones, do exist. Dance (chapter 9, this volume) talks about the forms of spoken language, identifying two: external and internal. In his schema, the external and internal forms of spoken language can each occur on the intrapersonal level. I find it helpful to add a consideration of purpose and function to Dance's lucid taxonomic structure of form. For clarity and specificity, I am separating the occurrence of spoken language on the intrapersonal level into two operationally distinct phenomena: (a) a dialogue with the self, or self-talk, which may be internal or external, and (b) a process of coding thought into language or decoding perceived language into meaning, which is one of the functions of inner speech.

Self-talk and inner speech are both spoken language phenomena occurring at the intrapersonal level. They differ, however, in both form and function. Self-talk can be either overt or covert, so it is both external and internal in form; inner speech is only internal by all definitions. Consequently, self-talk is a phenomenon embodying the contrast between internal and external existence, similar to the initial perception of contrast on a purely vocal level that Dance (1979) and Yingling (chapter 6 this volume) assert eventually gives rise to consciousness. It also entails a semantic dialectic between subjective and objective meanings as well as individual and cultural perspectives. These juxtapositions will be discussed in more detail in the section on the development of self-talk.

Operationally, I define *self-talk* as a dialogue with the self existing in two forms: (a) the silent, internal dialogic process of inner speech, and (b) the audible, external dialogue addressed to self although others may hear it. In self-talk, the self is both the source and the object of interaction. Both silent, internal and audible, external forms call forth an interpretive response or feedback, and the existence of both is based on the coding/decoding process of inner speech. The distinctive attributes of self-talk, given this definition, are: (a) self-awareness or what Mead (1934) termed reflective consciousness; (b) its dialogical nature—addressing the self as the object of one's talk whether vocalized or silent; (c) a stimulus, either sign or symbol, originating from the self; and (d) an interpretive, symbolic response or feedback from the self. Self-talk may be intentional or unintentional, silent or vocalized. Neither intentionality nor audibility affects its distinguishing self-awareness nor that the self is eliciting a response from itself as it would from others on the other levels of human communication. The level of self-awareness may vary qualitatively from one occurrence to another, but some minimal level is necessary in order to address the self as an object.

Self-talk, then, is essentially a speech act (Searle, 1969) for the self. The act may be deliberate or scripted/automated, and the result may be cognitive understanding or an overt change in behavior, but the evocation of an interpretive response from the self must be there for the communication to constitute self-talk as defined earlier. This definition excludes vague impressions, sensations, images, fragments of thought, and natural sign behavior responses (Faules & Alexander, 1978), such as blushing, from the domain of self-talk, thereby rendering it more accessible for study.

Johnson (chapter 8, this volume) maintains that human intrapersonal communication serves both an expressive function (the revelation of meaning) and a generative function (the creation of meaning). Any consideration of such semantic purposes mandates also a consideration of the phenomenon of inner speech, the complexity of which has further obfuscated a clear understanding of intrapersonal level functioning. Vygotsky (1934/1986) utilized the term *inner speech* to refer to both a dialogue with the self and the process of a thought being realized in words. However, his idiosyncratic writing style and the actions of various translators (Van der Veer, 1987b) make securing a clear, precise definition from Vygotsky difficult for all scholars, especially so for non-Russian speakers. In contrast, Luria, who became a neurologist and an aphasia expert after Vygotsky's death in 1934, used inner speech to refer primarily to the encoding/decoding process that connects pure thought with an expanded utterance. The difference in their inner speech emphases was influenced, no doubt, by Vygotsky's literary penchant in contrast to Luria's search for a precision compatible with his neurological orientation.

Wertsch (1980) believed that Vygotsky considered both egocentric speech and inner speech to be dialogic in nature although Vygotsky's explicit comments on dialogue were limited to external social speech. In support, Wertsch cited Vygotsky's emphasis on the symbiotic relationship between social activity and mental activity, his concept of "internal collaboration with oneself," and the possible influence of Mikhail Bakhtin, the eminent Soviet philologist who viewed all verbal communication as dialogic, including literary texts. Bakhtin was a contemporary of Vygotsky, but there is no clear evidence that Vygotsky drew upon his work, although Kozulin (1990) noted that Bakhtin and Vygotsky's cousin, David, belonged to the same Leningrad intellectual circle in the 1920s. It is logical to assume that David served as a source for Vygotsky with respect to the latest thinking in linguistics and literary theory. Given Vygotsky's sociogenetic roots, as well as his active participation in discussions of semiotics in the Soviet Union during the 1920s and early 1930s, one must concur with Wertsch's perception of an emphasis on dialogue by Vygotsky. That does not mean, however, that Vygotsky and Luria used the same term to reference different concepts. I see Vygotsky and Luria as each simply emphasizing different operational aspects (dialogue and coding) of inner speech, though not denying the existence of the other process.

DEVELOPMENT OF SELF-TALK

Intrapersonal's self-talk, or dialogue with the self, however, cannot occur until such time as inner speech exists and a "self" has been constituted. Human speech and symbolic interaction play vital roles in this development. Vygotsky and Luria (1930) delineated a developmental progression of speech that moves from external speech to egocentric speech to inner speech. Mead (1934) did not discuss the phenomenon of inner speech, but he did provide us with an explanation of how the self is created via speech and social interaction. The child first internalizes the perspectives or attitudes common to the community and takes those views for its own because it is not yet aware of itself, and consequently is unable to develop any unique, individual outlook. It is my interpretation that spoken language is the vehicle for this assimilation of the group's attitudes, which includes ideas about self and the world as seen through the eyes of others—Mead's "Me" or Royce's "non-Ego." In a sense, the self begins simply as an abbreviated clone of its social milieu. The catalyst that modifies this passive state of affairs according to Mead is the vocal gesture. The spoken language of the child acts as a stimulus to him or her and evokes a response from the self just as it calls for a response from others. Both responses are then incorporated as new facets of the "Me." Thus, the self is constructed from the results of interactions simultaneously occurring with self and with others. It is the interaction with the self that prevents one's personality from being a compliant recording of input from one's social environment or culture.

Mead's (1982) description of personality as a miniature society facilitates our comprehension of self-talk. Rather than defining self in terms of static components such as Freud's Id, Ego, and Super-ego, he sees it as comprised of two processes—the "I" and the "Me." The former is the dynamic, spontaneous, creative action-taker with biological origins, whereas the "Me" is the internalized, organized aggregate of attitudes and perceptions garnered from others. The "I" does, and the "Me" monitors the doing. Any reaction or response to oneself thus results from a social interaction between the two—the "I," or actor, and the "Me," or critic. Each response to the "I" results from the monitoring of the "Me" and then becomes an element in the memory of the "Me" to be used in the next interaction. This interactive process is the means by which self-consciousness is accomplished: The self reflects upon the self. Consequently, the individual is an active contributor to his or her own construction or development, but the "Me" originally defined by society provides the basic structure to be reshaped. Thus, every interpretive process produces a synthesis that results from the interaction of the individual and the internalized other.

The stimulation of the "I" followed by its action and the interpretation of that experience by the "Me" is referred to as the process of self-indication (Fisher, 1978). Self-indication establishes new information and memories; it may also involve "role-taking," that is, deliberately reviewing one's actions from a specific role attendant to a social act. The "Me" integrates the role expectations and views of the self garnered from specific others as well as from the "generalized other" that reflects the attitudes of the entire social group or community to which the individual belongs. In sum, the self becomes for itself, an object to which it responds and upon which it reflects and thereby achieves self-consciousness.

Self-Talk as a Dialectic

Building on Mead, but rejecting his social behaviorism with its emphasis on the behavioral act, I envision self-talk as essentially a dialectic between the individual and the society (and its culture) embodied in the internalized other. The dialogue may originate from either facet of the self, individual or societal, but the one addressed always responds on an interpretive, symbolic level. For example, the "other" formed by society may critique the values of the individual, or the individual may choose to remain deviant from cultural values internalized as a component of the "other." The interpretive process of identifying, defining, and evaluating any value constitutes self-talk because it is characterized by the level of self-awareness necessary to address the self as an object, and an interpretive, symbolic response from one of the facets of self. Thus, a dialogue has occurred, albeit with different aspects of a single person, that produces a new synthesis of the two.

Talk—the spoken word—is essential to the development of self. As explained more specifically in the section on inner speech, it is the internalization of spoken language in hearing individuals that creates inner speech and thereby provides the means for human interaction with others or with self. Mead (1982) contends that the role of the vocal gesture is so crucial to the creation of personality that "if this is lacking, some substitute must be provided, if self-consciousness is going to be built up. This other means of intercourse must have the same mechanics as that of speech, stimulations calling out responses to which the child can respond" (p. 59). Thus the voice and its symbolic utterances build not only personality but also self-consciousness. Mead's vocal gesture is not mere vocalization, the oral production of sound; rather, it incorporates language so that it is human talk or spoken language that has a semantic as well as a physical aspect.

Talk physically creates a new awareness of self and others and gives awareness a form for internalization. The symbolic dimension of talk elevates consciousness to the uniquely human level of self-reflection, thus creating intellect and inner dialogue. Vygotsky distinguished between pure intellect and consciousness by maintaining that consciousness, by its very nature, "is necessarily dialogical" (Kozulin, 1990, p. 271). Similarly, it was Mead's (1982) belief that "anything that can be vocalized is a part of the self. The self is confined to fields of consciousness where there is communication" (p. 175). It might appear from reading Mead that the act of simply responding creates self-consciousness, but the crucial element for self-talk to exist is the mediation engendered by symbolic speech (Vygotsky, 1934/1986). A mere response could be the reflexive scratching of an itch, but the necessary element of self-awareness, or monitoring, is possible only if the linear, direct response of a reflex is mediated to permit alternatives or choices in how one responds.

PURPOSES AND FUNCTIONS OF SELF-TALK

Creation of Meaning Purpose

The purpose, however, of the process of self-talk is not just the creation of an entity called the self, but also the creation of meaning for the self. From Mead's (1934) view, it is the behavioral response that gives the communicative act its meaning. The response may be merely a tendency to act, for example, thinking of sitting in a chair rather than the overt act of actually sitting down. This seems a behavioral oversimplification because constraining one's response to action alone seems insufficient to account for the creation of meaning. Any realistic explanation needs to be expanded to include the dialectical perspective of Vygotsky (Kozulin, 1990), which transcends the behavioral and can be applied to abstractions as well as activity.

Prior to any response, however, Mead (1934) stated that the creation of meaning requires a state of reflective consciousness that occurs only when the self is an object to itself. This state of consciousness, according to Luria (Vocate, 1987), is possible only when the symbolic linkages of inner speech have mediated the individual's mental connections so that a choice to view oneself from a nonegocentric perspective can be made and the resultant objectivity can be exercised. Self-awareness, therefore, results from internalizing the language of one's social community. This internalization of language also entails the internalization of word meanings as they are then understood, although such meanings are dynamic and subject to frequent revision. The subsequent inner speech coding process, engendered by the internalization of language, involves shaping thought into words, thereby imbuing it with meaning. Once inner speech exists, the self-talk made possible by it becomes the chief vehicle by which new meaning is created by the self. This is because the interpretive response of self-talk requires intentional intervention in the inner speech coding process, thereby creating a new synthesis of subjective and objective meaning. The specifics of the process are discussed in a later section on the coding process of inner speech.

Consciousness is a functional process derived from the interaction of the organism and its environment from Mead's (1982) perspective. Similarly, self-consciousness occurs only when an individual interacts with him or herself. Such self-talk is critical not only for the establishment of reflective consciousness, but also for an awareness of meaning. Mead maintained that we have *no* consciousness of meaning except when we can indicate symbols to ourselves. Consequently, neither subjective nor objective meaning exists for us until symbols become functional for us via inner speech and self-talk.

I find that it clarifies the creation of meaning to think of self-talk not merely as responding or providing feedback to oneself, but also, originally, as a dialectic between individual and society. As a result of those different experiences (biological vs. cultural), it also becomes a dialectic between Vygotsky's (1934/1986) "sense" and "meaning." "Sense" is subjective or connotative meaning and "meaning" is objective or denotative meaning; thus, the first is derived from personal experience and the latter from the culture, or the experience of society. For example, in self-talk, each instance of subjective interpretation could be reviewed also in terms of society's meaning for the same event—a monitoring of consistency with the cultural norm—which leads to a decision to either adjust or to continue the level of nonconformity. The dialectic, with its contrast and tension between distinctive elements, always produces a new synthesis, thereby accounting for changes in meaning.

The process of self-talk on the intrapersonal level may occur simultaneously with the levels of interpersonal or public communication, but it provides the richest input for human consciousness when intrapersonal is the exclusive level of communication taking place. The reflective consciousness enacted in the self-talk process is crucial if we are going to adjust or modify ourselves, whether the goal is a change in attitude or one in behavior. Personal growth or change can occur only through self-talk. In Mead's (1982) social behaviorist terminology,

> first of all, there is that checking of activity which is essential to reflective consciousness; the necessity for adjustment to the changed situation. Further continuation of that process is one in which we ask ourselves what the completion of the act indicated in the gesture will be. If we are in doubt we have several tendencies to respond, which mutually check one another. What is present in consciousness are these tendencies to respond in different social ways to gestures of other persons. Interpretation takes place in its simplest form in our tendency to respond. *We adjust ourselves before we can act* [italics added]. (p. 45)

Cognitive Adaptation Purpose

I believe that Mead's statement identifies the primary social purpose of self-talk: adaptation of the self. Using Mead's schema, the "I" makes choices, and the interpretive, critical process that follows from the "Me" allows us to adapt ourselves mentally, physically, or both before we think or act further. Thus, self-talk constitutes a cognitive version of Piaget's process of adaptation, an interaction whereby the organism uses its environment to enhance and benefit itself. Dance (Dance & Larson, 1976) maintained that any such interaction is inevitably accompanied by entropic reduction and change. This happens because the adaptation process that increases the organization of the organism requires adjustments in either the individual, or the items to be ingested, or both. "Adaptation" identifies the overall interactive process, which is comprised of two subroutines: (a) assimilation, which refers to adjustments in the environment, and (b) accommodation, which refers to adjustments by the organism. The degree of adjustment in each subroutine may vary, but the interaction itself mandates at least some change by both organism and environment. The simplest manifestation of the process of adaptation is physical—such as eating or breathing—but it also occurs on the mental plane.

Cognitive adaptation is a process familiar to teachers at any level. Concepts and principles often have to be restructured to facilitate internalization by the student. This is done by simplifying relationships and using language that the student can understand, constituting Piaget's subroutine of assimilation. On the other hand, the student too must adjust (subroutine of accommodation) by remaining open-minded and by attempting to understand the material. The interaction of student and concept is an example of cognitive adaptation, which entails the two subroutines of (a) assimilation, which requires change in the material being studied, and (b) accommodation, which is the adjustment of the student him or herself.

The self-indication process itself is also an example of adaptation, in that the "I," which acts, has been changed by its previous interactions with the "Me," and, in turn, the latter also adjusts as a result of its interactions with the "I." Thus, self-talk integrates individual and society into a unique *intertextuality,* to borrow a term from literary theory (Kozulin, 1990). Intertextuality refers to a synthesis of meaning wherein the antecedent literary texts continue to exist because the reactions or interpretations of the consequent new text preserve their existence in it. The same model can be used to understand the creation of an idiosyncratic personality from the interaction of individual and culture in self-talk. Both the individual and the internalized other continue to exist in the subsequently changed self because it is a response to its predecessors ("I" and "Me") and retains elements of them as part of itself. Consequently, to define self-talk as a dialogue with the self that calls forth an interpretive response is to provide it with a domain essential to the adjustment of the self that acts in any communicative setting. It also makes self-talk a phenomenon crucial to any understanding of human communicative behavior, and defines self-talk as a manifestation of the speech communication function of linking. Purposes differ from functions, in this discussion, in that they are intentional, goal-directed behaviors, whereas functions are intrinsic, involuntary consequences.

Speech Communication Functions

Self-talk on the intrapersonal level communication shares three functions with the other levels of speech communication: (a) the linking of the individual and his or her environment, (b) the development of higher mental processes, and (c) the regulation of the behavior of self and others (Dance & Larson, 1976). As Dance indicated, these may vary in degree from person to person, but they are functional or inevitable consequences of the existence of spoken language in the individual. However, it is in self-talk that qualitative variation is most crucial for individual success in the social, mental, or behavioral realms.

The internalization of language in and of itself provides the individual with ties to his or her social community because language is comprised of significant symbols that have a shared meaning with other members of the language community. However, the interaction of the individual and societal components of the self also entails an interdependency between the individual and the environment because the "Me" originates in the attitudes of specific others and the community and then evolves into a new synthesis of self as it responds to the activities and views of the "I." Consequently, the social environment is always present and has a role in any act of self-talk, as does the sensory experience of the individual. The dialectic between the individual and the society intrinsic to self-talk means that self-talk is inherently a linkage between the individual and his or her environment. How well this function is enacted in the adult is of vital concern to interpersonal communication theorists because self-talk manifests itself in the social realm as competence.

Rod Hart's concept of rhetorical sensitivity (Hart, Carlson, & Eadie, 1980) provides an example of the functioning of self-talk in interpersonal communication. Hart looks at communicators as being a combination of three basic styles: (a) noble selves who see themselves as possessing the truth and communicating with others merely to inform them; (b) rhetorical reflectors who spend their interaction time trying to reflect back to their partner the personality and opinions that will be pleasing to the partner, and (c) rhetorical sensitives who take into consideration the context in which the interaction is taking place as well as the background, values, and attitudes of themselves *and* their partner to the interaction. Obviously, the noble self, because he or she makes no effort to adapt or adjust to the other person, has no need to engage in self-talk to accomplish such an adjustment. On the other hand, both the rhetorical reflector and the rhetorical sensitive must utilize self-talk in order to adjust to the partner and to enact the dominant/preferred communication style.

Self-talk functions to benefit the individual in the mental realm as well. As Cole points out in chapter 4, the cognitive schema acquired by the individual are incomplete, so an interpretative process is always necessary to augment and clarify the same. Similarly, any of the consistency theories, such as Festinger's (1957) cognitive dissonance, would require a process of self-talk in order to assess the cognitive elements that may be evaluated as irrelevant, consonant, or dissonant. Cognitive complexity, as delineated by Jesse Delia (Hale, 1980), requires that one be able to assimilate constructs to organize one's perceptions of people or events, and thus have the capacity to make more distinctions in such perceptions.

Mead's social behaviorism sees voluntary behavior as resulting from an interruption of the act before its consummation. Luria (Vocate, 1987) portrayed volition in neurological terms as the provision of afferent feedback so that the behavior is halted and noted that in adults this feedback can be provided internally by the symbol, or what I would term self-talk. Dance (Dance & Larson, 1976) pointed out that attempts to regulate behavior go through developmental stages: (a) regulation of self by others, (b) regulation of self by self, and (c) regulation of others by self. The first stage reflects the signal influence of the spoken word whereby the mere sound of the word interrupts and thereby regulates behavior. Once inner speech exists and the norms of significant others and the community at large are internalized into the self, then the second stage of self-regulation becomes possible via self-talk. And, as we become more sophisticated, we are able to at least attempt to control the behaviors of others, but again it is the functioning of self-talk that makes any intentional or scripted attempt possible.

Inner speech is the phenomenon that enables us to engage in all human communicative behaviors regardless of the level on which they occur, the sophistication of their performance, and the number of individuals involved. Let us look now at inner speech, the underlying competence that makes speech communication of any kind possible.

DEFINITION OF INNER SPEECH

Vygotsky (1987) noted the emphasis of French philosophers and Von Humboldt (1836/1988) on an "inner form" of language. Von Humboldt, however, did not operationally define the same or provide examples, no doubt because he had great difficulty writing clearly and his financial independence eliminated any need to overcome it (Aarsleff, 1988). It appears, however, that the concept intrigued the Ukrainian linguist, Potebnya, who brought the idea to Russia and developed it (Kozulin, 1990). Vygotsky, who was familiar with Potebnya's work, then elaborated on the concept of inner speech, maintaining that its development is an ongoing process, and that even in adults it is constantly undergoing modification.

In various writings, Vygotsky defined *inner speech* as both speech *and* thought. For example, in *Thought and Language* (1934/1986) he called it a "distinct plane of verbal thought" (p. 248); but he also stated that "inner speech is speech for oneself. External speech is for others" (p. 255). In another section, Vygotsky spoke of inner speech as thinking in pure meanings (p. 249); in yet another, he stated that inner speech is mediated internally by word meanings (p. 252). The variety of his definitions, added to Vygotsky's style of writing, serves to obfuscate any clear delineation of what constituted inner speech for him. Was it self-talk, the encoding of verbal thought, or both? Wertsch (1980) saw it as self-talk, whereas for some readers (e.g., Luria) it is primarily the encoding/decoding process that moves us from a nonsymbolic motive to a symbolic, communicative, external utterance and back. Thus for Luria, it is the internal act of becoming for verbal thought. Given the manuscripts currently available, it appears that it encompassed both functions for Vygotsky, although writing style and health problems kept him from being as specific or detailed in his presentation as we might wish.

Inner speech in both its processes (dialogue and coding) is closer to thought than external speech, so it encompasses more rudimentary levels of verbal processing than those forms of external communication that have been encoded for another person. Vygotsky (1978, 1934/1986, 1987) noted that inner speech is silent, egocentric, and characterized by condensed meaning, ellipsis, syntactic incompleteness, and predication or the omission of known information such as the subject— qualities that would render understanding by another person quite difficult. These attributes are discussed in more detail in the section on the process of inner speech.

The coding process of inner speech most clearly exhibits its symbiotic relationship to external speech communication if we examine it from the sociocultural perspective articulated by Vygotsky and Luria rather than from the mechanistic information processing point of view more common in the United States. This is because the sociocultural view includes a consideration of social interaction and cultural influence, permitting a more humanistic view of inner speech than the mechanical, reductionistic approach of information processing. It is also a view more compatible with other areas of speech communication study (e.g., interpersonal communication) in its emphasis on the role of social interaction.

My study of Luria resulted in a definition of *inner speech's coding process* as a cognitive process linking thought and utterance that consists of three stages characterized by increasingly deliberate semantic and syntactic relationships that may eventually result in the overt production of words in syntactically complete expressions. The entire process from the motive of pure thought to external utterance is presented by Luria (1982) as consisting of five stages; it is my interpretation that inner speech involves only three of the five. The coding process of inner speech is primary and must occur before it can serve functionally as an internal dialogue with the self—self-talk.

DEVELOPMENT OF INNER SPEECH

Inner speech, according to Vygotsky, originates with an individual's internalization of the transitory stage of egocentric speech. At the Ninth International Congress on Psychology held at Yale in 1929, Luria presented a paper coauthored with Vygotsky on egocentric speech, and announced that the developmental schema of inner speech is: (a) external speech, (b) egocentric speech, and then (c) inner speech (Vygotsky & Luria, 1930). Egocentric or "speech for oneself" is paradoxically acquired through social interaction with others and constitutes a normal stage in a child's language acquisition. Initially in the external speech stage, an adult attributes communicative intent to the infant who is not yet capable of such intent, and responds to the infant accordingly. Those children who are denied such initial social interchange will not progress to the subsequent stages of egocentric and then inner speech. That original stage of adult–child interaction has an organizing function with respect to behavior as demonstrated in Luria's studies of the verbal regulation of behavior (1959a, 1959b, 1960a, 1960b, 1961a, 1961b, 1963, 1967, 1982; Zivin, 1979), in which speech's effect moves from the impelling to the significative aspect of the word as the child develops. The continual organizing function of speech in subsequent stages is illustrated in the more recent finding that task difficulty significantly increases the amount of task-relevant egocentric speech (Hewes & Evans, 1978). Once the inner speech stage is well established, Lurian theory, as delineated by Vocate (1987), maintains that all human (conscious and voluntary) behavior is organized through it.

Subsequent to its initial organization of behavior through being a physical stimulus, speech moves inward to serve as the organizing base for mind as well. As a result of inner speech's ties to the language of one's culture and to the interaction with others by which one acquires that language, Vygotsky (1966, 1934/1986) saw inner speech as having both social and cultural roots. Luria supported this premise with his field studies of peasants in a remote area of central Asia (Luria, 1931, 1933, 1976b); then, based on neurological evidence, he expanded Vygotsky's concept of inner speech to maintain that inner speech has a vital role in *all* higher mental functioning (Vocate, 1987). This relationship between mind and social speech was anticipated, however, in Vygotsky's (1978) early theoretical prediction:

> Every function in the child's cultural development appears twice: first, on the social level, and later, on the individual level; first, *between* people (*interpsychological*), and then *inside* the child (*intrapsychological*). This applies equally to voluntary attention, to logical memory, and to the formation of concepts. All higher functions originate as actual relations between human individuals. (p. 57).

Thus, what later becomes the phenomenon of inner speech is spawned via social interaction between adult and child, and the subsequent internalization of word meanings and principles of language from the adult's particular language and culture. In maturity, the locus of the process of inner speech is *within* the individual, but it retains the social dimension: Any modification of the denotative aspect of its meanings is always acquired via an interactive mode whether it be with a text, an individual, or the self. The cultural dimension endures too because such interaction continues to be accomplished by means of language, that system of signs and symbols that "carries within it the generalized concepts that are the storehouse of human knowledge" (Luria, 1979, p. 44) and that reflect cultural conditions. The influence of culture on inner speech is presented in some detail in Luria's *Cognitive Development: Its Cultural and Social Foundations* (1976b), should the reader wish to pursue it further. The possibility that cultural input could be deterministic is ameliorated by the fact that inner speech is easily influenced and can be changed or augmented by training (Luria, 1957; Luria & Yudovich, 1959) or by self-talk.

INNER SPEECH AND THOUGHT

Moving the focus from the origins of inner speech to its characteristics, I think some of the confusion about what constitutes inner speech is exacerbated by the tendency to view inner speech and thinking as synonyms. Inner speech gives rise to verbal thought and its process may augment nonlinguistic thought, but thought can exist apart from inner speech. Basic motives or urges as well as presemantic color or tone perceptions are outside its realm, whereas automatized or habituated reactions were in its domain during their inception, but no longer require its participation in their reflexive enactment. The study of inner speech in and of itself does not force us into a theoretical domain beyond a concern with human communication. That happens when and if we make an inferential leap to equate all types of thought with inner speech. Defining inner speech and thinking as identical processes shifts the focus of scholarly inquiry from inner speech to thought and gives rise to the argument that creative or scientific people such as Einstein do not "think" in words. Recognizing inner speech's dependence on verbal meaning, we then assume that somehow *intentional* thought must precede inner speech. If we accept this proposition that logical thinking is not always linguistic in mode, then the value of studying inner speech is disparaged for us because it cannot possibly inform a concern with intentional *interaction* if it is even unnecessary for intentional *thought*.

It is my position that inner speech is a higher mental process in neurological locus, but it is not thought in general, although it is necessary for problem solving, evaluation, and most mental activities that are in loose terminology simply labeled "thought." Luria (*passim*) devoted most of his lengthy career in neurology and psychology to a consideration of inner speech and never used the terms *thought* and *inner speech* as interchangeable. Unfortunately, such differentiation is not typical of the majority of Western scholarship today; the equation of thought and inner speech is not limited to speech communication but is expressed by theorists in several fields, including linguists.

Having equated the two concepts originally, some theorists then attempt a belated precision and modify their equation by claiming that inner speech is synonymous *only* with thinking in words—one modality of thinking. Based on such deductions, even someone as familiar with Vygotsky's inner speech as linguist Vera John-Steiner (1985) came to the conclusion that "condensed thought is not limited to inner speech and to the inner processes of those who think in words" (p. 215). In her *Notebooks of the Mind* (1985), John-Steiner postulated a plurality of modes of thinking based on interviews with over 50 individuals that she termed "experienced thinkers" ranging from Anais Nin to Basil Bernstein. She argued that the dichotomizing of thought into either verbal or visual thinking is a gross oversimplification and suggested that dependent on one's experience, thought may be based also on movement or sound: "I would suggest that the internalization of experience and of the modality-specific ways in which experience is shaped are not mirror images of the external communicative process. The notion that thought is subvocal speech is strongly contradicted by the information provided by experienced thinkers" (p. 213)

One result of equating subjective reports of nonlinguistic thinking with inner speech is that some communication scholars begin to view inner speech as the concern of other academic disciplines, thus taking it outside of its legitimate domain, speech communication. Viewing inner speech as *just* a particular mode of thought is the consequence of abandoning our consideration of the phenomenon of inner speech to examine instead what others, "experienced thinkers" or not, construe to be thought. It is this focus that led John-Steiner to use the methodology of subjective introspection that Vygotsky rejected in 1924 to denigrate the importance of inner speech. By ignoring Vygotsky's emphasis on the internalization of external speech, she made inner speech a comparatively trivial phenomenon meriting study only by rather esoteric scholars interested in this particular form of thought.

For Vygotsky and Luria human thought is always *verbal,* but it is not literally thinking in words. It is dependent on language in that it draws upon word meanings and the organizing principles of language, but it is not constrained structurally to *words* only. Perhaps one of Vygotsky's (1934/1986) definitions of inner speech can provide some clarification of the relationship between inner speech and thinking:

> Inner speech is not the interior aspect of external speech—it is a function in itself. It still remains speech, i.e., thought connected with words. But while in external speech thought is embodied in words, in inner speech words die as they bring forth thought. Inner speech is to a large extent thinking in pure meanings. It is a dynamic, shifting, unstable thing, fluttering between word and thought, the two more or less stable, more or less firmly delineated components of verbal thought. Its true nature and place can be understood only after examining the next plane of verbal thought, the one still more inward than inner speech.
>
> That plane is thought itself. As we have said, every thought creates a connection, fulfills a function, solves a problem. The flow of thought is not accompanied by a simultaneous unfolding of speech. The two processes are not identical, and there is no rigid correspondence between the units of thought and speech. . . .
>
> Thought has its own structure, and the transition from it to speech is no easy matter. . . . Thought, unlike speech, does not consist of separate units. . . . A speaker often takes several minutes to disclose one thought. In his mind the whole thought is present at once, but in speech it has to be developed successively. A thought may be compared to a cloud shedding a shower of words. Precisely because thought does not have its automatic counterpart in words, the transition from thought to word leads through meaning. . . . Direct communication between minds is impossible, not only physically but psychologically. Communication can be achieved only in a roundabout way. Thought must pass first through meanings and only then through words. (pp. 249–252)

Obviously, Vygotsky himself did not view all thought and inner speech as synonymous, nor did he equate inner speech with what John-Steiner termed *subvocal speech,* because he specifically stated that thought "is not accompanied by a simultaneous unfolding of speech" (1934/1986, p. 249). A more detailed consideration of the relationship between thought and inner speech is given later in the discussion of the process of inner speech.

The equation of inner speech with thinking in general is a perspective built on superficial logic. It also has a negative impact on attracting speech communication scholars to the study of inner speech: Some will ignore it because a consideration of all forms of thought is outside of our domain, whereas others more psychologically oriented will minimize the importance of inner speech to our field because it's *only verbal* thought. Both perceptions are erroneous for the following reasons: First, I am convinced that inner speech is not just linguistic thinking, with all of the assumptions of syntactical ordering that "linguistic" connotes today thanks to Chomsky's influence. Rather, it is primarily a semantic phenomenon in its initial stages that may or may not subsequently entail syntax, depending on whether its coding process progresses to an expanded utterance or remains at a relatively pure meaning stage. This makes it an essential component in all symbolic interpretation regardless of how or if it is expressed. Inner speech's participation is not, however, required for the performance of reflexive behavior or practical trial-and-error problem solving that does not incorporate symbolism. Second, because of its role in the creation of human consciousness or self-reflexiveness, inner speech is the phenomenon that precedes all uniquely human cognition and makes it possible regardless of the mode—visual, musical, or whatever. Luria defined "human" consciousness as characterized by rational, volitional behavior and dominated by the system of semantic associations engendered by language, whereas mere "animal" consciousness is instinctive behavior and passive sensory awareness (Vocate, 1987). Third, inner speech is a necessary attribute for all human communication theory, especially intrapersonal theory, because its absence would eliminate any human ability to attach meaning, thus precluding human intentionality as well as any faculty for influencing or communicating with others regardless of number, context, or mode.

Having been one of the editors for Vygotsky's *Mind in Society* (1978), John-Steiner was familiar with his concept of inner speech and she explained it by drawing a parallel between the expansion of the early abbreviated utterances of a child by a nurturing adult and the expansion of inner speech into communicable language accomplished alone by the mature speaker. She saw both as involving a movement from a holophrastic, "sense" (subjective meaning) filled single word to a more sequential expanded utterance.

A more detailed description of inner speech was attempted by Johnson both in "Spoken Language and Vygotsky and Sokolov's Concept of Inner Speech" (1981) and in chapter 8, this volume. He notes its four major characteristics: (a) it is always silent, (b) it has high levels of semantic complexity, (c) it has predication or syntactic synthesis, and (d) it is very egocentric. In Johnson's view, inner speech is an intrapersonal process with the special function of decoding external speech into thought. Thus, discussions of inner speech by both a linguist and a speech communication scholar talk about it in mental process terms that often lead to the equation of inner speech with verbal thinking, which many readers then construe as simply thinking in words. This definition of verbal thought engenders the typical explanation of the inner speech coding process, exemplified by John-Steiner's definition mentioned earlier; namely, that it begins with a single word and progresses via a syntactically ordered progression to the final product of an external utterance produced for the decoding of others. This explanation is inadequate in that it describes only the last stages of the coding process of inner speech and totally ignores its dialogic function as self-talk.

PROCESS OF INNER SPEECH

The realization that inner speech is in its essence semantic rather than syntactic is probably the most important factor in understanding the essential relationship of inner speech to human communication. In the excerpt from *Thought and Language* (1934/1986) quoted previously, Vygotsky asserted that inner speech is largely the process of "thinking in pure meanings." How that can occur is clarified if we read Luria, with his penchant for making Vygotsky intelligible while building on his theory, and if we discard our Chomskian bias for seeing grammar as the quintessence of language.

Treating the fact that inner speech originates from external speech as a given, Luria initially described the subsequent internal process of inner speech as a rather pedestrian movement from motive to completed utterance

> involving at least four stages—motive of the utterance, thought (frequently described as a semantic graph including both theme and rheme), inner speech, and finally, the expanded speech utterance. Having been rather definite about their characteristics in his earlier works, we find him much more tentative about these stages in his final writings in this area (Luria, 1982). Luria is quite candid, in fact, about saying that there is insufficient reliable data to definitely characterize these stages, and that much more investigation is needed. However, he suggests that the initial semantic graph includes the subjective sense of the utterance, which is then converted into a sequentially organized speech utterance via the means of inner speech. Thus, the essential element in the progression from motive to complete external utterance is the transformation of Vygotsky's "sense" into "meaning" and Luria sees inner speech as having the vital role in recoding subjective sense into a syntagmatic [linear] schema. So rather than humans having any innate coding mechanism for syntax, it comes into being via the psychological process of inner speech, which has sociocultural origins. (Vocate, 1987, p. 122)

Modifying this description of the motive-to-utterance process to encompass Luria's thought at the end of his career, the progression from thought to external speech expands to involve at least five hypothetical stages: (a) motive, (b) semantic set, (c) deep structure, (d) surface structure, and (e) expanded utterance (See Fig. 1.1). In keeping with current Western language theory, a cursory reading of Vygotsky and Luria would lead one to believe that in understanding the process of inner speech, our emphasis should be placed on the successful attainment of the syntactical aspects of deep and surface structure. I now think that we (myself included as the previous quote demonstrates) have been in error in that assumption, and that instead the emphasis should be placed on the semantic set component of the process, the locus of Vygotsky's pure meanings—both his "sense" or connotative meaning, and his "meaning" or denotative meaning.

The first stage of the progression, motive, is limited to three types of nonverbal thought according to Luria (1982): -mand, the desire to request something; -tact, the desire to transmit something; and -cept, the desire to understand, clarify, or classify something in a system of concepts. According to Luria, those speech utterances that

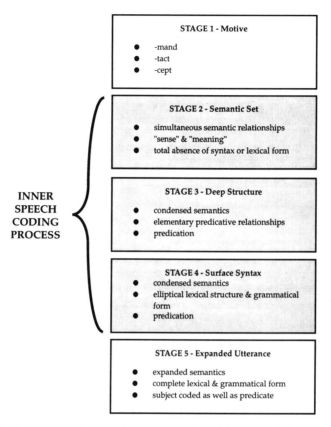

FIG. 1.1.   Stages of processing from pure thought to expanded utterance.

do not begin with a motive, such as profanity or affective exclamations, *are not* examples of higher mental functioning, because they are not conscious and voluntary. In his schema, such "mindless" utterances are not truly speech utterances because the activating force of a motive is absent. Similarly, dialogic responses that simply repeat the question rather than requiring active creation do not entail motives either, and Luria (1982) cited research with frontal lobe patients as evidence that motives are not needed for such responses. Thus, motives are necessary for the conscious and voluntary higher functioning that characterizes intentional communication, which is uniquely human communication.

In the progression, any of these motives will be linked to the highly personal and experientially based "sense" and/or the culturally derived "meaning" available in the next stage of the process, the semantic set. As quoted earlier, Vygotsky pictured inner speech as "thinking in pure meanings," which is speech, or "thought connected with words"; but thought is portrayed as "more inward than inner speech" and creating connections, and so on. Hence, Vygotsky's concept of "thought" appears to combine what Luria later separated into "motive" and "semantic graph or set." The latter stage combines and preserves "sense" and "meaning" in a synthesis unique to a particular person. "Sense" is subjective and closely related to the individual's motives, affect, and sensory experience, whereas "meaning" is objective and tied to the culture's "system of objective associations represented by the word and reflecting the real phenomena irrespective of the needs to which these associations correspond" (Luria, 1976a, p. 8).

The semantic set operates with semantic elements, including a set of relations designated by them, but not with words, so it has no grammatical form. These relationships are simultaneous, and Luria postulated that there are only 40–50 main types such as finality, inception, causation, function, operation, and so on (Luria, 1976a). Thus, thought as simultaneous linkages of pure meaning must take place in Luria's semantic set, which in its processual nature ties motive to subjective meaning (entailing emotion, sensory perceptions, etc.) and to word meaning in a gestalt of total meaning. This becomes the initial stage of the inner speech process rather than being simply a lexical storeroom on which inner speech draws. If the encoding process of inner speech stops here, we have that phenomenon we have all experienced of knowing what we mean or intend as a gestalt, but are unable to express because we have not yet given it a linear or sequential ordering, that is, the structure of syntax. Inner speech, or Vygotsky's "thinking in pure meanings" may, however, proceed to the deep structure stage with its rudimentary sequential relationships, or beyond to a more syntactically sophisticated stage so that expression is possible.

In the deep structure stage, inner speech retains its properties of semantic representation although at the same time it begins to include sequential relationships. It is at this point that inner speech becomes viable to support self-talk because it has sufficient syntactic form to be used as communication with the self, although it is still too incomplete for communication with others. Luria suggested that the sequential relationships in this stage are limited to a few predictive relations that do not exceed ten in number such as "relationships corresponding to the question who?/what?, whom?/what?, to whom?/to what?, of whom?/of what?," and so forth (Luria, 1976a, p. 22). The surface syntax stage expands the sequential ordering to include lexical structure and grammatical forms but is characterized by ellipsis because it is still coding for oneself. Beyond inner speech, in Luria's fifth stage in the progression from motive to external speech, we have the production of an overt, syntactically expanded, verbal expression that typically is used to communicate with another person and consequently adds the heretofore unidentified but understood subject of the thought.

The phenomenon of inner speech, in my opinion, consists of stages two, three, and four of the progression from motive to expanded, external speech. In other words, inner speech may progress through semantic set, deep structure, and surface structure or it may be arrested at any of these and not continue. For some self-talk messages, coding at the level of deep structure may be sufficient to address the self. I would anticipate, however, that self-talk serves its cognitive adaptation purpose optimally at the competence level of inner speech's surface syntax stage, whether it is silent or audible, because that stage would facilitate an equal consideration of "sense" and "meaning."

While Luria categorized the stages of inner speech according to syntactical completeness, the semantic development that accompanies this progression is crucial to human communication. This semantic development is essentially Mead's interpretive process. A dialectic exists between personal meaning or "sense," which includes physical and emotional data as yet uninterpreted, and the cultural interpretation or "meaning" of an event/topic that one acquired by internalizing the language of the culture. Any expression of thought requires some resolution or synthesis of these personal and cultural accounts of the event/topic. The expansion of syntactic completeness and linguistic form realized as one moves from the stage of deep structure to surface structure increases the role of one's culturally determined language and imbues the message automatically with increased denotative meaning. I postulate, however, that the encoder can intercede in the deep-structure or surface structure stages of the process by shifting to the dialogic function of inner speech, thereby taking an active role in his or her interpretive process. It is this self-talk to achieve the desired synthesis of subjective and objective meaning that determines one's communication effectiveness or competence. It also resolves the conundrum of whether communication is "mindful" or "mindless" (Langer, 1992) because the dialogic process of inner speech requires some self-consciousness, whereas the encoding process can occur passively below the level of self-awareness as in a scripted or exclamatory utterance.

PRODUCTS OF INNER SPEECH

Luria noted that the human brain is capable of both simultaneous and successive synthesis, and that these result from inner speech's retention of the associations and principles inherent in language (Vocate, 1987). It seems quite probable that simultaneous synthesis is first realized in the semantic set of inner speech with its gestalt of "sense" and the various levels of "meaning," whereas the capacity for sucessive synthesis is derived from the serial nature of sequential language organization with which thought is shaped in the more syntactically structured stages of inner speech. Luria even identified for us the brain systems responsible for each of these abilities (Vocate, 1987), but such information exceeds the requirements of this discussion.

It is also the semantic set component of inner speech that gives it a role in the creation of human consciousness or self reflexiveness. This premise is based on the work of Luria as well. He asserted that human consciousness does not exist as an innate quality of the human brain but occurs as the second of two developmental stages. The initial stage of consciousness is animal consciousness, or mere sensory awareness of reality that is dependent on the elementary sensory systems of the brain and the role of the upper brain stem in maintaining a state of wakefulness. Human consciousness or self-reflexiveness, when it occurs, retains this dependence on the physiological system supporting wakefulness, but must have human language to make that *"leap from the sensory to the rational world,* which is essential for human consciousness" (Luria, 1982, p. 41). This "leap" is made possible by the word's function as a mediating factor between the stimuli of the environment and the response of the individual, thereby permitting human choice.

In order for human intentionality or volition to occur, there must be some means by which to mediate and organize an individual's response. Drawing on his neurological expertise, Luria discovered that even the simplest motor reflex requires some afferent feedback to signal that efferent impulses should be discontinued when the needed action has been accomplished. Building on this observation while researching voluntary behavior, Luria noted that experimenters could utilize a contravening movement by a young child in response to verbal commands as the afferent signal to end diffuse motor impulses, but true volition could not occur until the child had developed inner speech and was able to use its semantic aspect as self-generated feedback to end motor impulses. The reader who desires more detail on the role of inner speech in intentionality is referred to Vocate (1987) or Zivin (1979), but the point is that inner speech provides the intervening neurological signal that permits intentionality by freeing consciousness in humans from a direct, isomorphic linkage to naturally occurring phenomena.

As the basic unit of language, the word has two linguistic functions in the reflection of objective reality. The most basic of these, and the first one acquired, is the word's referential function, meaning that it can substitute for an object, act, property, or relationship. As a result of this, humans can expand their functioning to include things that are not present, and transmit knowledge from one person to another. This ability to elicit images apart from the thing permits humans to regulate their perception and memory, and to act internally. Despite the freedom from passivity granted by the referential function, it is the second function of the word that is most significant in the achievement of human consciousness: its abstracting and generalizing function. It is this function that permits the singling out of the essential properties of things, and then generalizes those properties by relating them to other things or properties in a category. Thus, the meaning of the word cannot be limited to its referential function, because one word may have many associations and, as a result, numerous meanings.

Consequently, word meaning, which is internalized in inner speech's semantic set, encompasses all of the associative meanings that are included in the word's semantic field apart from any consideration of syntax. These associations include phonetic, morphological or visual, and conceptual associations and may be drawn from one of two systems: (a) denotative meaning or the stable system of association that is the same for all speakers of a particular language, or (b) connotative meaning or the unique system of relationships and associations that may be salient to a particular speaker in a particular situation. It is my premise that these associations are first accomplished and maintained within the semantic set of inner speech and then are combined in unique ratios for each utterance composed for oneself or others.

Luria saw abstraction and generalization as being the most important function of human thinking, and thus considered the word, because it provides this ability, a "*unit of thought*" (Luria, 1982, p. 38) as well as a unit of language. It is a major principle of Lurian theory (Vocate, 1987) that the evolution of word meaning in ontogenesis parallels the evolution of the capacity of individual consciousness to reflect reality; Luria held that changes in word meaning are accompanied by psychological changes as a result of the word's role in forming mental connections.

Ontogenetically, the most salient characteristic of word meaning is first affect, then concrete image, and then the system of logical connections that stand behind the word. The latter stage of development permits the word to acquire a "paradigmatic" character that refers to the location of its meaning "in an hierarchical system of abstract operations" (Luria, 1982, p. 52). In other words, we all attain a dominance of semantic linkages in the course of our natural development, although the "sense" aspect of inner speech's semantic set continues to preserve the affective and sensory components of meaning, which may be either expressed intentionally, or involuntarily if our cortical tone is reduced by a pathology or a decrease in wakefulness.

> Due to their close ties, the evolution of consciousness follows a path similar to that of word meaning, and we see that during the earliest stage of ontogenesis, consciousness has an affective character. Words, through which the world is reflected, evoke a system of practically actuated connections. It is only at the final stage that consciousness acquires an abstract verbal–logical character, which differs from the earlier stages both in its meaning structure and in psychological processes, although even at this stage the connections that characterize the previous stages are covertly preserved. (Luria, 1982, p. 53)

Thus, the developmental level of an individual's linguistic competency will influence the consciousness that he or she manifests. The fact that differentiation precedes generalization in an individual's mental development has been known for some time, and Luria asserted that "differentiation is characterized by *concretely based thinking*" (Luria, 1982, p. 59). Our initial dependency on concrete personal experience is reflected in Vygotsky's observation that the young child thinks by remembering and the adolescent remembers by thinking (Luria, 1976a). In summary, the level of linguistic (primarily semantic) competency currently achieved by an individual will influence the mental linkages or meaning that can occur in his or her semantic set as well as the subsequent stages of inner speech.

Self-reflexive consciousness and intentionality are impossible without the mediation of inner speech between stimulus and response, and meaning cannot be attributed without the existence of inner speech's semantic set. It follows that none of the various definitions of speech communication describe an activity that could occur without the coding process of inner speech. If that is a valid conclusion, then obviously inner speech constitutes an essential attribute for any theory attempting to explain or predict human communication with any specificity across various situations. Inner speech coding is particularly salient to understanding self-talk, because two of its stages, including the more rudimentary deep structure stage, are sufficient for the occurrence of intrapersonal dialogue, whereas other levels of communication, for example, interpersonal and public, are inadequate if not impossible until thought has progressed to the production of a syntactically expanded external utterance.

INTRAPERSONAL THEORY AND COMPETENCE

Luria frequently criticized Western scholarship for its lack of theory. The criticism is valid in the case of intrapersonal communication studies, which presently reflect an aggregate of relatively gratuitous assertions rather than any integrated theoretical paradigm. The complexity of intrapersonal functioning makes an inductive approach to theory construction problematic in that it could perpetuate current fragmentation. In addition, intrapersonal communication phenomena are not easily observed/measured with current measuring instruments (see Stacks & Sellers, chapter 5, this volume), which renders a data-to-theory approach difficult. Therefore, I think a deductive, or theory-to-data, approach will better serve to organize our research efforts. The verification problem remains, but it is alleviated somewhat by having a logical formulation of what it is that one is attempting to observe and/or measure. This chapter was conceived as an initial step toward developing such an integrated theory.

A coherent deductive theory of human intrapersonal communication would transcend its own focus to inform other crucial areas of interest in the field of communication such as interpersonal competence. Because the inner speech processes of coding and/or dialogue underlie speech communication performance at any level, understanding them better is essential if we are to progress in either explaining or improving communication competence. The study of interpersonal competence to date vividly illustrates the problems of a research area without a unifying theoretical paradigm. A review of the literature (Spitzberg, 1987) reveals that the field has not identified any consistent set of components necessary for competence, or even how the various components that have been identified are interrelated. A lot of time and energy has been devoted to assessing qualities of the "competent" individual while ignoring another integral aspect of communication—the message. The dependence of inner speech's coding process on language could provide us with a touchstone by which to bring some order to our understanding of competence. A knowledge of the semantic and syntactic structuring of inner speech and their affect on self-talk could restore an emphasis on symbolic messages to competence study and integrate it with the currently prevalent stress on individual skills and/or personality traits.

Spitzberg reported on two studies that found that almost 43% of competence variance was explained by motivation. Investigating that could be more feasible if our initial investigation of intentional communication were limited to the three motives of Luria's (1982) view (demand, contact, and concept) rather than trying to encompass an infinite number of possible purposes. Also, if competence were directly connected to the source's intent, then the problem of who is a valid observer of competent behavior would be resolved, and we would not be subjected to the multiplicity of variables on which raters may vary. We know that judgments of "competent" communicative behavior can vary by situation and perceiver. This problem might be eliminated if we began our assessment of competence at the level of inner speech, or at the level of self-talk, when it is relatively context or relationship free. Then we could build a knowledge base about competence from which to assess performance in any context, because all performance is guided by the abilities of inner speech and will be influenced by self-talk if it occurs.

In short, the integrated theory about uniquely human intrapersonal communication presented in this chapter could have widespread ramifications if it serves to increase our understanding of other communicative phenomena that are dependent on the core functioning of inner speech and self-talk.

RESEARCHING SELF-TALK
AND INNER SPEECH

If one concurs that self-talk and inner speech should be studied, the difficult problem of how to do it still remains. If inner speech were, as some believe, structurally limited to words, then we might use vocabulary assessment and argue that such measures are empirical indicators of the semantic relationships of inner speech. No doubt an individual's vocabulary influences the quality of his or her inner speech, but research limited only to vocabulary study is inadequate because inner speech as outlined previously involves constant change, two functions, and is characterized across its three stages by increasingly deliberate semantic and syntactic relationships rather than being limited to a static lexical structure. In other words, such a method would lead us into the problems articulated by Powers, Jordan, and Street (1979) in their assessment of techniques for measuring cognitive complexity. Namely, the "assumption that the constructs present in one's verbalizations of interpersonal impressions represent the constructs present in the cognitive system" (p. 70). Such an approach is based on the fallacious assumption that overt production is isomorphic with the semantic competency of inner speech. The distinction between competence and performance has been articulated by many others, such as childhood language experts, who have pointed out that comprehension in children always exceeds their performance capabilities during language development. To equate vocabulary with the various levels of semantic relationships extant in inner speech is to make that same kind of error of confusing performance and competence.

Remember too, inner speech may be rendered an intentional process by the activation of self-talk at the deep or surface structure stages. Therefore, inner speech could be investigated through a consideration of self-talk because the latter can utilize stages of inner speech not available to us in interpersonal or public communication data. Self-talk, of course, is a phenomenon worthy of study on its own merits because its dialogue shapes all intentional discourse. Methodologies that can be employed to study either inner speech or self-talk are discussed in other chapters in this text.

SUMMARY

Talk is the quintessence of human communication, and on the intrapersonal level it entails both self-talk and inner speech, which are not identical phenomena, and neither is simply thinking. Inner speech's coding process is the competency that underlies the performance of human communication at any level. It utilizes the multiplicity of meanings internalized from social interactions, both those inherent in the culture and those derived from the personal experience of the self, to build thought into the communicative form of verbal thought.

Inner speech coding is dynamic and processual in nature but never communicative. Self-talk, on the other hand, involves a dialogue between elements of the self—"I" and "Me," "Ego" and "non-Ego," or individual and culture. Its communication also may constitute a dialectic between subjective and objective meanings— Vygotsky's "sense" and "meaning"—which produces a synthesis that still retains elements of both. Inner speech in its semantic set stage embodies both natural sign and symbolic meanings as well as both idiosyncratic meanings and cultural meanings. These pure meanings must progress in consolidation to at least the deep structure stage of inner speech before they have a symbolic form that can be used to respond to the self in internal or external dialogue. Of course, the surface structure stage of inner speech and beyond that, the expanded, external utterance itself could also be used for self-talk, but the deep structure stage is minimal for self-talk to occur. The point of contrast is that inner speech coding can be devoid of syntax in its first stage whereas self-talk, in order to accomplish its communicative purpose, must have some degree of syntactic ordering or structure.

Inner speech's semantic set, therefore, is closer to pure thought than self-talk and requires no self-awareness to occur. The syntactic ordering of the later stages of inner speech also can take place in an automatic fashion without any monitoring by the self. The mere process of incorporating more syntactic structure mandates an incorporation of more denotative meaning without the individual's intent. One can via self-talk, however, intervene in the process and actively determine the ratio of subjective and objective meaning that will occur in a specific message. It should be noted that although the discussion throughout this chapter has focused on the coding process, the same inner speech process in reverse is involved in decoding a received message. In other words, one can *intentionally* decide to be more or less egocentric in encoding one's message, or in decoding the message of another via self-talk. On the other hand, if no self-talk is utilized in preparing or receiving a message, then the communicator is left with the happenstance ratio of subjective/objective meaning resulting from passive coding or decoding. No deliberate decentering or consideration of other perspectives (monitoring by the "Me") occurs, and one enacts a "noble self" communication style with its attendant social insensitivity or misunderstandings. A similar passive coding process occurs during the stage of childhood speech known as egocentric speech, which developmentally precedes the reflective consciousness of self-talk, which is not yet available to the child.

Adult self-talk, in contrast to inner speech coding and childhood egocentric speech, requires sufficient self-awareness to treat the self as an object that one addresses or to which one responds. Consequently, self-talk may vary qualitatively as to the degree of decentering or movement away from an egocentric perspective, but it must have a minimal level of self-awareness in order to exist. It is this inherent self-awareness of self-talk that should facilitate our further investigation of its functioning and/or that of inner speech, and subsequently permit us to improve our performance as human communicators.

REFERENCES

Aarsleff, H. (1988). Introduction. In W. von Humboldt, *On language: The diversity of human language-structure and its influence on the mental development of mankind* (P. Heath, Trans.). Cambridge: Cambridge University Press. (Original work published 1836)

Chautauqua: Mindfulness-mindlessness and communication. (1992). *Communication Monographs, 59*(3), 288–327.

Cunningham, S. B. (1989). Defining intrapersonal communication. In C. V. Roberts, K. W. Watson, & L. L. Barker (Eds.), *Intrapersonal communication processes: Original essays* (pp. 82–94). New Orleans: SPECTRA.

Dance, F. E. X. (1979). Acoustic trigger to conceptualization: A hypothesis concerning the role of the spoken word in the development of higher mental processes. *Health Communication Informaties, 5*, 203–213.

Dance, F. E. X. (1990, March). *A taxonomy of primitive terms for a speech theory of communication.* Unpublished taxonomy.

Dance, F. E. X., & Larson, C. E. (1976). *The functions of human communication: A theoretical approach.* New York: Holt, Rinehart & Winston.

Faules, D. F., & Alexander, D. C. (1978). *Communication and social behavior: A symbolic interaction perspective.* Reading, MA: Addison-Wesley.

Festinger, L. (1957). *A story of cognitive dissonance.* Stanford, CA: Stanford University Press.

Fisher, B. A. (1978). *Perspectives on human communication.* New York: MacMillan.

Hale, C. (1980). Cognitive complexity-simplicity as a determinant of communicative effectiveness. *Communication Monographs, 47*(4), 304–311.

Hart, R. P., Carlson, R. E., & Eadie, W. F. (1980). Attitudes toward communication and the assessment of rhetorical sensitivity. *Communication Monographs, 47*(1), 1–22.

Hewes, D. E., & Evans, D. (1978). Three theories of egocentric speech: A contrastive analysis. *Communication Monographs, 45*(1), 18–32.

Johnson, J. R. (1981, November). *Spoken language and Vygotsky and Sokolov's concept of inner speech.* Paper presented at the meeting of the national Speech Communication Association, Anaheim, CA.

John-Steiner, V. (1985). *Notebooks of the mind: Explorations of thinking.* Albuquerque, NM: University of New Mexico Press.

Kozulin, A. (1990). *Vygotsky's psychology: A biography of ideas.* Cambridge, MA: Harvard University Press.

Langer, E. (1992). Interpersonal mindlessness and language. *Communication Monographs, 59*(3), 324–327.

Langer, S. K. (1972). *Mind: An essay on human feeling* (Vol. 2). Baltimore, MD: Johns Hopkins University Press.

Luria, A. R. (1931). Psychological expedition to Central Asia. *Science, 74*(1920), 383–384.

Luria, A. R. (1933). The second psychological expedition to Central Asia. *Science, 78*(2018), 191–192.

Luria, A. R. (1957). The role of language in the formation of temporary connections. In B. Simon (Ed.), *Psychology in the Soviet Union* (pp. 115–129). Stanford: Stanford University Press.

Luria, A. R. (1959a). The directive function of speech in development and dissolution: Part I: Development of the directive function of speech in early childhood. *Word, 15*(2), 341–352.

Luria, A. R. (1959b). The directive function of speech in development and dissolution: Part II: Dissolution of the regulative function of speech in pathological states of the brain. *Word, 15*(3), 453–464.

Luria, A. R. (1960a). Experimental analysis of the development of voluntary action in children. In

H. P. David & J. C. Brengelmann (Eds.), *Perspectives in personality research* (pp. 139–149). New York: Springer.

Luria, A. R. (1960b). Verbal regulation of behavior. In M. A. B. Brazier (Ed.), *The central nervous system and behavior: Transactions of the third conference February 21, 22, 23, and 24, 1960, Princeton, NJ* (pp. 359–423). New York: Josiah Macy, Jr. Foundation.

Luria, A. R. (1961a). The genesis of voluntary movements. In N. O'Connor (Ed.), *Recent Soviet Psychology* (pp. 165–185). New York: Liveright.

Luria, A. R. (1961b). *The role of speech in the regulation of normal and abnormal behavior.* J. Tizard (Ed.). New York: Liveright.

Luria, A. R. (1963). The role of speech in the formation of temporary connections and the regulation of behaviour in the normal and oligophrenic child. In B. Simon & J. Simon (Eds.), *Educational psychology in the U.S.S.R.* (pp. 83–97). Stanford: Stanford University Press.

Luria, A. R. (1967). The regulative function of speech in its development and dissolution. In K. Salzinger & S. Salzinger (Eds.), *Research in verbal behavior and some neurophysiological implications* (pp. 405–481). New York: Academic Press.

Luria, A. R. (1973). *The working brain: An introduction to neuropsychology.* New York: Basic Books.

Luria, A. R. (1976a). *Basic problems of neurolinguistics.* The Hague: Mouton.

Luria, A. R. (1976b). *Cognitive development: Its cultural and social foundations.* Cambridge, MA: Harvard University Press.

Luria, A. R. (1979). *The making of mind: A personal account of Soviet psychology.* M. Cole & S. Cole (Eds.). Cambridge, MA: Harvard University Press.

Luria, A. R. (1982). *Language and Cognition.* J. V. Wertsch (Ed.). New York: Wiley.

Luria, A. R., & Yudovich, F. (1959). *Speech and development of mental processes in the child.* J. Simon (Ed.). London: Staples Press.

Mead, G. H. (1934). Mind, self, & society: From the standpoint of a social behaviorist. C. W. Morris (Ed.). Chicago: University of Chicago Press.

Mead, G. H. (1982). *The individual and the social self: Unpublished work of George Herbert Mead.* D. L. Miller (Ed.). Chicago: University of Chicago Press.

Powers, W. G., Jordan, W. J., & Street, R. L. (1979). Language indices in the measurement of cognitive complexity: Is complexity loquacity? *Human Communication Research, 6*(1), 69–73.

Roberts, C., Edwards, R., & Barker, L. (1987). *Intrapersonal communication processes.* Scottsdale, AZ: Gorsuch Scarisbrick.

Searle, J. R. (1969). *Speech acts: An essay in the philosophy of language.* Cambridge: Cambridge University Press.

Spitzberg, B. H. (1987). Issues in the study of communicative competence. In B. Dervin & M. J. Voigt (Eds.), *Progress in communication sciences* (Vol. 8, pp. 1–46). Norwood, NJ: Ablex.

Valsiner, J., & Van der Veer, R. (1988). On the social nature of human cognition: An analysis of the shared intellectual roots of George Herbert Mead and Lev Vygotsky. *Journal for the Theory of Social Behavior, 18*(1), 117–136.

Van der Veer, R. (1987a). The relation between Vygotsky and Mead reconsidered: A comment on Glock. *Studies in Soviet Thought, 34,* 91–93.

Van der Veer, R. (1987b). Review of *Thought and language.* Lev S. Vygotsky (newly revised, translated, and edited by A. Kozulin). Cambridge, MA: MIT Press. *The Journal of Mind and Behavior, 8,* 175–178.

Van der Veer, R., & Valsiner, J. (1988). Lev Vygotsky and Pierre Janet: On the origin of the concept of sociogenesis. *Developmental Review, 8,* 52–65.

Vocate, D. R. (1987). *The theory of A. R. Luria: Functions of spoken language in the development of higher mental processes.* Hillsdale, NJ: Lawrence Erlbaum Associates.

Von Humboldt, W. (1988). *On language: The diversity of human language-structure and its influence on the mental development of mankind* (P. Heath, Trans.). Cambridge: Cambridge University Press. (Original work published 1836)

Vygotsky, L. S. (1966). Development of the higher mental functions. In A. Leontyev, A. R. Luriya, & A. Smirnov (Eds.), *Psychological research in the U.S.S.R.* (pp. 11–45). Moscow: Progress Publishers.

Vygotsky, L. S. (1978). *Mind in society: The development of higher psychological processes* (M. Cole, V. John-Steiner, S. Scribner, & E. Souberman, Eds.). Cambridge, MA: Harvard University Press.

Vygotsky, L. S. (1986). *Thought and language* (A. Kozulin, Ed. and Trans.). Cambridge, MA: MIT Press. (Original work published 1934).

Vygotsky, L. S. (1987). *The collected works of L. S. Vygotsky: Vol. I: Problems of general psychology* (R. W. Rieber & A. S. Carlton, Eds., N. Minick, Trans.). New York: Plenum.

Vygotsky, L. S., & Luria, A. R. (1930). The function and fate of egocentric speech. Proceedings of the *Ninth International Congress of Psychology: Proceedings and Papers—New Haven, September 1–7, 1929* (pp. 464–465). Princeton, NJ: The Psychological Review Company.

Watzlawick, P., Beavin, J., & Jackson, D. (1967). *Pragmatics of human communication: A study of interactional patterns, pathologies, and paradoxes.* New York: Norton.

Wertsch, J. V. (1980). The significance of dialogue in Vygotsky's account of social, egocentric, and inner speech. *Contemporary Educational Psychology, 5,* 150–162.

Zivin, G. (Ed.). (1979). *The development of self-regulation through private speech.* New York: Wiley.

2 Phylogenesis: Understanding the Biological Origins of Intrapersonal Communication

Samuel C. Riccillo
University of Texas at El Paso

It seems somewhat premature to label a chapter on the origins of communication and a specific level called intrapersonal with the term *phylogenesis*. Phylogenesis suggests a family history that documents succeeding lines of decendency emerging with each successive generation. The epistemology of phylogeny suggests that a systematic change through adaptation or selection yields a set of characteristics or properties that can be at once identified and demonstrated. Within that same epistemology also exists the inference that the selective pressures for such changes were easily identifiable and complete. The notion of origins, or the completion of a natural history (Plotkin, 1982), has always been a preoccupation of serious scholars; almost all histories of various cultures possess accounts of the antecedent conditions for the capacities of the human organism (Hamilton & Moser, 1988).

For Western thought, the biological origin of communication may be viewed within three prevailing theories: (a) the Darwinian view that selective pressures and adaptive structures changed over time, thereby allowing more complex adaptive organisms to survive; (b) the creationist's view that some divine intervention took place, by some divine being causing those characteristics commonly associated with humanness; or (c) the Claddist or Agnostic claim that neither of the previous positions for origins is complete, for neither a direct line of descendence nor a divine cause has been demonstrated. Yet phylogenetic scholarship requirements push us toward a search for verifiable evidence from the hard sciences.

The falsification of the major tenet of evolution, that is that all organisms have parents, has not occurred thus far because no organism has been discovered to date that has not had a parent or parents as its antecedent. We may not know many of the antecedents as yet, but the work for each species under consideration is continuing vigorously in biology (Bowler, 1989). For communication theorists, although the issue may be premature, establishing parameters for a biological perspective is essential for theory development on a hard science base. A biological perspective can make extensions from selective systems present in other mammals. It can also provide points of departure for change in anatomical, physiological, neural, and of course cultural features, that suggest a relationship to antecedent structures in other species (Delbruck, 1986; Lenneberg, 1967; Pribram, 1971).

Although evolutionary theory cannot give a clean line of ancestry for the human communication system, it does provide an epistemology from which to explore, describe, and perhaps falsify the proposition that some line of descent exists for the many similarities and differences among living organisms. Whether from fossil or from mitochondrial DNA, the origin and development of specific structures provides a data base for comparisons as well as numerous hypotheses to falsify. It is important to note that empirical investigations of origins, particularly those involving humans, are not complete, and that investigations will continue as new structures are discovered for some time to come. Therefore, one need not be overly concerned with the inconclusive debates between Johansen and the Leakeys as to which lineage Lucy may fall into, for that debate promises to continue. For communication scholars, our concern must focus on how we have developed and extended the communication process. What characteristics have we inherited from our varied ancestry? What biological features emerged as a result of adaptation or natural selection? These questions can only be answered by the examination of anatomy, physiology, and neural structures that we use to communicate.

There are a variety of biological structures, such as anatomic features and neural mechanisms, that may influence the origins of intrapersonal communication. In particular, I attempt to identify the common set of structures that can be associated with communication in general, and more specifically the means or functions of communicating that developed from selective pressures and adaptations in a biological frame.

Taking a biological perspective, I cannot help but note the relevance of biology to key concepts in the discipline of communication. We are confronted today with an "information age," a concept that has been widely used to describe the current impact of technology on the human nervous system (McLuhan & McLuhan, 1986). And yet the very etymological basis of this concept has yet to be explored in any detail. The very word "in-form," implies the activity of creating some structural relationship between what is external, and taking whatever that is and making it internal: hence, "in-forming." Ultimately, what form is taken in, and the selective processing of any stimuli, is an internal process involving neurosocial interaction. There are, consequently, transformations accomplished by the interaction of biological structures with sociocultural structures. This chapter is too brief in extent to provide a lengthy review of this process of "in-forming." It will focus instead on those biological structures that are characteristic of the species and necessary to accomplish such interactions.

There are several important phylogenetic features that need clarification in order to understand how the human organism accomplishes complex interactions. The most obvious are those features tied to maturation and other developmental patterns necessary for communicative acts. Many are not present at birth but emerge on a biological time scale. Many of these are accomplished, of course, through speech and language. This chapter examines the process of communication, and intrapersonal communication in particular, reviewing the phylogenetic history of those characteristics that have evolved and can be considered a part of the natural history of the species.

INTRAPERSONAL COMMUNICATION:
A BIOLOGICAL PERSPECTIVE

It has been theorized that communication occurs simultaneously at multiple levels in the organism, and in multiple systems, while at the same time being viewed as central to the overt activity of the organism. In general, communication theory has numerous theorists (Berlo, 1960; Dance, 1967; Ruben, 1988) that have constructed arguments for the existence of levels of communication. Generally defined, a *level* is a point of observation from which to view or hypothesize about the activity labelled communication. The communication process may be seen as occurring either internally, externally, or both. Whether considered from the level of the cell or from the level of complex interactions mediated by electronic systems, intrapersonal communication has been viewed as an activity that is processed internally with various levels of awareness or consciousness. Yet it may occur simultaneously with external manifestations of communication behavior such as those occurring at the interpersonal or public levels.

Intrapersonal communication can be operationalized as a process involving the activity of the individual biological organism's capacity to coordinate and organize complex actions of an intentional nature. This activity occurs as a result of the long complex interaction of the organism's biologically endowed systems of perception and sensation with its complex sociocultural environment. For the human organism, such complex interactions are anchored in the signalling processes known as symbolic languages. In the epistemology of the communication field, these signalling characteristics have been operationalized further as signs and symbols (Cronkite, 1986; Dance & Larson, 1972).

These efforts to operationalize the biological and socio-cultural interaction resulted from observing the functioning of complex systems and the subsequent outcomes of these systems in both actions and artifacts. These actions include the initial vocalizations in the precognitive/prelinguistic period that are taken as indicators of language emergence. They also appear as resultant actions or movements in relation to utterances directed toward the organism during the same developmental period. These outcomes become dependent on symbolic systems, language in particular, but require a biological base to occur. It is well accepted in the literature that the capacity to organize and coordinate these processes is governed by an internalized symbolic system (Lempert & Kinsbourne, 1985; Piaget, 1970; Vygotsky, 1962). The outcomes involve overt behavior associated with neuromotor operations that eventually become internalized (Sokolov, 1972; Vygotsky, 1962). The outcomes are also dependent on those emergent operations such as attention, cognitive stages, phonation and articulation, and various language acquisition specifics characterized in the developmental literature (Bates, Bretherton, Shore, & McNew, 1983). These outcomes seem to be operating on the complex emerging biological systems in the organism and also seem to be influenced by the sociocultural activity outside the organism. The organization and coordination of the internal systems rely on the external environment progressing from quite simple reflexive operations to more coordinated operations as the organism progresses along a defined biological timetable. These complex organismic actions result in formal operations characterized as language and thought.

Bronowski (1978) characterized human communication systems as having the capacity for reconstitution and internalization of the external environment. One of the key functions for this operation is the organism's capacity to monitor with existing sensory motor operations the production and reception of this process. We are able to see ourselves as if we are part of the outside world. An additional product in this process is what Bronowski labels, in his evolutionary view, the "prolongation of reference." It is directly tied to the physical characteristics of speech. It is a reference to time, both in the production and reception of signaling, which grants a capacity to the species to transcend time. It includes a reflective capacity to be preoccupied with not only the present, but also to be able to reflect on the past and anticipate the future.

I have often characterized the nature of time in utterances called "sentences" as having a biological dependence. The etymology of "sentence" has two root words based on the physiological properties of acoustics: sensation and time, hence sensation plus tense. There is a remarkably slow response by humans to their signalling system; this response relies on acoustic energy so that in the production and reception of the signal, ample time is present for both cognition and affect. The processing time for these mental and emotional communicative operations also provides the opportunity for the individual organism to carry on an internal dialogue: intrapersonal communication. "Human beings have a wholly unique gift in the use of language, and that is that they can talk to themselves. Everybody does it, all the time" (Bronowski, 1978, p. 35). Implied in Bronowski's statement is a view of talk and thought being interrelated. We internalize our talk for reflection through our speaking and hearing operations. We reconstitute our thought through an internal dialogue with ourselves. Our external modal systems enhance and organize our thought for internal self reflection.

The individual organism internalizes symbols together with experience acquired through the senses. Each organism reconstitutes this experience symbolically through sociocultural interaction. Whereas there are disagreements in some operational accounts of various theorists, there is a general acceptance of Piaget's and Vygotsky's view that overt action is fundamental to the evolution of language in general as a symbolic system. The developmental literature seems to confirm that children's first words are tied to action or behavior. The action or behavior of children rests on the emergence of the human communicative system rooted not only in visual and tactile stimuli, but also in an acoustic, aural, and oral environment.

The biological structures present in the human organism that accomplish human communication are a direct result of selective pressures and adaptations of sensory motor operations and anatomical adaptations. Although each biological system contributes to the communicative process, the most significant of these are associated with the capacity to hear and speak. It is the convergence of such systems that becomes essential to the phylogenetic scheme. As yet not all of these system's roles are integrated theoretically, many roles being assumed under labels such as "prelinguistic or precognitive" actions in the communicative process. But intrapersonal theorists wishing to comprehend the sophistication of this scheme and its structures must begin to integrate those observations into our theories. For communication scholars, in my opinion, the most fertile issue is one focused on how the organism has acquired the intrapersonal communication process and developed a set of behaviors that can be attributed to biological inheritance or genetic factors. If one follows this path of research, one is directed toward the question of what is genetic and inherited versus what is sociocultural and acquired from the environment. This type of investigation requires an examination of ontological and epistemological assumptions before it is undertaken. Theorists must confront the underlying assumptions about "reality" and how reality is characterized in their theories. When we refer to internal or external activity, do we treat these references as related to one another or separate from one another, such as a Cartesian division of mind and body? When we make knowledge claims such as "communication is a process," what do we accept as evidence for our claims? Both reality assumptions and knowledge claims need clarification.

Ontological Assumptions

Bronowski was quoted earlier as making the observation that a uniquely human behavior is talking to one's self. It is both common to talk to one's self and also to reflect upon that "conversation." There has been some common concern among theorists of communication processes about whether or not stretching the concept of communication to this internal level distorts the fundamental tenets of theory construction (Infante, Rancer, & Womack, 1990). Although quoting Cronkite (1986)— that human symbolic activity defines communication—these theorists exclude intrapersonal processes on the grounds that it could distort the characteristic of intentionality. The assumption here is that communication is primarily social and interpersonal. The justification of this point rests on the assertion that if one views communication as having descriptive adequacy for more than social interaction, one level of observation, the concept is extended too far and becomes meaningless. In response, I must note that the attributes of communication in general should be functional from multiple perspectives in order to be metatheoretically adequate to explain the phenomenon. In biology, for example, micro and macro perspectives are permitted as observations of reality. Similarly, depending on one's level of observation, sender, receiver, message, and channel in communication can be used to indicate a multiple perspective about the process of interaction.

Pribram (1986) devoted considerable attention to a new ontological perspective he called "neutral monism" (this concept will be explained in greater detail later).

He suggested that any attempt to explore complex human behavior would need to consider such a position or face the philosophical entanglements often associated with dualism. For communication scholars to argue from a monistic perspective that communication occurs only in a social perspective, that is defined as interactive and involving another human being, reduces the acceptance of observations about the phenomenon to only those that involve at least two people exchanging messages of one kind or another in a particular context. Asserting the existence of a self or mind under such constraints of scope would necessitate the observation of a phenomenal experience that exists independent of observation, while relying on the consensual validation of others who may have had the same experience. These two observations provide information viewed on the one hand as objective, having to do with matter; and viewed on the other as subjective and having to do with mind. A classic dualism is raised that inevitably restricts our conception of reality.

Similarly, descriptions from a phylogenetic perspective alone utilize observations of a biological nature and lead to dualism also (Brown, 1978). Neither a materialistic nor a mentalistic view of reality alone can sustain for long a position that is truly adequate for holistic descriptions of human behavior. Delbruck (1986) devoted his final lectures at Berkeley to trying to resolve these ontological issues. He noted that phylogenetic descriptions of DNA and RNA, anatomy and physiology, neural transmitters and brain organization all have something to do with the evolution of mind from matter (the title of his text was *Mind From Matter*), but all are inadequate explanations. Ontological claims about the object of reference and the object of experience thus present many complex issues. Many of these biological characterizations rest on fundamental ontological assumptions in physics (Capra, 1975).

The observations made from a biological perspective tend to rely on primarily physiological data. Descriptions of various neural and physiological mechanisms seem far away from descriptions of symbolic systems and mentalistic or cognitive structures. These descriptions too, often create a dualism that is irreconcilable. For example, Rosenbleuth (1970), in order to explain neural activity, created a philosophical position called "parallelism," with mind and body on two separate planes. Physiological data about the activity of the brain was correlated with specific cognitive activity or other mental processes. The data was relational, that is, as specific cognitive tasks were given subjects, corresponding physiological data were recorded as having occurred simultaneously. He asserted the existence of a mentalistic phenomenon, and at the same time he accounted for the materialistic processes of the brain. He stated that "we invent or postulate a material universe in order to rationalize our perceptions. The universe is necessarily anthropomorphic in the sense that it has to adjust to the mental processes (perceptions and inferences) through which we judge its structure" (p. 115). Rosenblueth's ontological assumptions were deliberately dualistic. He admitted a cognitive reality, and accounted for its existence on a separate plane from materialism.

To bridge the gap between dualism, phenomenal versus material, Pribram (1971, 1986) devised a structural realism that transcends the ontological assumptions of material or mechanistic determinism. He called his perspective neutral monism: Mind is a structure of neural data. Mentality is structured and developed in a stepwise progression through brain processes. The primary structures are the resultant outcomes of "communicative acts," interactions between language and culture. Pribram asserted that humans can distinguish clearly between the process of experiencing and the contents of that experience. He identified the very act of perception as akin to the matter–energy transfer process in modern physics. Matter and energy are not identical, but matter is constituted of energy. These transformations of material experience in the process of perception are routine. Each receptor organism is converting sound waves and light waves on a regular basis. The experience of such conversions is a matter–energy transform. It is the configurations of these minute energy systems that organize the basis of experience that each living organism encounters. Both phenomenal experience as well as reductive materialist perspectives are required for this position. Pribram (1986) said the following:

> I propose that dualism can be transcended by carefully combining the techniques and results of both the reductive and the phenomenal approaches to enquiry. Structure having been made the central and enduring, single quality of a pluralistic monism, both reductive entities and phenomena are seen as realizations of identical structures derived from a more basic existential given. (p. 518)

In other words, by working from both perspectives, the world of personal experience and reductive materialism can be made to converge into a single perspective of descriptions of similar phenomenon. Experience begins with the senses and is often thought of as an imposition of order or structure from the mind. In this case, the grouping of sensations through spectral arrays provides a perspective of reality for each procedural view. The grouping, sorting activity of the brain provides a basis for a realism that accounts for both positions. The mind and body from this ontological perspective are not viewed as separate entities, but rather transform back and forth in structure via a matter–energy transform. Both mental and material observations of similar phenomena are viewed as complimentary and not antagonistic from a neutral monistic perspective. The view taken for a phylogenetic perspective presumes this ontogenetic position.

Epistemology

Any phylogenetic review of biological origins has to be concerned with basic observations of change over time. What constitutes knowledge from this perspective has several epistemic bases. Most perspectives of change accounting for a given adaptation ultimately rest on the reductionistic perspective of what constitutes the most simple or primitive organized form of life, the cell. One result is that the 20th century has been embroiled in a controversy over whether or not all life forms are reducible to their basic DNA–RNA structures. Advocates for this position would assert that cellular arrangement into more complex systems has been the result of continual evolutionary changes resulting from selective pressures. In this process, some organized systems failed to adapt to changing environmental pressures, which resulted in their eventual extinction. Such a view of the cellular level developed out of the early comparative work of Darwin and has enjoyed its share of controversy (Bowler, 1989).

The wealth of information present today regarding various adaptations about human evolution is overwhelming. For example, the research regarding anatomical divergence has focused on the emergence of bipedalism for upright walking behavior and raised new issues for classification of lines of decent (Johansen and Shreeve, 1989). At the cellular level, the issue of cellular communication (Stendt, 1972) is both informative and directive. In fact this data becomes the basis for much of our definitional notions of life itself. Cellular change and evolvement have at least three time schemes in their genetic time table: (a) cellular activation is almost immediate, (b) DNA/RNA in the developing fetus requires 9 months, and (c) hormonal emergence may be on a sequential schedule and appear at different periods of lifelong development. The size, shape, and capacity of human-like skulls has raised various issues about brain function, where no evidence of the brain itself is involved (Crelin, 1987). What becomes accepted as "knowledge" derived from the many disciplines that have contributed to phylogenetic theorizing has not yet been integrated into any unified whole. Most biological evidence rests on what has been systematically inherited, namely genes, and whether or not there is a transference of these characteristics to the offspring that follow (Wilson, 1983). The claim that the origin of the human race resides in ancestry traceable to an African origin has been recently challenged by two replicative studies of the original genes in the recent issue of *Science* (Templeton, 1992; Hedges et al., 1992).

Rather than the cell, the focus of research on the phylogenesis of human communication has been directed toward those communicative mechanisms that reveal their epistemic roots in behavior associated with specific communication features or morphologies (Edelman, 1992; Lenneberg, 1967). Morphologies are specific structures that allow the organism to perceive stimuli from its environment; or coordinated actions that allow the organism to signal other organisms in its environment. Most theorists have adopted developmental perspectives at different points in time. Many have also embraced Earnst Haeckle's theorem regarding the systematic emergence of select behaviors that provide descriptions of the relationship of phylogenetic or family inheritance of species-specific behaviors to individual development. This acceptance is due in part to the lack of fossil evidence to sustain comparisons of change. The Haeckle proposition for discovering biological evolution is one that is easily falsifiable and provides both predictive and explanative power.

Haeckle asserted that ontogeny is a brief, rapid recapitulation of phylogeny. In essence, this proposition asserts that in the development of an organism from its infancy to adult maturation, a resume is manifested of those selected features that resulted from selective pressures confronting the species. The list of features should provide a history of what the family or phylum contains. From this list, hypotheses are constructed about the phylum's genetic code and adaptation strategies.

Recapitulation in the ontogeny of a given species thus suggests that if one systematically observes the development of the single organism (or a group in the same time period), the observer should be able to record changes in selected features or behaviors from which to construct this species' natural history. The record of the observations should yield a cladistic account of those behaviors and some step-wise progression of the change to a preferred selected behavior from some other less adaptive structure, which will provide an advantage for survival. It should also yield a description of what behaviors tend to be culturally dependent and delineate the variation that exists from one culture to the next. Such an epistemic base requires one to work systemically to tease out those structures that can indicate choices for various complex mechanisms. In the case of the human species, this process becomes a time-consuming exploration that usually is slower to produce results than observations of less sophisticated or less complex organisms. For human evolution, the complexity in both structure and function is at times overwhelming. Selecting a set of behaviors and recording their structure and function can precipitate extensive and often confounding consequences. In the case of communication as a main phenomenon, this exploration can be both hazardous and rewarding.

The epistemic record of the many fields reporting research on the biological origins is becoming almost voluminous and unmanageable. Anthropologists, geneticists, linguists, ethologists, and neuroscientists have all made contributions to the productivity of various conceptualizations. They have also contributed to a variety of controversies, fueling feuds regarding the nature/nurture controversy. What one chooses as a phenomenon to investigate is tied directly to various knowledge claims. For human communication, it has been theorized that selective pressures have been responsible for the distinctive neural features of the brain and the anatomical features of audition and vocalization. Both are used interactively in a common observable communicative behavior called speech and its necessary perceptual counterpart called audition or hearing.

In some circles, epistemic arguments targeted speech as performance and removed it as a distinctively human process. These arguments attempted to identify speech in some cases as an overlaid function operating as a convenience for the production of language (Chomsky, 1968; Dance, 1982; Gardner & Gardner, 1969; Lenneberg, 1967; Routhier, 1979). Arguments have been raised on both sides as to whether or not it is significant that a language is spoken. Selective pressures for most of these arguments were primarily sociocultural in nature. In the case of the Gardners (1969), for example, the primary purpose was to show a direct line of descendence to our mammalian cousin, the chimpanzee. Knowing that chimpanzees would not be able to use aural/oral systems, they attempted to teach a chip sign language by operant conditioning. The research direction was not to start with ontogenetic behavior and corresponding mechanisms associated with chimp behavior, but to rush into comparisons about language acquisition for which many of the underlying and emergent adult chimp behaviors had not been adequately researched from a biological perspective. There is still a residue and a large list of hypotheses that need falsification.

The most controversial hypothesis is one identified as the innate language-acquisition device theorized to be located in the neural mass of the brain (Chomsky, 1967). With the removal of speech, a behavioral, performative noncompetence in the rational dualism of Chomsky and others, performance or behavior was relegated to a second-rate concern, or omitted entirely. In fact, for communication theorists, sociocultural features of the communicative process required an extension of the mentalistic concept of competence to account for context variations that produced a communicative competence (Hymes, 1971; Riccillo, 1982). With a syntactical rule base for linguistic competence, Chomsky left the speaker with little or nothing to say, no message, just syntactical form in the various contexts in which a speaker of a language has to function. Attention was focused on competence, not performance or action. Little attention then was paid to the overwhelming fact that almost all human languages are spoken and heard. Nor was much attention paid to the role that speech or listening might play in the acquisition and development of various language functions. If there is an innate language-acquisition device, it would certainly have to be associated with biological structures and emerge in the many sociocultural contexts of human interaction.

The issue of syntax, or grammar, as a universal having a specific center in the brain may be more of an ontogenetic characteristic than a phylogenetic one (Lieberman, 1991; Piaget, 1970). Delbruck (1986) hypothesized that there are two kinds of learning: ontogenetic and phylogenetic. A phylogenetic example would be that during the course of evolution, the human organism has evolved sophisticated machinery for perceiving the real world. This is primarily associated with the change in vision, in which the organism was exposed to a variety of signals affecting the neurophysiological processes in each hemisphere, and interhemispheric consensus was achieved via the emergence of the corpus callosum. This structural change was probably due to selective pressures and the resultant neurostructures were altered in the brains of our ancestors. The corpus callosum was then inherited as part of our neurostructures. In ontogenetic learning, various species acquire characteristics that are primarily concerned with specific cultural, linguistic, and scientific knowledge. This type of learning is not transmitted via genetic endowment to succeeding generations. The more appropriate question regarding language than the innate language-acquisition device from a phylogenetic perspective might be what interhemispheric relationships could account for the capacity to produce nominalization and predication in human language systems?

Phylogenetic knowledge, such as understanding the hearing/speech process, requires a careful observation of biological mechanisms along with the corresponding genetic factors associated with them. This does not mean that the theorizing about mentalistic generative cognitive grammers was not important; quite the contrary. It worked to solidify the effort to find those areas of theorized "competence" that might indicate the structures supporting the evolution of a human language (Pribram, 1971). More specifically, the developmental research of Menyuk (1971) and others has clarified several important characteristics in the ontogenetic development of language: (a) that comprehension precedes production because the speech apparatus lags behind in development; (b) that phonological development proceeds in accordance with the control of the tongue and other physiological structures, developing from the back vowels sounds in the rear of the oral cavity to the front vowels; and (c) that sophistication in grammatical structures and complex sentences can be correlated with age and, hence, development of the brain. Clearly, the process cannot be accelerated and must also be on a biological timetable not unlike those identified by Stendt (1972) mentioned earlier. It should be quite obvious that a phylogenetic perspective involving the role of aural/oral perception and production, as well as related brain mechanisms, is critical to the development of a phylogenetic base for human communication theory. If comprehension precedes production because of a biological delay in development, then intrapersonal processes for acoustic analysis of sounds and development of discrimination for phonological pairs of sounds necessary to create phonemes are proceeding in the development of critical listening skills. If lexical development for labelling objects in one's environment proceeds in a stepwise progression from objects, nouns, to action words or verbs, then significant intrapersonal development is occurring regarding the organization of perceptual and cognitive categories. Thus a biological perspective becomes essential in describing the phylogenesis of human communication at various levels of the organism.

We have reviewed two important perspectives necessary for understanding phylogenesis: an ontological perspective that asserts that our view of reality is "neutral monistic" and not Cartesian; and, an epistemological one that identifies those kinds of knowledge claims associated with the biological sciences. In the next section, I identify those phylogenetic factors that contribute to our understanding of the intrapersonal process at this time.

A PHYLOGENETIC BASIS
FOR INTRAPERSONAL COMMUNICATION

Although nearly 99% of our DNA/RNA is similar to that of chimpanzees, our structural morphology is different. Our physical features do not resemble theirs, nor do we behave in a manner that can be perceived as isomorphic. Edelman (1992) asserted that the gene-level similarities do not account for the variation in morphological structures that is obvious in the performance of human behavior. The shape, size, and structure of human cells, organs, and tissue are of primary importance in evolution, and it is this "morphogenesis," Edelman theorized, that shapes the natural selection and sustains the development of the species. In the next sections, we examine those anatomical speech mechanisms, auditory features, and neurological features that can be attributed to morphogenesis. These changes in structure comprise the phylogenetic basis of the human communication process as we currently understand it.

There is a proposition that exists in my own ontological assumption for this paper: "homo loquens ergo homo sapiens" (The speaking organism therefore the wise organism). We are an articulate mammal, with anatomical features for the production and reception of aural/oral language that allow us to communicate and organize our existence in a "wise" manner. It is an obvious structural deviation from our nearest known ancestors. Although sharing nearly 99% of our gene pool with another species, the arrangement and choices of the display of our genetic features, morphogenesis, becomes a primary concern. Both Delbruck (1986) and Edelman (1992) asserted that the morphology of structures associated with various biological structures of the human organism is responsible for our structural and behavioral differences. This suggests that in the phylogeny of human behavior, the pursuit of understanding morphological characteristics for communication behavior play a central role in understanding adaptation. Our overt behavior, speaking, is tied intricately to our covert behavior, thinking. Although we do not have a complete understanding of all of the relationships that exist between our overt actions, we are beginning to understand how these actions are intricately tied to the processes in our brain that resulted from selective pressures in our environment. Crelin (1987) clearly identified in his research that the anatomical structures that are associated with the vocal tract clearly preceded the changes in the brain of the modern human. The selective pressures that were encountered by our ancestors in their environment resulted in brain change and eventually in an integration and expansion of the human communication system.

A speaking organism requires a structural base for the production of sound. It also by necessity requires a perceptual mechanism to monitor the sound production. The interaction of these two structures should yield a data base to substantiate that a species, labeled by Linnaeus as homo sapiens, can achieve some wisdom or be contemplative only by acquiring morphological change first. The interaction also suggests that there is a time sequence in which one structure precedes the other, for neither are complete at birth. That is, the capacity to hear or perceive will necessarily precede the capacity to speak. Both are necessary before one can be a wise or cognitive organism. For these structures to fit into some clean, discernable sequence requires an examination of at least two sets of mechanisms: one for the production and reception of sound, and the other to process the acoustic stimuli. Both the production and reception mechanisms are properties of a variety of living organisms, especially in the mammalian phylum (Bekesy, 1957). Both a production mechanism and a reception mechanism are present at birth for the human organism. Neither, however, resemble the fully mature or developed system of the adult of the species.

Phylogenetically, two sets of research, one anatomical and the other neurological, are important for the descriptions of the behavior of the species. In the descriptions that follow, the emergent sequence will be placed in a time frame from birth. Embryonic development of the antecedent conditions will not be discussed. Each description delineates a morphogenetic structure that supports the emergent characteristics of the adult counterpart. This will provide a basis for observing the antecedent conditions as they are displayed in the ontogeny of those morphological characteristics. In particular, there are structural changes that account for the biological capacity of the human organism to communicate in a fashion quite dissimilar to that of other species. These morphological structures play a critical role in the development of human communication. The morphological structures are genetic, and the subsequent structures that depend on it are epigenetic.

For example, one could propose that speech has morphological structures that are genetic whereas language is epigenetic, depending on neural–social interaction for emergence. Or, because speech precedes thought (see Crelin, 1987), the subsequent morphological changes in the brain would lead to the epigenetic phenomenon known as mind. This biological proposition sustains the observations of previous research in language and cognitive development. Thus the organism is biologically structured in such a way that it can internalize and organize the external environment, as well as be equipped to socialize with other like species in its environment.

There are several morphogenetic structures that are specific to the human organism. These structures involve anatomical and physiological mechanisms, neural structures of the brain, and specific emergent behaviors that are species specific and central to the capacity of the human organism to communicate. These morphogenetic structures are necessary for many of the developmental mechanisms that serve as antecedent structures for specific communication processes. A review of these provides those characteristics that are part of our phylogeny at this point in time.

Anatomical Speech Mechanisms

The past few years have yielded important data (Crelin, 1969, 1987; Lieberman, 1977, 1991) regarding the evolution of the human vocal tract. Both Lieberman and Crelin had research teams engaged in the phylogenetic exploration of the human vocal tract. Basically, their research identified the anatomical changes in vocal tract development. Three essential characteristics of the human anatomy are compared: (a) length of the vocal tract or wind pipe as it extends from the larynx to the back of the roof of the mouth; (b) shape of the pharynx or angle of wind pipe from the larynx; and (c) location of the larynx position in the trachea structure. The eventual state of these structures in the adult vocal tract enables the human adult organism to produce acoustic frequencies in the range of common speech.

The average length of the vocal tract is 17cm for the adult of the species. The shape of the tract along the back of the neck is bent into a radical angle, thereby creating a chamber for the physical passage of air. The adult larynx moves to a location low in the trachea to complete the elongated system. Lieberman (1977) called this anatomical structure a "bent two tube system," which allowed for the manipulation of air molecules passing at a restricted rate and direction. It would be much like taking the stem of a balloon that contains air, and manipulating it so that you could control the passage of air and vary the sound, perhaps even producing a tune if you were talented. This anatomical structure allows for those sound frequencies associated with vowel sounds.

Crelin (1987) summarized over 10 years of anatomical research attempting to construct an anatomical replica of this vocal tract in his labs at Yale. He compared the physiological features of the adult human vocal tract with various homo skulls and discovered that an anatomical difference exists between many of the homo lineages, including the chimpanzee. Crelin then created "rubber" duplicates of the tract and was able to produce sound frequencies for the vowel sounds of the human tract. His comparative anatomical studies led him and his students to make general comparisons of humans with the chimpanzee. In those studies, he concluded that the vocal tract of the human infant was remarkably similar to that of the chimpanzee. Using various additional techniques, Crelin demonstrated that the positional descent of the vocal tract was important to the production of sound and that no other physiological benefit could be derived for this radical change in structure. The physics of sound production could be accomplished with his anatomical model. Vocal tract length and shape had been modified through some evolutionary change that allowed the human organism to phonate and articulate, to make sound in a fashion unlike previous related species.

What is also important is the comparison of the vocal tract of the human infant and the discovery of its amazing similarities to that of the adult chimpanzee. This provides physical evidence for earlier phenomenal observations of the human infant's inability to speak at birth although it is able to vocalize. Hence the development and decent of the vocal tract are important to the ontogeny of the organism and a first step in explaining phylogenetic differences. The production of sound is a common phenomenon among a variety of species. The production of a specific range of sounds now had descriptive validity from a physiological change in structure. Each species has a natural history of selective changes from which adaptations have taken place. The adaption to phonate and produce a certain range of sound frequencies is facilitated by a change in shape and length of the tract as well as the position of the larynx. The human organism's capacity to articulate was enhanced by developing the ability to manipulate the vocal mechanism and to restrict the flow of air through the anatomical structures. These abilities account for the consonant system produced by the control of these air signals. Both Crelin and Lieberman provided detailed descriptions of these anatomical changes and species comparisons, should the reader desire more information on the topic.

Auditory Features

The auditory systems and their subsequent physiology are almost identical for most mammals (Borden & Harris, 1984; Brown & Wallace, 1980). The peripheral system, with its ability to perceive sound, is generally complete by the sixth gestational month for humans. The auditory pathways, with their complete neural sophistication, continue developing until the 11th or 12th year of life. The auditory system has always shared critical research space in the speech and hearing research with the speech production system. The perception of discrete signals and their ramifications has been explored quite frequently. The associated behaviors with these studies are summarized in some very exhaustive treatments (e.g., Bekesy, 1957).

A significant functional problem that becomes obvious for humans is that if damage to this auditory receptor organ occurs, the resultant vocal production is impaired. Impaired production inhibits the normal development of speech in terms of anomalous production of phonated articulated sound (Lenneberg, 1962). Lenneberg noticed that vocal production emerged in congenitally deaf infants but ceased by the 6th month of life. The impact of this research led many researchers to believe that the loss of hearing or acoustic perception was indicative of a differentiation in species. To conclude that peripheral system damage in an ontogenetic instance is an indication of species specificity is reductionism at its worst. While the auditory mechanism is essential for vocal perception and development, the plasticity of other receptor mechanisms can come into play to provide communicative substitutes.

A rather substantial number of studies have emerged on the functional role of the auditory system in humans. Issues involving lateralization and asymmetries have dominated the literature. They indicate that the left hemisphere is involved in the discrimination of brief transient and temporal-order judgments, whereas the right hemisphere is involved with nonlinguistic stimuli (Ravizza & Belmore, 1979). The majority of these studies suggest that the auditory receptive mechanism for humans is well prepared for both continuous and categorical perception of discrete signals from the environment (Lieberman et al., 1971). In general for the human auditory system, both hemispheres perceive and analyze acoustic cues, but the left hemisphere is primarily involved with the perception of speech cues.

Let me digress a moment regarding the lack of acoustic perception and natural selection. The frequency of congenital deaf births is less than 0.1 of 1% of the population. Hearing impaired persons in a normal population with a variety of acoustic deficits comprise less than 15% of that population. The majority of impaired individuals usually acquired the deficit after the first year of life, with a majority acquiring their deficits after the critical periods of development (Poizner, Klima, & Bellugi, 1987; Sacks, 1989). In many cases, these individuals have developed alternative language systems based on visual/hand systems, which are effective methods of communication that utilize other perceptual mechanisms. It is also interesting to note from the research of Poizner et al., that the use of sign language is affected in pathologies in the same manner as vocalized language or speech. Aphasic disorders for production and reception of signed systems are the same following damage to the left hemisphere. That is, a production or reception disorder occurs with lesions in the left hemisphere for both signers and speakers of culturally based languages. The criterion for discussing phylogenetic characteristics is that a substantial portion of the population of a species must possess a set of characteristics for it to have a significant role in phylogenesis. A genetic occlusion that is present in such a small portion of the population does not exclude the role of auditory characteristics in phylogenesis.

From the research on deaf individuals, we see that the same regions of the brain associated with speech production are utilized by hearing and deaf people. The adaptation of the underlying neuromechanisms to a modal input change suggests considerable flexibility for the species. The organism in such cases is relying on substructures of an evolved biological system to acquire a cultural system. It is an adaptation to an input deficit that has not become genetic and species wide. The presence or absence of the acoustic system does play an important role in the selection of alternate perceptual modes, but it does not exclude neurosystems. Perhaps the choice of gestures or hand signals as a selective mechanism is a result of the location of the motor functions of the brain, which reside above the production centers for speech. Additional research like that of Poizner, Klima, and Bellugi will shed more light on the issue. Similarly, congenital defects to vision or locomotor behavior do not impede the results of phylogenetic theory. They merely demonstrate the plasticity of the biological system and display the diversity of human socio-cultural adaptation. However, it is the neurological system that seems to be the most crucial for human communication.

Neurological Systems

The human brain is a composite communication system in itself, coordinating afferent and efferent pathways to various peripheral systems. It regulates various systems through a variety of signaling devices. It develops slowly through the gestational period and is only approximately 25% of the size of an adult brain at birth. It is through the brain that innervation for the functional movement of the vocal tract is accomplished. It is also through the brain that the transformation of acoustic signals is accomplished. Geshwind (1970, 1972) and his research associates have been responsible for research synthesis thus far regarding the active integration of brain function. Geshwind's summary and description of the neural pathways of the cerebral cortex has been the most widely accepted and referenced.

The human brain is, in some respect a composite of neural evolution. The concept of the tripartite brain carries within it the metaphoric description of successive differentiation and change. Ornstein and Thompson (1984) provided one of the most readable descriptions of human brain evolution. Much of both the description and graphic art that compose this text are entertaining and instructive. The description is a history of evolution, with one system or structure built upon another. Each structure is a natural history of function. The hindbrain, the oldest part of the brain, is the brain stem, including the medulla and pons. The midbrain is a smaller section that sits on top of the brain stem. The forebrain contains some older structures in addition to much of what has recently occurred in evolution, including the cortex. The central and autonomic nervous systems are connected or wired to and through these basic divisions of the brain, ascending through the brain stem via a device called the reticular activating system (RAS). This is like a central pathway that sends a neural network of interconnected fibers to all regions of the brain. The RAS system is considered the origin of consciousness for its regulation of both ascending and descending control for the "thinking" or higher cortical control regions of the brain.

There are two cerebral hemispheres, evenly divided for the most part. The right is slightly smaller than the left side for many mammals, with language in the human population generally relegated to the left side. The cerebral cortex is the crowning mass of neural structures that covers the other two lower portions of the brain. Of all mammals, humans have the most density, causing the greatest enfoldment. This is generally due to the small size of the cranial cavity, hence enfoldment, in a sense, is a response to cramped storage space in the skull.

Left cerebral dominance in the humans has been determined primarily from studies of the pathology of the brain. Geshwind (1970, 1972) mapped out what is now a classic review of the neural pathways of the left cerebral cortex for humans. Localization of function in specific "centers" of the brain are well established for both speech production and reception. In the cortical region of the brain on the left side, are two centers that are labeled Broca's Area and Wernicke's Area. Broca's Area is located in the frontal cortex area, whereas Wernicke's is located in the temporal lobe in an area referred to as the auditory cortex. Generally for right-handed people, Broca's and Wernicke's Area of the brain are on the left side. Broca's Area is located at the bottom of the motor strip of the brain, in which the motor cortex controls movement of hands, arms, legs, lips, and other facial features. Given its location, Broca's Area is understandably responsible for the motor production of speech. Damage to this center of the brain results in production aphasias characterized by considerable difficulty, if not in some cases an inability, to produce speech.

Wernicke's Area is located in the temporal lobe to the posterior side of the motor areas of the brain and adjacent to various sensory areas. Wernicke's Area is responsible for auditory reception and language comprehension. Damage to this area causes reception aphasia, and speech perception is impaired. There is a small neural network of fibers that connects Wernicke's area with Broca's area called the arcuate fasciculus. Information from the hearing section is thereby connected to the speech production center and vice versa. The evolution of this interconnectivity is crucial because it allows both production and reception operations to communicate with each other. In addition, there is another neural pathway from Wernicke's Area to the visual cortex or occipital lobe in the rear of the neocortex. This fibrous connective pathway, called the angular gyrus, connects the visual centers of the brain with the hearing centers. The angular gyrus is located on both sides of the brain and connects the visual system to Wernicke's Area. Our reading functions are frequently associated with the motor cortex, as in reading aloud, and are referenced with neural processing of visual spatial stimuli through these centers. These centers are extremely important to normal speech processing and are not found in structural or functional relationships in other mammals. Each center's importance is amplified by the fact that the coordination and functional relationship of these centers is essential for normal audition/vocalization interaction. These language centers are species specific.

Index of Encephalization

In addition to the centers of the human brain that organize various functions, there is the morphogenetic factor of increased mass in the human brain. Size of the brain per se would not account for a morphogenetic difference. Jerison (1976) hypothesized a different calculation for comparing brain size based on proportionality of brain weight to body surface. His proposition relates structure to function by stating that the larger the body surface, the more innervation required to process these transactions. The logarithm turns out to be correct, that when a comparison of the proportion of brain weight in grams is made to body weight in kilograms, a slope line of $2/3$ power emerges. This suggests that the number of brain cells, their relative size, and volume of intercellular spacing all bear on brain size in relation to the surface area of the body. The formula developed by Jerison is defined as an encephalization quotient, or EQ. The lower vertebrates have EQs of about 0.07. The primates have EQs of about 1.2 to 2. The human has an EQ of 7, and the dolphin is right behind.

The correlation between brain weight and surface area of the body is not attributable to the dependance of one of these parameters on the other. Rather it seems to be attributable to their mutual dependance on some third hidden parameter such as relative intelligence. The EQ further suggests that in the evolution of the hominid, the increase in relative cranial space has been a recent phenomenon associated with functions requiring more sophisticated structures. The EQ also encourages conjectures about the development of extensive frontal lobes in the human brain, as well as the enfolding of the brain's surface in what is obviously a tight cranial structure for modern human brains. Both Crelin (1987) and Delbruck (1986) asserted that this cellular mass acquired in recent years of evolutionary history contributes to both speaking and cognitive functions in humans. The modern articulate mammal requires a greater EQ than the australopithecine, which has an EQ of about 3, in between modern apes, where EQ = 2, and the EQ of 7 for the modern human.

Consciousness and Phylogeny

Many neuroscientists have hypothesized about the role of signaling systems and their role in information processing (Edelman, 1992; Pavlov, 1960; Pribram, 1971, 1991). In each of these theoretical models, it has become clear that the process of communication links the complex interactions of the neurological system with the environment. Edelman theorized that these structures produce a higher order consciousness for humans as opposed to primary consciousness, which is a process in all mammals. Primary consciousness is a process of being aware of the objects or events in our environment and is associated with volition. Higher order consciousness involves recognition by thinking and processing and can be independent of external stimuli. It is responsible for those cognitive activities that can be accessed via other association areas of the brain that have been mapped by experience. Higher order consciousness is dependent on reentrant circuits for neural processing and evolved out of primary consciousness.

Edelman's theory of reentrant circuitry is based on the phylogenetic properties of human brain evolution and categorical operations in brain cells. It is dependent on the role of human language and categorization. With simple microbiological structures, Edelman demonstrated that the cells in the brain construct "maps" of their own activity that links cerebral areas of the cortex. Brain categorizing appears early in the cerebral cortex and is associated with perception. It is extended in humans because consciousness takes us out of the perceptual present that is associated with other mammalian brains. This is accomplished through our ability to reenter our consciousness via a human language system. Consciousness, both primary and higher order, is the result of natural selection.

This theoretical position on consciousness in the evolution of our awareness can be clarified biologically. Although still theoretical, the ontogenetic observations of individual development need to be further studied. If morphological structures such as the aural/oral system have evolved with corresponding neural mechanisms, it would seem reasonable that our intrapersonal communication processes have emerged through neural social interactions that are observable in the developing organism. One of the ways we map our external environment onto our neural structures may be more obvious than we think.

We begin our ontogeny with relative meager brain mass in infancy. We are more potential than reality, with our aural/oral structures barely able to vocalize, our visual system myopic, our taste buds mere potential, and so on. We take in information through our receptor organs and map the perceptual present. As our brain develops and our vocal and auditory systems emerge, we affect our own consciousness. Through our sociocultural interactions, we map new categories via a linguistic system as our perceptions are coded and structured for various mental operations. We internalize our experience via an evolved system of aural/oral interaction. Through various cognitive activities, we are thus able to reconstitute our individual experience. Phylogenetically, we have evolved a system that emerges externally and then is internalized via morphological structures. There is still much work to be done to clarify and explore our phylogenetic basis of communication and the role of intrapersonal processes. One of the areas where ontogenetic behavior can help explain the neural–social interaction will be described below.

ONTOGENETIC EVIDENCE FOR PHYLOGENESIS: AUDITORY–VOCAL INTERACTION

I began this discussion with the intent of exploring the biological basis of human communication. I have asserted that what is needed is a phylogenetic perspective. What I have presented thus far is a natural history of physiological and neurological characteristics of the species homo sapiens. At present, I have clarified that a complete phylogeny of communication is not available and have advocated the continuous systematic research necessary to accomplish this. I have asserted that ontogenetic descriptions of biological functioning were important to establish the place of communication in biological evolution. My own research interests and programmatic research have been directed to that end. The two characteristics, sound production and reception, that I have chosen to follow through this process are central to understanding those aspects of human communication that are crucial to human information processing and the acquisition of a spoken language. These initial interactive characteristics suggest that the organism gains voluntary control by suppressing a primitive vocal reflex. Morphogenetically, vocalization is present in all newborn humans. When presented with acoustic signals, the organism ceases to vocalize and attends to the acoustic environment.

Any interaction would be difficult with continuous vocalization because simultaneous perception of both one's own sound and that of other sound would not be efficient. It may be that suppression of vocalization in the presence of acoustic stimuli is the first voluntary attempt to listen. If this is the case, suppression of the crying reflex would represent the infant's first attempt to interact with its environment. As the primitive nervous system matures, crying would proportionally decrease in frequency. The decrease in cry frequency would then permit noncry vocalizations to develop in context-free situations. These vocalizations have the potential to develop symbolic meaning (Murai, 1963). Thus cry suppression may be the neurosocial mechanism that functions as the link between crying and other vocalizations. The lack of crying is more important to the development of vocalization than the act of crying because it is a precursor of volition.

The selection of the period of examination was quite simple. Our interest was to explore the behavioral acts an organism developed, and one that naturally completed the gestational process. We selected the human infant at birth (Riccillo & Watterson, 1984). Our project had four phases, and subsequent data is still under review. The vocal behavior of the organism at birth is characterized by the obvious vocalization identified as a cry. We did not induce this behavior, but rather waited for spontaneous vocalization. The human cry is part of a common set of reflexive, primitive behaviors present at birth. The sucking reflex and the startle reflex are others that are present.

The human organism's first signalling attempt in its environment is vocalic. This vocalic behavior is not linguistic in the sense of a developed or adult-like speech production. As reported earlier, the physiological development at this point is limited and there is no capacity for phonated and articulated sound. Hence we characterized this vocal signal as prelinguistic. The auditory mechanism, in terms of its peripheral characteristics, is developed, but its extensive neuropathways to the brain are minimal and less developed. The capacity of the perceptual system thus is less sophisticated than the more mature adult of the species. Hence, we called the reception of acoustic signals at this point, precognitive. We have, therefore, at birth for the human species an essentially immature system both neurologically and physiologically. We postulated it would provide a good beginning point for biologically oriented research to assess the capacity of the organism in terms of the origin of these two characteristics of sound production and reception. More specifically, a reflexive system such as an infant cry provides a good indication of the origins of the vocal system control.

The results of our first study (Riccillo & Watterson, 1984) were informative regarding initial audition and vocalization in that we found infants are able to suppress their vocalization behavior in the presence of acoustic stimuli.

The interaction of acoustic stimuli in the presence of vocalization was the focus of our study. We were not concerned whether or not the infant could produce a cry signal that was comparable to or similar to a linguistic event such as a vowel or consonant. Rather, our question was whether an infant at birth is able to control vocal behavior that is initially reflexive, out of voluntary control, in the presence of acoustic stimuli.

Some theories regard crying behavior as externally stimulated, reflexive responses to physical discomfort. Crying responses, for example, have been associated with manipulation, fatigue, pain, and hunger. If infant crying represents the state of the neonate, it could be regarded as the first communicative act. On the other hand, if crying is just part of the state itself, it is no different than any mammal's vocalization.

Infant crying has also been characterized as a reflexive response to acoustic stimuli, especially stimuli generated by the human vocal tract. That possibility is important because it implies that crying may be the first vocal response to a human voice, and therefore the first stage of speech and language development (Lewis, 1951; Lieberman, Harris, Wolff, & Russell, 1971). Morley (1967) theorized that reflexive crying in response to vocal stimuli may contribute to the onset of babbling. He suggested that reflexive crying could occur as a response to the cry of another infant or as a response to an infant's own cry. This would serve as a primitive precursor to reduplicated or circular babbling.

In our first examination we exposed the infant to two cry behaviors, his or her own and that of another infant. If neonates cry when exposed to their own cry and/or the cry of another neonate, this might suggest that crying is used as an auditory-to-vocal stimulus response. The neonates in this investigation did not respond to the test cry stimuli in greater or lesser amounts. They were unable to recognize their own cry under test conditions, nor were they startled by the cry of another infant as a distress signal. However, neonates heard the test stimuli of both cries and responded by stopping their own cry behavior, perhaps to listen. Whether the state of the tested infant was calm or crying, it was more likely to remain calm in the presence of the acoustic cry stimuli.

It is well known that a newborn infant is dominated by primitive reflexes that serve primitive needs (Gesell, 1945; Langer, 1969; Piaget, 1971; Wolff, 1969). As part of the process of maturation, these primitive reflexes must be suppressed, modified, and/or shaped into volitional behavior (Mysak, 1976). Crying behavior is present at birth, and like any primitive reflex it serves primitive needs. Those needs might include signalling caretakers, or obtaining respiratory exercise, or a variety of other possibilities. But in the course of maturation, the human infant must suppress crying because it would interfere with auditory/vocal development and the subsequent progression to more efficient means of communication.

Additional research was performed using a variety of acoustic signals (Watterson & Riccillo, 1983, 1985). In all test conditions, using a variety of stimuli, the infants were able to suppress their cry behavior. This research supports the proposition that auditory/vocal interaction is present at birth, and that the cry suppression is a mechanism that allows for voluntary control of the vocal mechanism. It demonstrates the capacity of the organism, only a few hours after birth, to respond to its environment through a neuro–social interaction of vocal/auditory mechanisms. The suppression of primitive reflexes allows for an efficient selective method for communicative interaction with an acoustic environment to begin.

This ontogenetic behavior of the human infant provides some interesting questions for future research. Developing a phylogeny of human communication will require a significant number of research efforts that cover the early human developmental period. My hope is that each will contribute to the phylogeny of communication and our further understanding of the biology of communication.

SUMMARY

A biological perspective is essential to understanding the phylogenesis of human communication. Though not complete, this perspective clearly identifies specific biological features essential to the communication process in general, and it may lead to insights into intrapersonal communication. This perspective mandates the recognition of the role of speech and hearing in specific identifiable mechanisms in phylogenetic development. Although it is obvious that no fossil evidence at present provides a record to support a phylogenesis of the communication process, the examination of specific biological features provides a resume of changes and adaptations by the human species over time.

Our ontological assumptions need to be changed from past dualistic perspectives to a more structured and functional neutral monism. The clumsy dualism of the past created difficult philosophical distinctions between mind and body. For communication theorists, a biological perspective forces the integration of mind and body into a structure that can explain matter–energy transformations. Any consideration of phylogenesis requires this kind of orientation.

For intrapersonal communication, biological structures that directly link the internal/external operations are important. Both production and reception mechanisms such as speech and hearing have always played a role in mental operations such as cognition. The early developmental theorists characterized early cognitive operations via a phenomenon called egocentric speech. It is the biologically inherited mechanisms that allow for the internalization of an external environment and thus may be responsible at least in part for an epigenetic phenomena called mind.

There are distinct biological features that characterize the phylogenesis of human communication. They are anatomical features such as size, shape, and length of the vocal tract. Cerebral dominance exists in the human neocortex. There are also specific localized neural structures such as Broca's Area and Wernicke's Area that regulate the production and reception of vocalized linguistic signals.

Ontogenetic studies are also providing examples of specific functions that are present at birth and demonstrate control of the auditory/vocal mechanisms. Suppression of primitive vocal reflexive behaviors, such as crying, provide insights into how the organism gains control of the biologically inherited speech and hearing mechanism shortly after birth.

A biological perspective is the only perspective that can yield a phylogenesis of human communication. Although attempting such a perspective is new to communication theorists, there is much from biologists and neuroscientists that can yield insights for a more complete phylogenesis of the human species.

REFERENCES

Bates, E., Bretherton, I., Shore, C., & McNew, S. (1983). Names, gestures and objects: symbolization in infancy, and aphasia. In K. E. Nelson (Ed.), *Children's language* (pp. 59–123). Hillsdale, NJ: Lawrence Erlbaum Associates.

Bekesy, G. V. (1957). The ear. *Scientific American Reprint,* 1–12.

Berlo, D. (1960). *The process of communication.* New York: Holt, Rinehart & Winston.

Borden, G. J., & Harris, K. S. (1984). *Speech science primer* (2nd ed.). Baltimore: Williams & Wilkins.

Bowler, P. J. (1989). *Evolution: The history of an idea* (rev. ed.). Berkeley: University of California Press.

Bronowski, J. (1978). *The origins of knowledge & imagination.* New York: Yale University Press.

Brown, H. (1978). *Brain & behavior.* New York: Oxford University Press.

Brown, T. S., & Wallace, P. M. (1980). *Physiological psychology.* New York: Academic Press.

Capra, F. (1975). *The tao of physics.* New York: Bantam.

Chomsky, N. (1967). The formal nature of language. In E. H. Lenneberg (Ed.), *Biological foundations of language* (pp. 397–442). New York: Wiley.

Chomsky, N. (1968). *Language and mind.* Cambridge, MA: MIT Press.

Crelin, E. S. (1969). *Anatomy of a newborn: An atlas.* Philadelphia: Lea and Febiger.

Crelin, E. S. (1987). *The human vocal tract: Anatomy, function, development and evolution.* New York: Vantage Press.

Cronkite, G. (1986). On the focus, scope, and coherence of the study of human symbolic activity, *Quarterly Journal of Speech, 72*(3), 231–246.

Dance, F. E. X. (1967). (Ed.). *Human communication theory: Original essays.* New York: Holt, Rinehart & Winston.

Dance, F. E. X. (1982). A speech theory of human communication. In F. E. X. Dance (Ed.), *Human communication theory* (pp. 120–146). New York: Harper & Row.

Dance, F. E. X., & Larson, C. E. (1972). *Speech communication: Concepts and behavior.* New York: Holt, Rinehart & Winston.

Delbruck, M. (1986). *Mind from matter.* Palo Alto, CA: Blackwell.

Edelman, G. M. (1992). *Bright air, brilliant fire: On the matter of mind.* New York: Basic Books.

Gardner, R. A., & Gardner, B. T. (1969). Teaching sign language to a chimpanzee. *Science, 165,* 664–672.

Geshwind, N. (1970). The organization of language and the brain. *Science, 27,* 940–945.

Geshwind, N. (1972). Language and the brain. *Scientific American 226,* 76–83.

Gesell, A. L. (1945). *The embryology of behavior.* New York: Harper.

Hamilton, V., & Moser, B. (1988). *In the beginning.* New York: Harcourt Brace Jovanovich.

Hedges, S. B., Kumar, S., & Koichiro, T. (1992). Human origins and analysis of mitochondrial DNA sequences. *Science, 255,* 737–739.

Hymes, D. (1971). Competence and performance: In R. Huxley & E. Ingram (Eds.), *Language acquisition: Models and methods* (pp. 67–99). New York: Academic Press.

Infante, D., Rancer, A. S., & Womack, D. F. (1990). *Communication theory.* Prospect Heights, IL: Waveland Press.

Jerison, H. J. (1976). Paleoneurology and the evolution of mind. *Scientific American, 234*(4), 90–101.

Johansen, D., & Shreeve, J. (1989). *Lucy's child.* New York: William Morrow.

Langer, J. (1969). *Theories of development.* New York: Holt, Rinehart & Winston.

Lempert, H., & Kinsbourne, M. (1985). Possible origin of speech in selective orienting. *Psychological Bulletin, 97*(1), 62–73.

Lenneberg, E. H. (1962). Understanding language without the ability to speak: A case report. *Journal of Abnormal Social Psychology, 65,* 419–425.

Lenneberg, E. H. (1967). *Biological foundations of language.* New York: Wiley.

Lewis, M. M. (1951). *Infant speech.* New York: Holt, Rinehart & Winston.

Lieberman, P. (1977). *Speech physiology and acoustic phonetics.* New York: Macmillan.

Lieberman, P. (1991). *Uniquely human: The evolution of speech, thought and selfless behavior.* Cambridge, MA: Harvard University Press.

Lieberman, P., Harris, K. S., Wolff, P., & Russell, L. H. (1971). Newborn infant cry and nonhuman primate vocalizations. *Journal of Speech and Hearing Research, 14,* 718–727.

McLuhan, M., & McLuhan, E. (1986). *Laws of media: The new science.* Toronto: University of Toronto Press.

Menyuk, P. (1971). *The acquisition and development of language.* Englewood Cliffs, NJ: Prentice-Hall.

Murai, J. (1963). The sounds of infants: Their phonemicazation and symbolization. *Studia Phonologica, 3,* 17–34.

Morley, M. E. (1967). *The development and disorders of speech in childhood,* Baltimore, MO: Williams & Wilkins.

Mysak, E. D. (1976). *Neuroevolutional approach to cerebral palsy and speech.* New York: Teachers College Press.

Ornstein, R., & Thompson, R. F. (1984). *The amazing brain.* Boston, MA: Houghton Mifflin.

Pavlov, I. P. (1960). *Conditioned reflexes: An investigation of the physiological activity of the cerebral cortex.* New York: Dover.

Piaget, J. (1970). *Genetic epistemology.* New York: Norton.

Piaget, J. (1971). *Biology and knowledge.* Chicago: University of Chicago Press.

Plotkin, H. C. (1982). *Learning, development and culture: Essays in evolutionary epistemology.* New York: Wiley.

Poizner, H., Klima, E. S., & Bellugi, V. (1987). *What the hands reveal about the brain.* Cambridge, MA: MIT Press.

Pribram, K. H. (1971). *Languages of the brain: Experimental paradoxes and principles in neurobiology.* Englewood Cliffs, NJ: Prentice-Hall.

Pribram, K. H. (1986). The cognitive revolution and mind/brain issues. *American Psychologist, 41,* 507–522.

Pribram, K. H. (1991). *Brain and perception: Holonomy and structure in figural processing.* Hillsdale, NJ: Lawrence Erlbaum Associates.

Ravizza, R. J., & Belmore, S. (1979). Auditory forebrain: Evidence from anatomical and behavioral experiments involving human and animal subjects. In R. B. Masterson (Ed.), *Handbook of behavioral neurobiology: sensory integration* (Vol 1, pp. 78–118). New York: Plenum Press.

Riccillo, S. C. (1982). Modes of Speech as a developmental continuum. *Western Journal of Speech Communication, 4,* 1–15.

Riccillo, S. C., & Watterson, T. (1984). The suppression of crying in the human neonate: Response to human vocal tract stimuli. *Brain and Language, 23,* 34–42.

Rosenbleuth, A. (1970). *Mind and Brain: A philosophy of science.* Cambridge, MA: MIT Press.

Routhier, M. (1979). *A critical analysis and examination of the issue of speech as an overlaid function.* Unpublished doctoral dissertation, University of Denver.

Ruben, B. (1988). *Communication and human behavior.* New York: Macmillan.

Sacks, O. (1989). *Seeing voices.* Berkeley: University of California Press.

Sokolov, A. N. (1972). *Inner speech and thought.* New York: Plenum Press.

Stendt, G. (1972). Cellular communication. *Scientific American, 227*(3), 42–51.

Templeton, A. R. (1992). Human origins and analysis of mitochondrial DNA sequences. *Science, 255,* 737.

Vygotsky, L. S. (1962). *Thought and Language.* Cambridge, MA: MIT Press.

Watterson, T., & Riccillo, S. C. (1983). Vocal suppression as a neonatal response to auditory stimuli. *Journal of Auditory Research, 23,* 205–214.

Watterson, T., & Riccillo, S. C. (1985). Stimulus frequency and vocal suppression in neonates. *Journal of Auditory Research, 25,* 81–89.

Wilson, A. C. (1983). The molecular basis of evolution. *Scientific American, 253,* 164–173.

Wolff, P. H. (1969). Crying and vocalization in early infancy. In B. M. Foss (Ed.), *Determinants of infant behavior.* New York: Wiley.

3
The Human Brain: Understanding the Physical Bases of Intrapersonal Communication

Gail Ramsberger
University of Colorado at Boulder

> *The rich range of behavior that we assume is specifically human, including the uniqueness of oral language, can ultimately be reduced to and equated with the mere ebb and flow of minute chemical and electrical changes in tiny, but intricate, synaptic mechanisms.*
>
> —Love & Webb (1992, p.53)

This chapter provides the reader with an introduction to the neural bases of human communication. To the nonneuroscientist, basic neuroanatomy is a difficult, but necessary prerequisite to our discussion of functional neuroanatomy as it applies to both interpersonal and intrapersonal aspects of human communication. For those who struggle to understand neuroanatomy, the task is made no easier by the fact that text books disagree in their use of terms and classification systems to help with the organization of basic neuroanatomy. This presents a special challenge when one seeks to supplement information presented in one source with that gained from another. With this in mind, I attempt to alert the reader regarding alternative labels, classifications, and/or definitions during the following discussion of basic neuro-anatomy.

MODELS OF CEREBRAL ORGANIZATION

Curiosity regarding the biological bases of human behavior has generated numerous theories throughout history. Hippocrates may have provided the first written record of such interest when he proposed that the brain was the organ of intellect and the heart, the organ of senses. Several centuries later, Galen attempted to relate mental functions to specific structures within the brain. He believed that the ventricles (spaces within the brain that are filled with cerebrospinal fluid) were the site in which mental processing occurred, and went so far as to suggest that there was a functional differentiation of the three ventricles. This then, was the beginning of a theoretical orientation to the study of brain–behavior relationships referred to as "localization." This effort to identify distinct neural tissue that could be related to specific mental functions was carried to the extreme in the early 1800s when Gall localized such behaviors as love of parents, courage, and domestic instincts. Gall's notions were met with strong opposition from physiologists who formed the "anti-localization" school. Flourens, however, in 1824, may have been the first to apply the scientific method to the question of the neural bases of human behavior. He conducted a series of experiments with birds in which he systematically destroyed different brain areas and then observed that all the birds, regardless of the specific lesion site, displayed similar initial behaviors and ultimately experienced the same total recovery of function. While Flourens' experimental results with birds cannot be disputed, we now understand that it was incorrect to have generalized these findings from lower vertebrates with very simple nervous systems to higher verte-brates whose brains are highly differentiated and complex.

Efforts to understand the neural bases of behavior turned towards the complex human behavior of communication in 1825, when Bouillaud published a paper in which he divided speech into several intellectual processes and then suggested that articulation of speech was a function of anterior portions of the brain. This hypothe-sis was untested until nearly 40 years later when Paul Broca addressed the Paris Anthropological Society and reported on the postmortem examination of a patient with an acquired disorder of articulated speech. This patient had a lesion in the anterior portion of the left hemisphere and this area was thus labeled the "center of motor forms of speech," later being referred to as "Broca's Area." Broca's work encouraged others to carefully observe the behavior of patients and relate these observations to postmortem examination of their brains. Ten years later, Carl Wer-nicke described a patient with very different symptomatology. This patient had no trouble with the articulation of speech, but had great difficulty understanding spo-ken language. In marked contrast to the lesion reported for Broca's case, Wernicke's patient had a lesion in the posterior portion of the left hemisphere, later to be known as "Wernicke's Area." These two remarkable cases caused a flourish of enthusiasm for the localizationist view of cerebral organization until the turn of the century when Lashley carried out ablation studies with rats and reported that lesion size rather than location was the critical variable in determining behavioral consequence.

Thus, efforts to correlate behavior with material substrate have been charac-terized by a struggle between the two opposing views: localization and antilocaliza-tion. These two views were synthesized in the mid-20th century by researchers such as Pavlov, Bernshtein, Filimonov, and Ukhtomski (cited in Luria, 1980), who proposed the concepts of "graded localization of function," "pluripotentialism," and "dynamic localization." No longer was there interest in assigning complex behav-iors to static, fixed areas within the brain. Rather, it was now thought that complex behavior involved the smooth execution of a series of simultaneous and successive neural connections throughout the brain and was, thus, thought to be localized within dynamic systems. For example, a complex behavior such as stating the name of an object might be disrupted by lesions to any part of the system of connections that are necessary for correct naming performance. Accordingly, naming disorders may result from lesions that interfere with visual perception of the object to be named, from lesions that interfere with regions involved in the matching of a semantic representation with the concept, from lesions that interfere with regions involved in the selection of phonemes to match the semantic representation, from lesions that interfere with areas responsible for the motor planning and sequencing of articulation, or from lesions that disconnect these components of the naming system.

Current thoughts regarding the biological bases of complex human behaviors such as communication include several important concepts. First, no area of the brain is thought to be solely responsible for a complex human behavior. Rather, specific areas are believed to be responsible for the processing of component information involved in performance of multiple complex behaviors. This concept has cast a shadow on theories of strict lateralization of function, and we no longer think of the right and left hemispheres as having totally independent roles. Secondly, in the context of focal brain damage, complex behaviors are not destroyed or lost, but the system of simultaneous and sequential events that normally takes place is disrupted and thus restoration of complex behavior may be possible via "reorganization" into a new dynamic system. Such a reorganized system might yield overt behavior that is undifferentiated from the premorbid behavior, but the neural bases for this behavior are, necessarily, different from the original. Finally, it is now known that the brain's dynamic organization does not remain fixed during different stages of development. Thus, the effects of a lesion in a specific area of the brain will not be the same at different ages. Evidence of this is provided when one compares the speech and language deficits that result from similar lesions in the left, language dominant hemisphere of adults and children. Whereas lesions to different areas within the left hemisphere in adults result in a set of fairly predictable patterns of spared and impaired speech and language characteristics, children exhibit a more generalized depression of all language processing regardless of where the lesion occurs within the left hemisphere.

NEUROANATOMY, NEUROPHYSIOLOGY AND FUNCTIONAL CORRELATES

A detailed description of the anatomy and physiology of the nervous system is not within the objectives of this chapter. However, a basic understanding of cellular, physiologic, and gross anatomic components of the brain is a logical place to begin a discussion of the physical correlates of communicative behaviors.

The neuron is the basic functional unit of the nervous system. Neurons vary in size, but all consist of a nucleus, dendritic projections that receive information, and a longer axon that conducts impulses away from the nucleus (Fig. 3.1). The neuron is surrounded by a membrane with the intracellular area containing relatively high

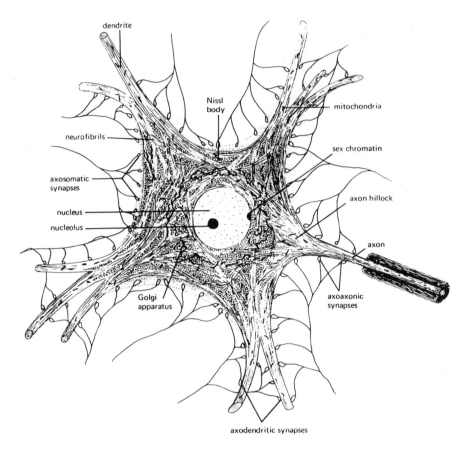

FIG. 3.1. Semidiagrammatic representation of the constituents of a nerve cell. From Barr and Kiernen (1993). *The Human Nervous System: An Anatomic Viewpoint.* Hagarstown, MD. Harper & Row, Publishers, Inc. Reprinted with permission.

levels of potassium and low levels of sodium and chloride, whereas the opposite conditions are found in the extracellular environment. This difference in chemical concentrations on either side of the membrane creates a small electrical potential known as the resting potential. Neural impulses are conducted when there is an abrupt change in the electrical potential, referred to as the action potential. At the peak of the action potential, there is a transient reversal of the polarity of the electrical potential across the membrane and the chemical concentrations within and outside of the cell become exchanged. The neural impulse travels along the axon until it reaches the junction with another neuron. This juncture, or space, between neuronal axons is referred to as a synapse. Transmission of the impulse across the synapse requires the release of one of several neurotransmitters (acetylcholine, dopamine, norepinephrine, serotinin, γ-aminobutyric acid) and the subsequent release of neurotransmitter deactivators.

Specific neurotransmitters are known to be active in discrete sites within the central and peripheral nervous systems and this is why certain pharmacological agents that simulate neurochemicals may be administered with very specific effects. This also explains why certain neurochemical disorders, such as Parkinson's disease, in which there is reduced levels of dopamine, may result in highly specific behavioral effects while having little-to-no impact on other neurological functions.

Because the nervous system is constantly receiving neural impulses, it must operate via a system of selectivity. That is, through a system of excitatory and inhibitory chemical influences the nervous system chooses which signals to respond to or ignore. Disturbances to this system of sensory selectivity are implicated in developmental disorders such as autism and attention deficit disorder (ADD). Many of these children may benefit from pharmacological treatments that facilitate a better balance between excitatory and inhibitory neurochemicals found within the nervous system.

The nervous system is divided into two major components. The peripheral nervous system (PNS) is, as the name suggests, the portion that makes the link with the peripheral effectors and affecters. It consists of 12 pairs of cranial nerves that exit the central nervous system at the base of the brain and 31 pairs of spinal nerves emerging along the length of the spinal cord. It is the peripheral portion of the nervous system that is responsible for the final transmission of neural commands for movements of the body's muscular system, including those movements involved in the production of speech.

It is important in our discussion of human communication to differentiate the physical act of speech production from that of language processing. The processing of language involves the application of a set of rules that govern the phonology, morphology, syntax, semantics, and pragmatics of the language. Speech is but one mode of expressing language. Thus, the patient with a PNS disorder that affects the movements involved in respiration, phonation, resonation, and articulation of sound will experience a speech disorder known as dysarthria, but will not have any language difficulties because language processing is a function of the central nervous system. This patient would be able to demonstrate language competence in a different output modality such as writing.

The PNS also is responsible for the initial reception of all types of sensory information, including hearing. These sensory inputs constitute the only means by which the mind is in contact with the external world. Peripheral sensory disorders to the hearing mechanism may have a significant effect on language development in children because audition is the primary input modality for language learning. However, it is possible for the profoundly deaf child to develop normal language competence if alternative input modalities are utilized. Furthermore, the adult who has fully developed language proficiency will experience no language effect as a result of acquired hearing loss.

The central nervous system (CNS) is comprised of the brain and spinal cord. Although the PNS and the spinal cord have an important role in the initial reception of communicative stimuli (e.g., hearing, vision, etc.) and in the final expression of communication (e.g., articulation, writing, moving the arms or face when gesturing, etc.), it is the brain that is critical to our understanding of higher mental processes. This discussion of basic neuroanatomy will, therefore, focus on the amazing organ that controls all human behavior, including the processing of language.

The human brain weighs approximately 1,400 g and constitutes only 2% of total body weight, yet it has ultimate control of all those higher mental functions that distinguish human beings from other species. The brain consists of over 10 billion cells and consumes 750 ml of oxygenated blood per minute to maintain normal activity. Vascular disruptions of only 5 to 10 seconds will result in temporary disturbances of normal neuronal activity and irreversible brain damage will occur after only 5 to 10 minutes. Neither cellular architecture nor metabolic activity is uniform throughout the brain. Rather, structural and metabolic variations are prominent within the brain, and these physical differences are related to the differing functions associated with neuronal tissue in various regions (Carpenter, 1991; Diamond, Scheibel, & Elson, 1985).

Neuronal tissue throughout the brain is categorized as either white or gray matter. The cerebral cortex, or surface, consists of gray matter made up of nerve cells, dendrites, and portions of nerve fibers. The core of the brain is primarily made up of fibers connecting regions within the hemisphere (association fibers), between the hemispheres (commissural fibers), and between the surface (cortex) and the subcortical/peripheral portions of the nervous system (projection fibers).

Myelin, with a fatty whitish appearance, encases most connecting nerve fibers. Thus, portions of the nervous system that are comprised of connecting nerve fibers are referred to as white matter. The function of the myelin sheath on connecting nerve fibers is to enhance the transmission of neural impulses. The rate of transmission is approximately 50 times faster in the myelinated fiber than in the unmyelinated fiber. Unmyelinated fibers are more commonly found in the smaller nerves of the PNS, whereas the neural fibers of the cranial nerves and CNS are mostly myelinated. The process of myelination in the nervous system is not complete at birth but continues into the early childhood years. Some researchers have attempted to relate the achievement of major developmental milestones, such as babbling and the use of words, with the development of myelination within the nervous system. Multiple sclerosis is, perhaps, the most common disorder of myelin. These patients exhibit a variety of neurologic symptoms including motor speech disorders and cognitive deficits.

The brain consists of five major anatomical divisions, each representing a gross horizontal level: telencephalon, diencephalon, mesencephalon, metencephalon, and myelencephalon. The uppermost or superior level is the telencephalon, comprised of the two cerebral hemispheres, each divided into six lobes: frontal, parietal, temporal, occipital, insular, and limbic. The two hemispheres are partially separated by the longitudinal fissure. This separation is complete in the frontal and posterior (occipital) regions, but in the more central portion or core, the division extends only to the level of corpus callosum, a deep thick plate of nerve fibers that serves as the major connection between the two halves of the brain.

The first observations regarding the unique functions of the two cerebral hemi-spheres were provided from clinical studies of patients with naturally occurring lesions to either the left or right side of the brain. Marc Dax presented a paper to the medical society in Montpellier, France in 1836 in which he reported 40 cases in which patients experienced a loss of speech following brain damage. In all 40 cases, the patients had sustained damage to the left side of the brain. Because these were unselected cases representing the entire population of patients seen in this physi-cian's clinical practice, Dax concluded that each side of the brain controls different functions, with speech being controlled by the left hemisphere. Although Dax's paper was not well received in his day, his conclusions are not inconsistent with modern knowledge about the interhemispheric lateralization of brain functions.

Today we know that over 95% of right-handed persons and 70% of left-handed persons have language localized within the left hemisphere. Of the remaining left-handed persons, half show a clear reversed pattern of lateralization for language processing, whereas half appear to have bilateral representation of language (Rasmussen & Milner, 1977). The right hemisphere came to be referred to as the "nondominant" hemisphere because of its limited role in the processing of lan-guage.

Although the role that the left hemisphere holds in control of linguistic behavior was recognized by the later part of the 19th century, it took nearly 70 years longer before empirical evidence was gathered regarding the "dominant" role that the right hemisphere plays in the control of other neuropsychological processes (Weisenberg & McBride, 1935). Patients with right hemisphere lesions were noted to do poorly on nonverbal tests requiring visuospatial abilities. Functionally, these patients were often so spatially confused that they found it difficult to find their way around even familiar environments. These patients often neglected the left hemispace and would consequently read only one side of the page, dress only one side of their body, or only eat the food on one side of their plate. These visuospatial deficits also effected performance on language tasks when the tasks required visuospatial mediation such as in giving oral directions regarding how to get from one location to another, or responding to logicogrammatical questions (John is bigger than Bill. Bill is bigger than Sally. Who is the biggest?).

Additional evidence regarding the lateralization of cognitive processing within the right hemisphere was provided not only in the observation of impaired abilities in right-hemisphere damaged patients, but also in observations of the preserved skills exhibited by patients with left-hemisphere damage. One such observation had to do with the processing of musical stimuli. Often, patients with left-hemisphere damage, who are otherwise unable to produce any speech, retain the ability to sing melodies. Still others, who may have profound difficulties understanding spoken or written language, may be able to understand the affective meaning carried in the melody of the speech. In marked contrast, right-hemisphere damaged patients sometimes exhibit aprosodia, or the loss of the ability to use suprasegmental varia-tion (e.g., changes in inflection, rate, stress, etc.) to carry linguistic or affective meanings. These remarkable observations suggest that melodic aspects of spoken output may not only involve different neural substrates than the linguistic processing necessary for speech production, but that the neural bases of melodic aspects of speech may be found within the intact right hemisphere.

Most researchers agree that the right hemisphere is essentially "silent" in that it appears to have very limited capability for carrying-out the processing involved in the expression of language. Several studies do suggest, however, that the right hemisphere may have the ability to comprehend certain types of linguistic information.

Graves, Landis, and Goodglass (1981) sought to test the hypothesis that the emotional quality of words would facilitate the recognition ability of the right hemisphere. In order to test this hypothesis, words were presented to neurologically normal participants via tachistoscopic presentation. That is, emotional, nonemotional, and nonsense words were very briefly flashed in either the left or right visual field and patients were asked to depress a key when a real English word appeared. The construct behind this procedure was based on what is known about the visual pathways. Information presented to the either the right or left visual fields is transmitted to the opposite cerebral hemisphere and later shared with the ipsilateral hemisphere by way of intrahemispheric connections (i.e., corpus callosum). Thus, if a stimulus is presented in the visual field opposite the hemisphere in which linguistic processing occurs, then the response reaction time should be shorter than if a stimulus is presented in the visual field opposite the hemisphere in which linguistic processing occurs, then the response reaction time should be shorter than if the information had to be transferred to the contralateral hemisphere for processing the left. One can then conclude that the aphasic pattern of reading comprehension observed by Landis, Graves, and Goodglass (1982) was the same as that of neurologically normal male participants when they read with their right hemisphere.

Landis, Graves and Goodglass subsequently studied the reading comprehension of aphasic patients who had single lesions within the left hemisphere. They found that these patients were able to demonstrate significantly better understanding of emotional abstract words (e.g., fear, kill, pain, etc.) as compared to nonemotional abstract words (e.g., time, view, form, etc.). These results combined with those from the earlier study with normal persons, suggest that aphasic patients may utilize right-hemisphere language processing for aspects of reading comprehension.

Patients with focal pathology in either the left or right hemisphere are not the only clinical participants who have provided information regarding interhemispheric lateralization of cognitive functions. In the 1940s physicians began studying the efficacy of a surgical treatment for patients with unretractable seizures that began in one hemisphere, but rapidly spread to the other. The so-called split-brain procedure involved separating the two cerebral hemispheres by cutting the corpus callosum. Unfortunately, the surgery had only limited success in relieving seizures. Although these patients appeared to have little if any functional residual effects from the procedure, they did provide researchers with a unique opportunity to investigate the performance of each cerebral hemisphere in isolation. Utilizing a rather elaborate testing procedure that included a special contact lens that ensured that only one hemisphere received visual stimuli, Zaidel (1975, 1978) conducted a series of investigations with split-brain participants.

Split-brain studies have provided invaluable information. However, some restraints may be warranted in the generalization of these results. Geschwind (1985) cautioned that patients with epilepsy severe enough to warrant such radical management may have had atypical cortical organization either as a result of (a) early brain lesions that may have actually precipitated the epilepsy to begin with, and/or (b) subsequent effects of long-standing seizures. Thus, it is uncertain as to what degree the results of split-brain investigations reflect normal interhemispheric lateralization of function.

In addition to that which is known about interhemispheric specialization of cognitive functioning, a vast amount of research focus has been placed on the investigation of specialized functions within each of the cerebral hemispheres.

The surface of the cerebral hemispheres appears convoluted, as if they were composed of coils. The high point of these coils are referred to as gyri, whereas the sulci are the separating clefs between adjoining gyri. As shown in Fig. 3.2, prominent gyri and sulci not only form the boundaries between the six lobes of the cerebral hemispheres but also serve as major anatomical landmarks for the identification of functional areas. (Note: Only four lobes are visible on the lateral view of the cerebral hemisphere shown in Fig. 3.2).

The frontal lobes are the most anterior portion of the brain, extending posteriorly to the central sulcus or fissure of Rolando (Fig. 3.2). This region is more developed in human beings than in any other species and does not achieve full maturity until late adolescence. This portion of the brain is the most recently developed in an evolutionary sense and its development is thought to have played a critical role in the human achievement of superior mental capacity. The frontal lobes are not only unique in terms of their relative size, but also in terms of proliferation of connections they have with other parts of the brain. Luria (1973) suggested that a dynamic background level of "cortical tone" is essential for the successful completion of any mental activity. This cortical tone must be modified depending on the activity being performed, and such regulation is thought to be a primary function of the frontal lobes. Thus, the frontal lobes are thought to be involved in all of the highest levels of mental activity or conscious behavior. Sohlberg and Mateer (1989) reported that patients with frontal-lobe pathology display difficulties in anticipation, goal selection, planning, self-regulation, incorporation of feedback, and completion of intended activities. The well-known case of Phineas Gage, who suffered frontal damage as a result of having a railroad spike penetrate his brain, offers a compelling example of how critical the frontal lobes are to the human personality.

> Although he appeared to make a complete physical recovery, his emotional behavior and personality were greatly changed. Following his accident, he was described as fitful and irreverent, indulging at times in the grossest of profanity (which was not previously his custom), manifesting but little deference for his fellow, impatient of restraint or advice when it conflicts with his desires. . . . (Harlow, 1868)

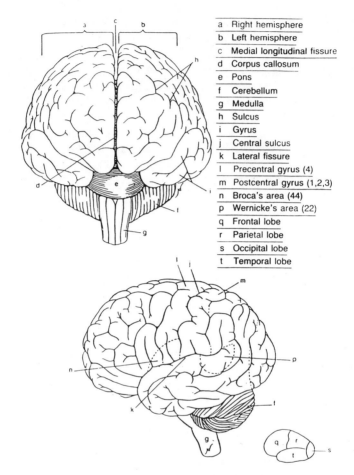

a	Right hemisphere
b	Left hemisphere
c	Medial longitudinal fissure
d	Corpus callosum
e	Pons
f	Cerebellum
g	Medulla
h	Sulcus
i	Gyrus
j	Central sulcus
k	Lateral fissure
l	Precentral gyrus (4)
m	Postcentral gyrus (1,2,3)
n	Broca's area (44)
p	Wernicke's area (22)
q	Frontal lobe
r	Parietal lobe
s	Occipital lobe
t	Temporal lobe

FIG. 3.2.   Cortical landmarks. From McKeough (1982). *The Coloring Review of Neuroscience.* Boston, MA: Little, Brown. Reproduced with permission.

Interestingly, the behaviors we associate with frontal pathologies in adults are similar to the normal behaviors observed in children and adolescents. Thus, our perception of a young adult having achieved maturity may be based, in part, on their having developed these, so called, "executive functions" of the frontal lobes.

In the posterior portion of the frontal lobe is a prominent gyrus immediately anterior to the central sulcus. This, precentral gyrus or primary motor area, is commonly referred to as the motor strip (Fig. 3.2). The cells in this region are responsible for the control of voluntary movement on the contralateral, or opposite, side of the body. The premotor, or supplementary motor, area is located just anterior to the primary motor area and it also controls muscular movement, but to a lesser extent. The motor strip is organized in such a way that one can map the anatomic regions being innervated. This upside down representation of the body along the motor strip is referred to as the *homunculus*. The amount of cortical surface area associated with particular body parts is not related to the size of the body part, but rather is reflective of the amount of motor control required by that region. Thus, the face, lips, tongue, and jaw, which are involved in the complex motor activity of speech production but constitute a relatively small part of the body, take up a relatively large part of the lower portion of the motor strip. Patients with brain damage to the motor strip will display weakness or paralysis of the corresponding body parts on the opposite side of the body. Lesions to either the left or right motor strip may cause difficulty in the physical act of producing speech.

Broca's Area is located at the base of the motor strip in the left, language-dominant hemisphere, in close proximity to the area responsible for movement control for the right facial area. Although lesions to the motor strip result in a motor speech disorder, damage to Broca's Area causes a specific form of language impairment known as Broca's aphasia. Patients with a lesion in this region have difficulty with specific aspects of language processing. These deficits appear in all language input and output modalities (e.g., speech, listening, reading, and writing). Patients with Broca's aphasia produce slow, effortful speech with frequent errors in the selection of correct speech sound and/or written letters (literal paraphasia and literal paragraphia). Their speech and writing consists of short phrases that are lacking grammatical structures. Although they produce very little language, the language that is produced is disproportionately loaded with words that carry important content. The resulting output is often described as being telegraphic because it resembles the form that is used in a telegram when one is trying to convey a message in a highly efficient manner. One such patient when asked to describe what was happening in the Cookie Theft Picture (Fig. 3.3) produced the following language sample:

"Water. The girl down. Washing the dishes. Cookies. Fall down. He cookies. Watch out!"

The patient with Broca's aphasia is said to have relatively intact listening and reading comprehension in comparison with their impressive difficulties in spoken and written expression. These patients do have trouble understanding meaning that is carried by grammatical structure and word order, however. For example, when hearing or reading the passive sentence, "John was hit by Jane," patients with Broca's aphasia may be unable to ascertain who was doing the hitting or who was being hit. The lesion producing Broca's aphasia often extends to the lower portions of the motor strip. Consequently, patients with Broca's aphasia often will experience both speech and language difficulties and may also exhibit paralysis of the right side of the body with greater involvement of the arm than the leg (Albert et al., 1981).

The parietal lobe is immediately posterior to the central sulcus, extending to the occipital lobe, posteriorly, and the sylvian fissure or lateral sulcus, inferiorly (Fig. 3.2). There are at least three important landmarks within the parietal lobe critical to our discussion of human communication. First, is the primary sensory cortex, or somesthetic area, located on the postcentral gyrus in the most anterior portion of the parietal lobe. Here, somesthetic sensory information (pain, temperature, touch, pressure) from the opposite side of the body is processed.

FIG. 3.3.   Cookie theft picture. From Goodglass and Kaplan (1983). *The Assessment of Aphasia and Related Disorders.* Philadelphia, PA: Lea & Febiger. Reproduced with permission.

The supramarginal gyrus curves around the posterior end of the lateral fissure and immediately posterior to the supramarginal gyrus is the angular gyrus. Together, the supramarginal and angular gyri form a portion of the posterior language zone. There areas appear to be related to the perception and interpretation of spoken and written language, as well as with the processes involved in word finding and mathematical calculations.

The lower and lateral portions of each hemisphere make up the temporal lobes, with the upper boundary being the lateral sulcus, and the posterior limits being defined by an imaginary line that marks the parietal–occipital juncture (Fig. 3.2). The temporal lobes are thought to play a primary role in the processing of auditory signals and thus serve an important role in the processing of language. The primary auditory cortex or Heschl's gyrus is not readily visible from a lateral view of the brain because it is located on the floor of the lateral fissure in the anterior temporal gyrus. The auditory association area, also known as Wernicke's Area (in the left hemisphere) and the planum temporali, are found in the more posterior portion of the superior temporal gyrus. This region is more highly developed in the left hemisphere and it is believed that this normal pattern of asymmetry is one example of how anatomical differences found throughout the brain reflect the functional uniqueness of different regions.

When a patient acquires brain damage in the auditory association area and the areas in immediate proximity to this region, they display a form of language impairment known as Wernicke's aphasia. The language characteristics of this form of aphasia are in striking contrast to those already described in association with a lesion in Broca's Area within the frontal lobe. The patient with Wernicke's aphasia generates an abundance of easily produced speech and writing. This output takes the form of sentences with a normal variety of grammatical constructions. Although these patients produce a great number of words, the words produced do not convey their intended ideas. At times real words are used incorrectly (verbal paraphasia). Sometimes these incorrect word choices share some meaningful relationship with the target word (semantic paraphasia). At other times word-like utterances are produced that follow the phonological rules of the language but that have no known meaning (neologisms). The following language sample was obtained by asking a patient to describe what was happening in the Cookie Theft Picture (Fig. 3.3).

> I see a girl gettin'. . apples or something like that because the cage is turned down at the bottom. And next one I see the particulars of a girl dressing clothes. I can't really say where she's at now. Is shows the particulars outside the shop. I can't tell for sure. Some water running off of that stove. I don't know why. She's wettin' her clothes. I don't know why but she is. Not much 'cause the drawer down here is bent over.

People with Wernicke's aphasia also experience great difficulty in understanding spoken and written language. Unlike the person with Broca's aphasia, for whom the understanding of grammar and word order present the greatest challenge, the person with Wernicke's aphasia has trouble understanding word meanings and processing critical phonological information (Albert et al., 1981).

It is interesting to note that aphasic patients with atypical asymmetry in the region of the planum temporali experience greater recovery of auditory comprehension following lesions in the left posterior language zone than do those with the normal pattern (Pieniadz, Naeser, Koff, & Levine, 1983). This observation suggests that people with atypical posterior asymmetry may have a corresponding functional asymmetry with greater bilateral representation of language.

Anterior and posterior language zones within the left hemisphere are connected via a band of cortical fibers referred to as the arcuate fasciculus. Geschwind (1965) hypothesized that a critically placed lesion involving the arcuate fasciculus and supramarginal gyrus would essentially result in the disconnection of Wernicke's and Broca's Areas. Such a lesion would spare these two primary language zones and the patient would experience retained auditory comprehension of language as well as the ability to produce internally generated speech. However, this disconnection would interfere with the patient's ability to repeat what was said to them. Clinically, this pattern of spared and impaired language functions is referred to as conduction aphasia. Patients with conduction aphasia have relatively spared auditory comprehension with some difficulty in the understanding of syntax. Their spontaneously generated speech and writing is fluent, but it contains frequent errors of sound/letter selection. The hallmark of this disorder is the remarkable inability to repeat what is heard and understood and what could be spoken in a spontaneous context.

Clinical observations of patients with unilateral left hemisphere lesions, studies

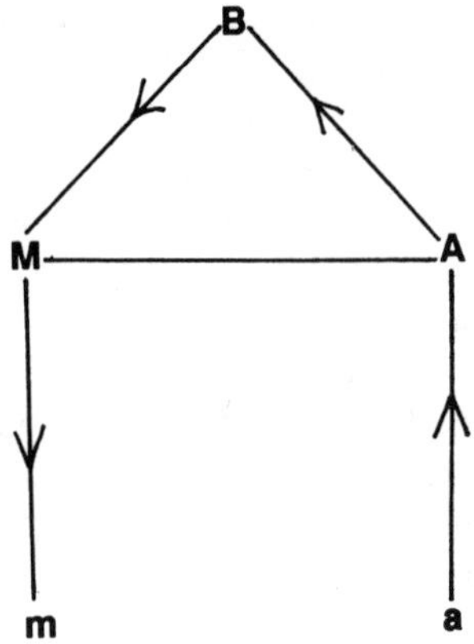

FIG. 3.4. Lichtheim's model of language processing. A represents the auditory word form center; B the concept center; M the center for speech planning; a the auditory pathway; m the motor pathway to the articulatory musculature.

of electrical and chemical activity within the brain while participants are carrying out linguistic tasks (Metter et al., 1985), and electrical stimulation of the brain during neurosurgery (Ojemann, 1983) have all contributed to the current knowledge base regarding the neural bases of language processing. These types of studies have led to the formulation of numerous models of linguistic processing. Interestingly, it is the Lichtheim model of language processing originally proposed by Lichtheim in 1885 and later revised by Carl Wernicke in 1874, and Geschwind in the later part of the 20th century that has best withstood the test of time. Despite its shortcomings, it continues to represent the most accepted conceptualization of language processing within the dominant perisylvian cortex. The model itself is of a connectionist orientation with several critical "centers," some of which are linked to specific anatomical locations and others that are more nebulous, and with specific neural pathways "connecting" these centers. The model identifies three primary centers.

The first, referred to as the "auditory word form center" and represented as "A" in Fig. 3.4, is the permanent store for the phonological representation of words and is thought to correspond with Wernicke's Area in the posterior portion of the left hemisphere. Auditory linguistic signals are transmitted to Wernicke's Area via the "auditory pathway," "a." Here, the auditory signal is matched to previously stored phonological representations of words. Once auditory representations for the sounds of words are recognized, this information is transmitted to the "concept center," "B," where meaningful concepts associated with the words are evoked. The concept center is thought to be diffusely represented in the cortex of the dominant hemisphere and may even involve portions of the nondominant hemisphere to some extent. Geschwind (1965) suggested, however, that a portion of the concept center is located in the supramarginal and angular gyri in the inferior parietal lobe. He proposed that it is in this location that there is a convergence of fibers projecting from somesthetic, visual, and auditory association cortices. The bringing together of multiple forms of sensory information allows for the connection between linguistic labels (e.g., words) and the sensory characteristics associated with those labels. Given the broad location thought to be associated with the concept center, it is not surprising to find that anomia, a condition in which patients have difficulty recalling linguisitic labels, may result from lesions in widely scattered sites within the language dominant hemisphere. It is also here within the concept center that self-generated expressive speech is thought to originate. Ideas to be expressed are related to concepts and these in turn are translated into phonological representations of words. Phonological representations of words to be spoken must then be trans- mitted to the center for speech planning, "M," which is thought to correlate with Broca's Area in the frontal region of the left hemisphere. Once the motor programs are generated, the actual movement commands are put forth by the motor cortex of both hemispheres and transmitted to the peripheral musculature via motor path- ways, "m."

This model of human linguistic processing fairly well predicts many of the aphasias, or linguistic deficit patterns, that have been observed in patients with acquired brain lesions. Three such forms of aphasia have been described above. Broca's aphasia results from a lesion in the center for speech planning, whereas Wernicke's aphasia results from a lesion in the auditory word form center. A lesion in the pathway that connects these two areas causes conduction aphasia.

Several other clinically observed syndromes of speech and language disorders are also predicted by the Lichtheim model. Lesions in the auditory pathway leading to Wernicke's Area cause a disorder called pure word deafness. These patients have normal self-generated spontaneous speech, reading, and writing, but profoundly impaired comprehension of speech and the inability to repeat what is heard. A lesion in the motor pathway, "m," leading out of the center for speech planning results in dysarthria or pure anarthria in which the patient has retained auditory comprehension, reading, and writing, but impaired ability to produce spoken lan- guage under any conditions.

Two very interesting additional forms of aphasia are predicted by the Lichtheim model. Both are characterized by a remarkable preservation of the ability to repeat spoken utterances that are presented auditorially. Lesions that disrupt connections between the auditory word form center, "A," and the concept center, "B," result in transcortical sensory aphasia. Patients with this form of aphasia are able to repeat despite severe comprehension disturbances. Transcortical motor aphasia is charac- terized by preserved repetition of speech in the context of severely impaired self- generated speech. This form of aphasia is thought to manifest when the concept center, "B," is disconnected from the center for speech planning, "M."

The strength of any model of cognitive processing is determined, at least in part, by its ability to predict what is observed clinically in patients with known lesions. No model, including that of Lichtheim as revised by Wernicke and Geschwind, is robust enough to withstand this test. For example, the Lichtheim model does not explain the reading disturbance that is often associated with Broca's aphasia. Fur- thermore, it does not predict the clinical phenomena observed in patients with anomia, the condition in which patients experience word finding difficulties in both spoken and written output while exhibiting no difficulty with auditory or reading comprehension for single words. Nor does it explain the reversed phenomena seen in transcortical sensory aphasia when patients may exhibit a single word compre- hension disorder with no anomia for expressive tasks. Perhaps most importantly, no model has successfully integrated nonlinguistic factors such as motivation, arousal, affect, and visuospatial processing, which are known to influence language performance. More recent dynamic studies of neural activity conducted while participants perform language tasks suggest that not only is it incorrect to ascribe complex linguistic processes to very specific regions within the left hemisphere, but also suggest that neural substrates in regions quite distant from the traditional cortical language zones may serve a critical role in the performance of language tasks.

Posterior to Wernicke's Area in the left hemisphere and its comparable region in the right hemisphere are the occipital lobes, and it is here that many aspects of visual processing, including those involved in reading, take place. The occipital lobes are relatively small and divided, medially, by the calcarine fissure into two major portions: cuneus and lingual gyrus. The primary visual cortex is located at the posterior pole of the occipital lobe in the cortex of the calcarine fissure and adjacent portions of the cuneus and lingual gyrus. It is here that the optic pathways leading from the eyes make their final projection. Lesions in the primary visual cortex will cause defects for vision in the opposite visual field. Such defects, referred to as homonymous hemianopsia, may also occur with lesions in the parietal or temporal lobes, which are in close proximity to the optic pathways. Homonymous hemianopsia is, thus, a common associated finding in patients with lesions in the posterior language zones.

Also located within the occipital lobe is the visual association cortex. It is here that meaningful interpretation of visual images occurs. Patients with lesions in this area exhibit a very rare, but interesting disorder called visual agnosia or cortical blindness. These patients are not blind in the classic sense, in that they are able to experience visual sensation. The patient with visual agnosia is able to visually navigate an obstacle course, match similar objects, and even describe the physical attributes of objects they see. What they are unable to do, however, is recognize or know what they are viewing. Visual agnosia is a modality-specific disorder, however, and patients with this disorder are able to recognize things that are sensed via another modality such as touch or taste.

The insula and limbic lobes are not visible from a lateral view of the cerebral hemisphere. The insula is found deep in the lateral sulcus and can only be viewed if the temporal and frontal lobes are separated. The limbic lobe is found on the medial surface of the brain and is part of the more extensive limbic system, which also includes the hippocampus and subcortical nuclei such as the hypothalamus, amygdala, epithalamus, and various thalamic nuclei. The limbic system has been linked to the regulation of emotional behavior. Electrical stimulation of this area may cause patients to have affective experiences such as very real feelings of hunger, thirst, cold, sadness, anger, reality, or unreality. MacLean (1949) suggested that the limbic system is the place in which internal and external experience are blended. Patients with disorders of the limbic system experience disturbances in affect, personal awareness, and an appreciation for reality.

Bilateral hippocampal lesions are associated with the inability to learn new information (recent memory). Because of this region's proximity to the boney protruberances of the cranium, it is especially vulnerable in traumatic brain injury where there is a rapid acceleration and deacceleration (such as in a car accidents). Consequently, patients who have sustained traumatic brain injuries often exhibit a profound memory disturbance for events subsequent to their injury with intact memory for events prior to their injury. The exact role that the limbic system plays in human communication is unknown. However, given its part in the mediation of memory and emotion, it seems plausible that limbic functions may not only influence the desire to communicate but also color the thoughts to be communicated.

Also found deep with the telencephalon are numerous structures including the corpus striatum, which appear to be important to our understanding of motor control and as such are implicated in certain motor speech disorders.

The inferiormost portion of the brain is the brain stem. It serves as the link between the mind and the external world. Its role in terms of the neurological underpinnings of intrapersonal communication is probably minimal, however. Thus the description that follows will be somewhat cursory. Textbooks disagree with regard to the structures that make up the brain stem or the base of the brain. Some include the diencephalon, whereas others include only the mesencephalon (midbrain), metencephalon (cerebellum and pons), and the myelencephalon (medulla oblongata). The diencephalon is comprised of the thalamus, hypothalamus, optic tracts, and the pituitary gland. The thalamus is the most important component of the diencephalon, serving at least four major roles in: (a) the processing of sensory information, (b) motor control, (c) regulation of cortical activity, and (d) higher level mental processing such as language. Thalamic syndrome is characterized by an alteration in sensory thresholds such that patients experience unpleasant and/or painful sensations in response to what are normally nondistressing stimuli. The thalamus also appears to play a role in the regulation of attention and in certain aspects of memory processing. Because normal language processing depends on both of these nonlinguistic cognitive functions and because the thalamus receives projections from both anterior and posterior cortical language regions, thalamic lesions, especially within the left cerebral hemisphere, have been shown to result in aphasia. Aphasia has also been found to result from lesions to several other critical subcortical areas within the left hemisphere including the putamen and internal capsule. The hypothalamus is important for the regulation of autonomic nervous system functions such as temperature control, emotional expression, and endocrinologic functions.

The mesencephalon, or midbrain, is the uppermost portion of the brain stem. The brain stem cannot be viewed unless the cerebral hemispheres are cut away, thus revealing the internal structures of the brain. The brain stem consists of a series of structures that form the conduit between the spinal cord below and superior portions of the central nervous system above. This area contains a great number of descending motor and ascending sensory fibers, as well as the cranial nerve (CN) nuclei for CN III (oculomotor, controlling eye movements and pupillary constriction) and CN IV (trochlear, controlling eye movements). Because all ascending and descending information must pass throughout this region, the integrity of the brain stem is integral to all overtly observable behavior. Of special importance is a portion of the central brain stem and adjacent superior structures that are collectively referred to as the reticular activating system. This system is known to play an important role in the initiation and maintenance of alert wakefulness. When its function is impaired patients will enter a state of coma.

There are patients who sustain brain stem injury that results in what is termed, "locked-in syndrome." These patients may have preservation of some or all functions of the reticular activating system but be unable to produce any response to external stimulation. Although testing is understandably extremely difficult, if not impossible, it is presumed that these patients have the potential for normal higher level cortical activity. It is, therefore, conceivable that these patients are in a state in which they are only capable of inner speech.

The cerebellum and pons collectively form the metencephalon. The cerebellum sits behind the pons and medulla in the posterior fossa of the skull. Consisting of two hemispheres joined at the midline, the surface of the cerebellum, like that of the cerebral hemispheres, contains many sulci and gyri. Each hemisphere also consists of an outer gray cortex and an inner core made up of deep gray nuclei and white matter. The cerebellum is phylogenetically new to the nervous system and serves a role in the coordination of rapid movements like those used in the articulation of speech. Three cerebellar peduncles connect the cerebellum to the brainstem at the level of the pons. Numerous ascending and descending pathways transverse through the pons like in the midbrain and cranial nerves V (trigeminal), VI (abducens), and VII (facial) emerge from the brain stem at this level.

Finally, the myelencephalon or medulla oblongata is the inferiormost portion of the brain stem with its lower boundary joining the spinal cord. The medulla contains the paired pyramids where descending motor pathways cross over ipsilateral to the side being innervated. Thus, lesions above this level result in motor deficits on the contralateral side, whereas lesions below this level cause motor signs on the same side as the lesion. Cranial nerve VIII (vestibulocochlear, controlling balance and hearing), IX (glossopharyngeal, controlling sensation to the tonsils, pharynx, and tongue and movement of the pharyngeal musculature), X (vagus, controlling sensation to the viscera of the neck, thorax, and abdomen and movement of the larynx, pharynx, and soft palate), XI (spinal accessory, controlling movement of the strap muscles of the neck), and XII (hypoglossal, controlling movement of the tongue) emerge at the level of the medulla. In addition, several important nuclei are found within the medulla, including the cochlear and vestibular nuclei having to do with control of hearing and balance, respectively.

SUMMARY

Much of what is known about human interpersonal communication and its physical bases has come from the study of neurologically abnormal individuals. Gardner (1974) suggested that studying the behavior of unfortunate victims of brain injury may offer those interested in neuropsychological research "the greatest potential for deepening our understanding of normal functioning" (p. 5). This text, however, is dedicated to the phenomenon of intrapersonal communication rather than interpersonal communication. What is the relationship between interpersonal and intrapersonal communication? One hypothesis is that the neurologic underpinnings for inner and public communication might be one and the same. Whereas interpersonal communication necessarily requires sensory and motor links with communicative partners, it may be possible for inner communication to take place in the absence of such connections to the outside world. Douglas Ritchie, a former British radio broadcaster, suffered a stroke at the age of 50 that resulted in aphasia. Several months later, after having made a significant recovery in his ability to carry-out interpersonal communication, he recalled his early experiences:

> There was, I observed, a wide difference between thinking about words and actually thinking in words and about words. I could daydream. . . . I could think, actively, . . without words. . . but. . . the minute I rehearsed speaking with my tongue, even though I kept silent the words would not come. . . . The inside of my brain (I call it that) worked better than the outside—the reacting, the speaking, the calculating, the writing, the humming and the understanding of writing or just speech. And it was the inside of my brain which was the most valuable and that could save me from drowning. (Gardner 1974, p. 405)

The intrapersonal communication experience described here took place during a time when many aspects of language processing were not readily available to Ritchie. And yet, his testimony suggests that although he had great difficulty availing words, the conceptualizations of those words were not inaccessible. Could this mean that once social speech has established inner speech than inner and public speech may share chiefly the "Concept Center" of the Wernicke-Lichtheim model, with the remaining centers relating primarily to the interpersonal transfer of concepts and secondarily to the maintenance of inner speech? I would hope that the reader would be encouraged to go beyond the various theoretical descriptions of inner speech and seek to understand the neurological bases of the phenomenon.

REFERENCES

Albert, M. L., Goodglass, H., Helm, N. A., Rubens, A. B., & Alexander, M. P. (1981). *Clinical aspects of dysphasia.* New York: Springer-Verlag.

Barr, M. L., & Kierman, J. A. (1993). *The human nervous system: An anatomical viewpoint* (4th ed.). Philadelphia: Harper & Row.

Carpenter, M. B. (1991). *Core text of neuroanatomy* (4th ed.). Baltimore: Williams & Wilkins.

Diamond, M. C., Scheibel, A. B., & Elson, L. M. (1985). *The human brain coloring book.* New York: Barnes & Nobel.

Gardner, H. (1974). *The shattered mind: The person after brain damage.* New York: Vintage Books.

Geschwind, N. (1965). Disconnection syndromes in animals and man. *Brain, 88,* 237.

Geschwind, N. (1985). The frequency of callosal syndromes in neurological practice. In A. G. Reeves (Ed.) *Epilepsy and the corpus callosum* (pp. 349–356). New York: Plenum Press.

Goodglass, H. & Kaplan, E. (1983). *The assessment of aphasia and other related disorders.* Malvern, PA: Lea & Febiger.

Graves, R., Landis, T., & Goodglass, H. (1981). Laterality and sex differences for visual recognition of emotional and non-emotional words. *Neuropsychologia, 19,* 95–102.

Harlow, J. M. (1868). Recovery after severe injury to the head. *Publication of the Massachusetts Medical Society, 2*, 327–346.

Landis, T., Graves, R., & Goodglass, H. (1982). Aphasic reading and writing: Possible evidence for right hemisphere participation. *Cortex, 18*, 105–112.

Love, R. J., & Webb, W. G. (1992). *Neurology for the speech-language pathologist.* Boston: Butterworth-Heinemann.

Luria, A. R. (1973). *The working brain: An introduction to neuropsychology.* New York: Basic Books.

Luria, A. R. (1980). *Higher cortical functions in man* (2nd ed.). New York: Basic Books.

MacLean, P. D. (1949). Psychomatic disease and the "visceral brain": Recent developments bearing on the Papez theory of emotion. *Psychomatic Medicine, 11*, 338–353.

McKeough, M. (1982). The coloring review of neuroscience. Boston: Little Brown.

Metter, E. J., Sepulueda, C. A., Jackson, C. A., Mazziotta, J. D., Benson, D. F., Hanson, W. R., Roege, W. J., & Phelps, M. E. (1985). Relationships of temporal parietal lesions and distant glucose metabolism changes in the head of the caudate nucleus in aphasic patients. *Neurology, 35* (suppl.), 120.

Ojemann, G. A. (1983). Brain organization for language from the perspective of electrical stimulation mapping. *Behavior Brain Science, 6*, 180.

Pieniadz, J. M., Naeser, M. A., Koff, E., & Levine, H. L. (1983). CT scan cerebral hemispheric asymmetry measurements in stroke cases with global aphasia: Atypical asymmetries associated with improved recovery. *Cortex, 19*, 371–391.

Rasmussen, T., & Milner, B. (1977). The role of early left-brain injury in determining lateralization of cerebral speech functions. *Annual New York Academy Science, 299*, 355–369.

Sohlberg, M. M., & Mateer, C. A. (1989). *Introduction to cognitive rehabilitation: Theory and practice.* New York: The Guilford Press.

Weisenberg, T., & McBride, K. E. (1935). *Aphasia: A clinical and psychological study.* New York: Commonwealth Fund.

Zaidel, E. (1975). A technique for presenting lateralized visual input with prolonged exposure. *Vision Research, 15*, 283–289.

Zaidel, E. (1978). Auditory language comprehension in the right hemisphere following cerebral commissurotomy and hemispherectomy: A comparison with child language and aphasia. In A. Caramazza & E. Zurif (Eds.), *Language acquisition and language breakdown*, (pp. 229–275). Baltimore: Johns Hopkins University Press.

4

A Conception of Culture for a Communication Theory of Mind

Michael Cole
University of California, San Diego

My goal in this chapter is to outline a way of thinking about culture appropriate to developing a theory of human cognition within the discipline of communication. I approach this topic from the perspective of a psychologist who has been dissatisfied with the role allotted to culture in mainstream cognitive psychology.

In attempting to formulate a theory of mind that places culture at its center, I have found it useful to work from the theoretical position known as "cultural-historical" psychology. I first encountered this perspective in the work of the Soviet psychologists, Lev Vygotsky, Alexander Luria, Alexei Leontiev, and their colleagues. Over time I have come to learn that their cultural historical approach was only one of many similar streams of scholarly thought throughout this century. In psychology the corresponding American thinkers included John Dewey, William James, and George Herbert Mead; In Germany Wilhelm Spranger, Norbert Elias, and the adherents of what they called "cultural psychology" (Stern, 1916/1990); and in France, it was the sociologists Emile Durkheim and Levy Bruhl who pursued the implications of a cultural-historical approach to human nature. I also came to learn that the ideas of the Russian psychologists were also influenced by a wide spectrum of Russian thinkers including Mikhail Bakhtin (literary and social theorist), Osip Mandelshtam (poet), Pavel Florensky (philosopher), and Sergei Eisenshtein (film maker). Those familiar with the history of communication as a scientific discipline can readily see in this list a somewhat unusual, but interesting cross-section of the people to whom the discipline owes its intellectual roots.

A common, if not universal, feature these thinkers share is the central importance they give to processes of communication in shaping human nature. For many, mind is quite literally created in communication, making it legitimate to speak of a "communication theory" of mind. This basic assumption is captured beautifully by Osip Mandelshtam in the fragment of a poem that serves as the epigraph to

Vygotsky's (1934/1987) meditations on the relation of language to thinking. Mandelshtam wrote,

> I forgot the word I wanted to say,
> And thought, unembodied,
> Returns to the hall of shadows. (p. 243)

Vygotsky, in conventional scientific language, expressed this idea by writing that "the thought is completed in the word" as part of the act of communicating. An uncommunicated thought, from this perspective, exists only in "the land of the shadows." It is not fully realized until it has been transformed from personal sense into culturally conventional meanings. Thinking, in short, is a culturally mediated social process of communication.

Arriving at this issue as a psychologist, I have found that in order to pursue its implications there is a pressing need to understand the properties of the cultural medium in which human communication takes place in far more detail and breadth than are contained in the writings of cultural-historical psychologists. Hence, my focus in this chapter is on the properties of culture and cultural mediation as essential elements in the process of communication viewed from the perspective of the "I" who does the communicating. After sketching out a way of thinking about culture from this perspective, I sketch out the directions a fuller elaboration of the topic needs to take in dealing with *joint* mediated activity, for example, communication. A full treatment of this topic would require a book-length treatment of great complexity.

A CULTURAL-HISTORICAL APPROACH
TO CULTURE

First, a word of caution in dealing with the term, *culture*. As Roy D'Andrade (1984) pointed out, competing definitions of culture are not, technically speaking, definitions (e.g., "a paraphrase that maintains the truth or falsity of statements in a theory when substituted for the word defined"). Rather, competing definitions of culture are more like theories in that they seek to make substantive propositions about an aspect of the world. The "definitions" one offers depend on what kinds of propositions about what aspects of the world one is interested in. I believe, however, that a cultural-historical approach to understanding culture has rather general utility, particularly for the discipline of communication.

Mediation by Artifacts

The crucial intuition that cultural-historical thinkers hold in common is that human life takes shapes and matures in a unique environment that includes the entire pool of artifacts accumulated by the social group in the course of its historical development. As a quasi-organized aggregate, the accumulated artifacts of a group, culture, is the species-specific medium of human development. The capacity to develop within that medium and to arrange for its reproduction in succeeding generations is the distinctive characteristic of our species.

The idea of cultural mediation is sometimes illustrated in terms of the concept of a tool, a prominent class of artifacts. In the words of the philosopher, Henri Bergson,

> If we could rid ourselves of all pride, if, to define our species, we kept strictly to what the historic and prehistoric periods show us to be the constant characteristic of man and of intelligence, we should say not Homo Sapiens but Homo Faber. In short, intelligence, considered in what seems to be its original feature, is the faculty of manufacturing artificial objects, especially tools for making tools, and of indefinitely varying the manufacture. (Bergson, 1911/1983, p. 139)

Tools, Luria (1928) wrote, change both the environment of human development and structure of psychological processes. Instead of directly acting upon the world, human beings act indirectly, through artifacts.

Precisely the same idea is to be found in the writings of C. H. Judd (1926), an influential psychologist writing at almost the same time. For example, Judd wrote that

> the tools which man has invented are powerful influences in determining the course of civilized life. Through the long ages while man has been inventing tools and learning to use them, his mode of individual reaction has been undergoing a change. He is no longer absorbed in direct attack on prey which furnishes him his food. He does not develop more skill in the use of claws and teeth in order that he may cope with his environment. He has adopted an indirect mode of action. He uses instruments which he has devised or borrowed from his forefathers or from his neighbor (pp. 3–3).

Judd, in a manner consistent with terminology developed by Durkheim (1915), referred to tool use (which includes language) as a social institution, by which he meant "all those accumulations of social capital which have been produced in the course of community life" (p. 3).

This new structural relation of the individual to environment has traditionally been pictured as a triangle, as in Fig. 4.1. Simplifying for purposes of explication, "natural" ("unmediated") functions are those along the base of the triangle; "cultural" ("mediated") functions are those where the relation between subject and environment (subject and object, response and stimulus, etc.) are mediated by some form of artifact, which Vygotsky and his colleagues referred to as auxiliary means.

It should not be thought that the emergence of tool use means that the mediated path replaces the natural one. One does not cease to stand on the ground and look at the tree when one picks up an axe to chop the tree down; rather, the incorporation of tools into the activity creates a new structural relation in which the cultural (mediated) and natural (unmediated) routes operate synergistically; through active attempts to appropriate their surroundings to their own goals, people incorporate

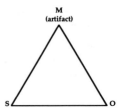

M
(artifact)

FIG. 4.1. The mediated structure of human action, in which mind is linked to the world both directly and indirectly through artifacts.

s   o

auxiliary means into their actions, giving rise to the distinctive, trinary relationship of subject–medium–object.

It also needs to be emphasized that what is taken as "direct" cannot properly be conceived of as "natural." Rather, the "direct" route, like the mediated route, depends on an environment modified by (prior) successful human actions and is to this degree suffused with human intentions. Consequently, what the early cultural-historical theorists referred to as "direct, natural" processes must be bracketed in quotation marks, to remind ourselves that the physical world is the world-as-conditionalized by culture and not entirely, "naturally given" (Sahlins, 1976).

The Dual Nature of Artifacts

The fact that Luria, Bergson, Judd, and others write about "tool" mediation may incline one to think that they had in mind such artifacts as hoes and plates. However, they all considered language to be a constituent of the cultural medium and part of the overall process of cultural mediation, the "tool of tools."

Cultural-historical theorists have a decidedly two-sided notion of how tool medi ation operates. As Vygotsky (1978) explained, what we conventionally call tools and what we conventionally call signs and symbols are two aspects of the same phenom-enon: mediational devices. Mediators thought of as tools appear to be more out-wardly oriented, as a means of changing aspects of the environment; mediators thought of as signs are more inwardly oriented, toward "the self." In reality, both potentialities operate as part of a single, dialectical "dance," as a result of which (to use a memorable phrase of Vygotsky's, 1978) human beings are able to "control their behavior from the outside" (p. 59).

An essential property of artifacts that underpins their double sided influence and provides a common grounding of language and culture is that artifacts are simul-taneously ideal (conceptual) and material. They are ideal in that they contain in coded form the interactions that they mediated in the past that they mediate in the present (e.g., the structure of a pencil carries within it the morphology of action appropriate to the forms of writing in the past). They are material in that they are embodied in material artifacts. This dual nature is as true when one is considering language/speech as it is for the more usually noted forms of artifacts such as tables and knives that are ordinarily thought of when discussing material culture. What differentiates a word, such as "language" from, say, a table, is the relative promi-nence of their material and ideal aspects. No word exists apart from its material instantiation (as a configuration of sound waves, or hand movements, or as writing, or as a pattern of neuronal and muscular activity), whereas every table embodies an order imposed by thinking human beings.

This dual nature of artifacts was emphasized by the American anthropologist, Leslie White, (1959) in terms that fit perfectly into the cultural-historical school's basic postulate of mediation (e.g., Leontiev, 1932; Luria, 1928; Vygotsky, 1987).

> An axe has a subjective component; it would be meaningless without a concept and an attitude. On the other hand, a concept or attitude would be meaningless without overt expression, in behavior or speech (which is a form of behavior). Every cultural element, every cultural trait, therefore, has a subjective and an objective aspect. (p. 236)

D'Andrade (1986) made this same point when he told us that "material culture—tables and chairs, buildings and cities—is the reification of human ideas in a solid medium" (p. 22).

The special quality of the kind of consciousness that arises with mediated activity is that human beings live in a "double world," simultaneously "natural" and "artificial." Luria (1981) described this double world in the following way:

> The enormous advantage is that their world doubles. In the absence of words, human beings would have to deal only with those things which they could perceive and manipulate directly. With the help of language, they can deal with things that they have not perceived even indirectly and with things which were part of the experience of earlier generations. Thus, the word adds another dimension to the world of humans . . . Animals have only one world, the world of objects and situations. Humans have a double world. (p. 35)

Again, we can find the same claim for the duality of human nature in Durkheim (1915), although it is couched in terms of the individual-social polarity:

> Man is double. There are two beings in him: an individual being which has its foundation in the organism, and the circle of whose activities is therefore strictly limited, and a social being which represents the highest reality in the intellectual and moral order that we can know by observation—I mean society. . . . In so far as he belongs to society, the individual transcends himself, both when he thinks and when he acts. (p. 29)

The Primacy of the Social

The final important implication of the principle of cultural mediation I discuss here is that other human beings, both those present to the senses and those of prior generations, play a crucial role in the formation of human cognitive capacities. It is not just that communication with human beings is necessary as an integral aspect of the completion of a thought. Because human beings are born helpless into a socially organized, culturally mediated human environment, the very existence of human thinking derives from its social nature. This emphasis is summed up in what Vygotsky (1934/1987) called the general law of cultural development.

> Every function in the cultural development of the child comes on the stage twice, in two respects; first in the social, later in the psychological, first in relations between people as an interpsychological category, afterwards within the child as an intrapsychological category. . . .
>   All higher psychological functions are internalized relationships of the social kind, and constitute the social structure of the personality. Their composition, genetic structure, ways of functioning, in one word all their nature is social. Even when they have become psychological processes their nature remains quasi-social. The human being who is alone retains the function of interaction. (Vygotsky, 1960, p. 197–198 quoted in Valsiner, 1988, p. 142).

At this point the affinity of Vygotsky's thinking to that of George Herbert Mead (1934/1956) becomes clear. "The importance of 'communication,'" wrote Mead, "lies in the fact that it provides a form of behavior in which the organism or the individual may become an object to himself" (p. 203). Such a self arises, according to Mead, in culturally/linguistically mediated joint activity involving the individual and the members of his or her society. The self is, in Mead's (1956) memorable description, "the internalized conversation of gestures which constitutes thinking or in terms of which thought or reflection proceeds. And hence the origin and foundations of the self, like those of thinking, are social." (p. 228)

A Provisional Summing Up

We can summarize the basic properties of the cultural medium and the associated structure of human thought and activity as follows:

1. Cultural mediation creates a species-specific, universal structure of human mind and associated morphology of action.

2. Cultural mediation has a recursive, bidirectional effect; mediated activity simultaneously modifies both the environment and the subject.

3. Cultural artifacts are both material and symbolic; they regulate one's environment and oneself. In this respect, they are "tools" broadly conceived, and the master tool is language.

4. The cultural environment into which children are born contains within itself the accumulated knowledge of prior generations. In mediating their behavior through these objects, human beings benefit not only from their own experience, but that of their forbearers.

5. Cultural mediation implies a species-specific mode of developmental change, in which the accomplishments of prior generations are cumulated in the present as the specifically human part of the environment; this form of development, in turn, implies the special importance of the social world in human development because only other human beings can create the special conditions needed for that development to occur.

CULTURE IN THE WORK
OF RUSSIAN CULTURAL-HISTORICAL
PSYCHOLOGISTS

During the 1920s and early 1930s, Vygotsky, Luria, and their colleagues studied the structural transformations in behavior that occur as people begin to incorporate auxiliary means into their actions. For example, Vygotsky carried out studies with young children modeled on Kölher's ape studies; the child was asked to achieve a goal (reach some cookies) that was beyond her reach and studied as potential tools were introduced into her environment (Levina, 1981). Luria demonstrated that the acquisition of self-control in simple choice situations is intimately related to the ability of children to mediate their activity through language. Such results substantiated his belief that "voluntary behavior is the ability to create stimuli and to subordinate [oneself] to them; or in other words, to bring into being stimuli of a special order, directed at the organization of behavior" (Luria, 1932, p. 401).

Just as studies with children could lay bare the way in which acquisition of mediational means is crucial to the evolution of behavior, so studies of the restoration of function following disease or injury to the brain illustrate the principles of mediated cognition used to guide therapy, that is, the remediation of behavior. In a well-known early example of this principle, Luria and Vygotsky carried out pilot work with a patient suffering from Parkinsonism. So severe was this condition that the patient could not walk across the floor. However, paradoxically, the patient could climb stairs. Vygotsky and Luria (reported in Luria, 1932, 1979) hypothesized that when climbing stairs, each step represented a signal to which the patient had to respond in a conscious way. When pieces of paper were placed on a level floor and the patient was asked to walk across the room stepping over them, the formerly immobile patient was able to walk across the room unaided. In a series of studies, Luria and Vygotsky showed that a variety of techniques that induced participants to regulate their behavior indirectly through artifacts produced the same kinds of remedial effects.

The principle of artifact/tool mediation is powerfully illustrated in these studies, but the cultural system of which it is a part was not systematically investigated; rather, it provided the taken-for-granted foundation that made it possible to highlight the principles of artifact mediation.

Culture conceived of as the patterning of a way of life was much more prominent in the expeditions made to Tadzhikistan, Kirgizia, and other remote parts of the then-Soviet Union designed to study how rapid changes from nonindustrialized to industrialized forms of life influence cognitive development and adult thinking (Luria, 1976; Valsiner, 1993). The Russians, like Durkheim, argued in favor of the view that cross-*cultural* comparisons could be used to assess cross-*historical* variations in human thinking (Wertsch, 1991). They did not speak of a "primitive mentality" *a la* Levy Bruhl (although they were familiar with his work in both French and Russian), but they did claim that the shift from a traditional, nonliterate, to a modern, literate mode of life was accompanied by a shift from "graphic-functional" to "theoretical" thinking.

This work can be criticized on a number of grounds (LCHC, 1983; Van der Veer & Valsiner, 1991; Wertsch, 1991). What most concerns me in the context of this discussion is that culture was treated very much as a package of "independent variables" rather than as a medium, and was not directly the object of analysis. Instead of an analysis of indigenous activities and understandings as the starting point of analysis, culture appeared as casual description or "significant dimensions" that, it was assumed, served as the cause of individual cognitive change. Dimensions such as literacy (vs. nonliteracy) or involvement in a collective farm (vs. traditional animal husbandry and farming practices) were employed to create a rough "traditional-modern" dichotomy that left cultural activities to be described by a rather crude folk theory of the culture, and the cognitive consequences of cultural differences were evaluated using tests devised for use with European children.

In short, the specification of culture that underpinned the empirical research of the cultural-historical psychologists was in certain respects too schematized and in other respects inconsistent. At the microlevel culture was schematized in terms of the artifact-mediated actions of individuals; at the macrolevel in terms of vague, society-wide patterns of cultural causation rather than as cultural mediation. What was missing was a way of talking about artifact mediation that allows the study of units of analysis that extend beyond individual actions to include larger patterns of structuration in a single conceptual framework.

Over the past decade, there has been enormous interest in extending the key ideas of the cultural historical approach both within psychology and to other disciplines (Bruner, 1990; Cazden, 1993; Emerson, 1981; Rogoff, 1991; Wertsch, 1985, 1991). This work contains many suggestions for ways to enrich the treatment of culture within a cultural-historical perspective. Because I cannot hope to encompass all of these extensions in this chapter, I will focus on getting beyond the principle of artifact mediation to a deeper understanding of how culture as medium enters into the organization of human thinking, relying primarily on the ideas of anthropologists, although some sociologists and literary theorists will appear in my discussion.

Identifying Structured Units
Within the Medium

Although artifact creation and artifact/tool mediation constitute culture, culture is not a random assemblage of such artifacts. The questions then become, how are we to identify structure within culture-as-medium and what are the effective units of culture vis à vis human thought?

Contemporary anthropologists are divided with respect to the issue of coherence in culture, taken as a whole. In a wide-ranging discussion of this issue a few years ago, Paul Kay suggested "semiseriously" that the supposed coherence of culture is really a coherence imposed on the anthropologist by the need to publish a coherent story: "if I go out and study the 'whoevers,' I've got to come back and tell a consistent and entertaining story about what the 'whoevers' are like—and everything they do better fit into this one story" (in Shweder & Levine, 1984, p. 17).

Kay was immediately challenged by Clifford Geertz, whose work may have been one of the sources of Kay's provocative remark. Geertz is justly famous for developing the notion that different parts of culture cohere such that, for example, one could use a Balinese cockfight or puppet theater as an organizing metaphor for all of Balinese society. In the early 1970s, Geertz cited with approval Max Weber's image of humankind as "an animal suspended in webs of significance he himself has spun," declaring that "I take culture to be those webs" (Geertz, 1973, p. 5). Later in that same volume, Geertz suggested that culture should be conceived of by analogy with a recipe or a computer program, which he referred to as "control mechanisms." The "webs of significance" metaphor evokes images of the beautiful patterning of a spider's web, whereas the "recipe" metaphor suggests that the patterning is quite local and specific to particular "ingredients," the rules for combining them, and their qualitatively distinctive "flavor."

When responding to Kay, Geertz sought a new metaphor to describe his sense that human beings' cultural medium is neither made up of unconnected bits and pieces, nor a perfect configuration: "the elements of culture are not like a pile of sand and not like a spider's web. Its more like an octopus, a rather badly integrated creature—what passes for a brain keeps it together, more or less, in one ungainly whole" (Shweder & Levine, 1984, p. 19).

These anthropologists' efforts to characterize the overall degree of cultural cohesion suggest two extremes to be avoided: Human life would be impossible if every event was experienced as *sui generis,* an isolated instance; it is no more helpful to believe that a single, uniform, configuration of cultural constraints is constitutive of all events within a culture. In addition, it is essential to take into account the fact that human activity involves elaborate and shifting divisions of labor and experience within cultures, so that no two members of a cultural group can be expected to have internalized the same parts of whatever "whole" might be said to exist (Schwartz, 1978, 1990).

Consequently, it is not possible to say, in general, how much cultural coherence and integration exists between the two extremes; in order to say anything useful, it is necessary to abandon broad metaphors, and to seek specific sources of coherence and patterning.

Cultural Schemas and Scripts.   One prominent approach to thinking about structured units within the overall medium of culture that has close links to psychological theories about thinking focuses on systems of meaning, organized according to a variety of different principles (as networks of semantic associations, as taxonomies, etc.).

This approach has been thoroughly summarized by D'Andrade (1990) as follows: "Culture consists of learned and shared systems of meaning and understanding, communicated primarily by means of natural language. These meanings and understandings are not just representations about what is in the world; they are also directive, evocative, and reality constructing in character." (p. 65).

The basic constituents of these systems of meaning are called *schemas,* a term used to refer to knowledge structures in which the parts relate to each other and the whole in a patterned fashion. A schema specifies how certain essential elements relate to one another while leaving other, less essential elements to be filled in as needed according to the circumstances. Some elements, so-called default values, may not be specified at all. For example, if I hear my cat mewing outside the door, the elements, "breaths," and "warm blooded" are plausible default values. I know they are true without having to think about them. Under some circumstances, such as when I see the cat lying under the car and it is not clear if it is dead or alive, those elements of the schema may be crucial to my reasons.

D'Andrade (1984, 1990) proposed that "meaning systems" operate as cultural "schemas." In D'Andrade's (1984) terms,

> Typically such schemas portray simplified worlds, making the appropriateness of the terms that are based on them dependent on the degree to which these schemas fit the actual worlds of the objects being categorized. Such schemas portray not only the world of physical objects and events, but also more abstract worlds of social interaction, discourse, and even word meaning. (p. 93)

D'Andrade (1990) referred to intersubjectively shared cultural schemas as cultural models that are used to interpret and to guide action in a wide variety of domains "including events, institutions, and physical and mental objects" (p. 108). He illustrated how adults use cultural models to reason about objects, such as cats, social institutions, such as marriage, and about general properties of human beings, such as how the mind works.

Given the ideal of grounding their theories in the everyday activities of people, it is no surprise that psychologists who focus on cultural mediation should concentrate on event schemas referred to as scripts, which specify the appropriate people who participate in an event, the social roles they play, the objects that are used, and the sequence of actions and causal relations that apply.

Both Jerome Bruner (1990) and Katherine Nelson (1981) started their analysis of mental life with such event representations. Nelson referred to scripts as "generalized event schemas." Scripts, she wrote, provide "a basic level of knowledge representation in a hierarchy of relations that reaches upward through plans to goals and themes" (p. 101).

Consider the following examples, the first from a 3-year-old, the second from a child a little under 5 years of age responding to the request to "tell me about going to a restaurant."

> Three year old: Well, you eat and then go somewhere

> Five year old: Okay. Now first we go to restaurants at night-time and we, um, we and we go and wait for a while, and then the waiter comes and gives us the little stuff with the dinners on it, and then we wait for a little bit, a half an hour or a few minutes or something, and um, then our pizza comes or anything, and um, [interruption] . . . [The adult says, "So then the food comes. . . ."] Then we eat it, and um, then when we're finished eating the salad that we order we got to eat our pizza when its done, because we get the salad before the pizza's ready. so then when we're finished with all the pizza and all our salad, we just leave. (Nelson, 1981, p. 103)

Several points about these child formulations stand out. First, they are indeed generalized, although grounded in particulars; the children are talking about a habitual event ("You eat," "We go"). Second, the descriptions are dominated by the temporal sequencing of actions. Third, the causal logic of the event inheres in the temporal ordering of actions (pizza is eaten after salad because it takes longer to prepare). Finally, there is a good deal left unsaid, in part because it is taken for granted (We open the door and enter the restaurant, We pick up our forks and use them to eat the salad, etc.) and in part because the child is not involved and most likely does not understand (e.g., that one pays for the food and leaves a tip).

According to Bruner (1990), narrative lies at the heart of human thought, people's "folk psychology." The representation of experience in narratives provides a frame that enables humans to interpret their experience. If it were not for such narrativized framing, he wrote, "we would be lost in a murk of chaotic experience and probably would not have survived as a species in any case" (p. 56).

The ways that notions such as script and narrative have been used to explain culture's role in thought often differ. Scripts have ordinarily been employed to account for the structure in children's narratives of single events (going to a restaurant), whereas narratives (such as the master narrative evoked in response to the question, "who am I?") ordinarily involve several linked scenes. But scripts and narratives are both examples of what D'Andrade referred to as cultural schemas.

Cultural Schemas as Mediators.   As Holland and Valsiner (1988) noted, the anthropological notion of "cultural model" is very similar to the cultural-historical notion of a mediator. This point was made in different ways by D'Andrade and Nelson.

D'Andrade referred to physically realized cultural models as "mediating structures," using as an example Hutchins' (1986) description of the way airline pilots use a checklist as a tool to insure that they are prepared to take off. He pointed out that when using such a mediator-cum-cultural model, "the user does not coordinate his or her behavior directly with the task environment, but rather coordinates with a mediating object that has a structure that is like the task environment in some important way" (p. 107).

After describing in detail all of the subroutines that must be mastered and executed in order for the checklist/script/model to be effective, D'Andrade concluded that "what might at first look like a simple device in fact turns out to be a complex of mediations—that is, of coordinations between structures" (p. 107).

In the case of the checklist it is essential that the model and the reality it represents be identical; a highly experienced pilot directly recalls the actions to be taken and their effects on the environment. There are cases, however, where mediating cultural models replace the reality they are supposed to model with nonveridical structures. An example of such substitution is provided by the work of D'Andrade and Shweder (D'Andrade, 1974, Shweder & D'Andrade, 1980) in which adult observers view people interacting. Some observers score behavioral characteristics (such as disagreement, criticism, joking, etc.) while making the observations, others observe and then score the same people shortly after the observation. Surprisingly, there is virtually no correlation between the two sets of scorings. However, the scores of the group who make their ratings shortly after they observe the behavior correlate rather well with scores produced by people who observe no behavior, but instead rate the similarities among the descriptive terms used by the other two groups (e.g., how similar are disagree and criticize, disagree and joke, etc.). Here we see a pervasive effect of cultural models of social interaction on remembered reality; the simplified model replaces the complex reality, yielding, among other things, the "reality" of stable personality traits in place of context-specific variability in behavior.

In her work on children's acquisition of event representations mentioned earlier, Nelson highlighted additional important properties of scripts as mediators. First, she suggested that scripts, like the cultural schemas discussed by D'Andrade, serve as guides to action. When someone enters a novel event, they must seek out an answer to the question, "What's going on here?" The presence of scripts, embodied in the language being spoken, makes this task easier. Once a person has even a crude idea of what the appropriate actions associated with going to a restaurant are, they can enter the flow of the particular event with partial knowledge, which gets enriched in the course of the event itself, facilitating later coordination. "Without shared scripts," Nelson wrote, "every social act would need to be negotiated afresh" (p. 109). Nelson (1981) also pointed out that children grow up within contexts controlled by adults and hence within adult scripts. By and large, adults direct the children's action and set the goals, rather than engage in direct teaching. In effect, they use their notion of the appropriate script to provide constraints on the child's actions and allow the child to fill in the expected role activity. In this sense, "the acquisition of scripts is central to the acquisition of culture" (p. 110).

From Scripts to Events: The Dramatic Metaphor.   Nelson's notion of children "growing up in other people's scripts" meshes nicely with the cultural-historical emphasis on the special role of the social world in human development. At the same time it suggests that it is important to identify additional sources of structuration at the level of the events within which cultural scripts and schemas are embodied in activity. Many suggestions for how to think about cultural structuration at the level of events and activities could be offered (Bourdieu, 1977; Engeström, 1987, Lave & Wenger, 1992; Ortner, 1984). For my limited purposes here, I will follow a path suggested by the script metaphor and suggest the usefulness of including the range of phenomena suggested by the dramatic metaphor (Burke, 1945; Goffman, 1959; Kaplan, 1983).

My starting point for this elaboration is Morse Peckham's (1965) discussion of the dramatic metaphor and human thinking. Peckham began from the assumption that "not even the most elaborate script provides nearly enough prescriptions to control all the behavior necessary to act a play" (p. 52). He then suggested how each element of the dramatic metaphor provides a part of the "prescription" (e.g., to script ahead of time).

The initiator of "the play" is the author, although Peckham suggested that the "author" is often best thought of as the bearer of the cultural tradition. The script contains the skeleton specifications for action. It provides the roles and a skeleton description of the action. "Script in hand," Peckham then proceeded to expand the metaphor in specifying additional sets of constraints/resources that are needed for the live performance.

First, there is the director, "the cultural transmitter or, in the largest sense, the teacher" who must fill in the gaps between the necessarily imprecise specifications of the script (cultural tradition) and the range of behaviors that are deemed appropriate. Second, there is still further specification that must be provided by the actor: Every person has slightly different organic characteristics and past experiences, slightly different mixes of abilities and preferences, all of which shape his/her interpretations. Then there are properties of the setting, whether one is on stage or back stage, and various objects and behaviors that cue one to behave in one or another way.

Pursuing the metaphor, Peckham suggested that the audience also plays an important role in structuring our behavior (a point central to Bakhtin's, 1981, dialogism). If we are physically present with others, the interpretation of audience is obvious. Drawing on Mead (1934) Peckham suggested that whether or not we are with others, "each of us is at once author, script, director, stage-designer, and styling and innovating author . . . Everyman is ultimately his own playwright, and Everyman is his own audience" (pp. 54–55). Last comes the role of the critic, the detached "other" (who may be a real "other" or ourselves in a moment of detachment from the dramatic production) where self-evaluation and possible psychological insight occur.

Putting Mediated Action Into Context

If we now consider all of the sources for structuring the artifacts that constitute culture as a whole, they are not unconsiderable. Individual artifacts either represent or enter into the representation of schemas and scripts; scripts and schemas are constituents of events, "scripts as produced," that themselves provide resources for their sequential arrangement and deployment in action, which is constituent of the ongoing drama of one's life. Simultaneously, the artifacts known as words enter into relations with each other that cut across scripts and events, in semantic networks of sometimes bewildering complexity.

It requires little reflection to realize that even under the most generous assumptions about mechanisms that link object schemas together into hierarchies or event schemas into sequentially ordered dramatic interchanges, such knowledge structures drastically underdetermine what one should think or how one should behave on any given occasion even assuming that one has acquired the cultural model in question.

D'Andrade (1990) made this point when he wrote that every schema "leaves out an enormous amount and is a great simplification of the potential visual, acoustic, sensory, and propositional information that could be experienced" (p. 98). And so it is with all manner of cultural artifacts: They provide some degree of structuration to thought and the organization of action, but they cannot act alone. Put a little differently, cultural models never so completely constrain one's interpretation of reality that they can be said to determine thought in a mechanical cause–effect manner. Additional contributions are needed.

Context.   An obvious, but problematic, place to search for cultural restraints on human thought is in the concept of context. The invocation of context is an obvious place to look in the sense that we can say "the meaning of a behavior depends on its context." The meaning of someone's "fire" mediates activity differently and means something different when shouted in a crowded theater or at an execution. But the invocation of context is also problematic because context is one of the most slippery concepts in the social sciences (Duranti & Goodwin, 1992; Erikson & Schultz, 1977).

D'Andrade's remark about culture holds equally well for the concept of context; definitions of context are really substantive propositions about the world whose appropriateness depends on the uses to which they are put (Goodwin & Duranti, 1992; Gumperz, 1992). Here I will be concerned with two competing visions of context, one that fits well into relatively standard forms of social science theory and research, and one that does not.

The definition of context one finds in use most often among social scientists identifies context as "that which surrounds." It is this meaning we invoke in such phrases as "The test was administered in a play context" or "You took my words out of context." This notion of context is often represented in a manner akin to Fig. 4.2 as a set of concentric circles representing different "levels of context."

A classic application of this notion of context is found in linguistics (Bateson, 1972; Jackobson & Halle, 1956). A fundamental property of language is the apparent hierarchical relationship among its levels: A phoneme exists as such only in combination with other phonemes that make up a word. The word is the context of the phoneme. But the word only exists as such—only "has meaning"—in the larger context of the utterance, which again "has meaning" only in a relationship to a large

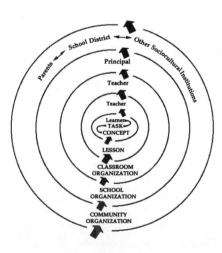

FIG. 4.2.   Context represented as a set of embedding relationships (in this case, referring to educational settings).

unit of discourse. As Gregory Bateson (1972) pointed out, "This hierarchy of contexts within contexts is universal for the communicational . . . aspect of phenomena and drives the scientist always to seek explanation in the ever larger units" (p. 402).

This same style of explanation is found in psychology, where attention is most often focussed on the unit "in the middle," some sort of event or activity engaged in by individuals. Psychologists seek to understand how the focal behavior is shaped by broader levels of context, understood more or less as levels of the environment of behavior. Many examples of this mode of explanation are to be found in Bronfenbrenner's (1979) monograph on the ecology of human development where, for example, the quality of mother–child interactions is linked to the "meso" and "exo" contexts of family, community, and work.

The particular example in Fig. 4.2 is taken from a monograph about the role of context factors in formal educational settings (Cole & Griffin, 1987). In that case, the focal event was a teacher–pupil exchange that was a part of a lesson that was part of a curriculum, and so on. We discussed how qualities of teacher–child interaction were shaped by the organization of the classroom, the school as a whole, and the school's links to its community.

Almost precisely the same image can be found on the cover of Jaan Valsiner's book, *Culture and the Development of Children's Action* (1987), which conceives of different levels of the environment in terms of embedded systems, with face-to-face interaction between children and responsible adults at its core. It fits also with Whiting and Edwards' (1988) periodization of childhood (borrowed from Margaret Mead) as proceeding from lap children to knee children to yard children to community children.

This notion of context is useful in keeping ever before us the fact that distal as well as proximal factors are important in explaining any particular form of behavior that we are interested in. But it has its difficulties.

The problem with evoking context as an explanation for the nature of the focal event (a phoneme, a test score) was pointed out by Bateson (1972) in the discussion to which I referred earlier.

> When we speak of an action or utterance as occurring "in" a context, [it] suggests that the particular action is a "dependent" variable, while the context is the "independent" variable. . . . It is important to see the particular utterance or action as part of the ecological subsystem called context and not as the product or effect of what remains of the context after the piece which we want to explain has been cut out from it. (p. 338)

Each part of this statement is significant. First, Bateson was denying the appropriateness of invoking "context" as a cause in the conventional sense. Such causal ascription assumes (incorrectly) a one-way, "top-down" relationship between levels of context. Second, he was challenging us to think of what we term "the act" or "the object" as somehow a part of the same system as what we term "the context." In short, "text" and "context" constitute each other.

A way to highlight the difficulty of assuming a simple temporal ordering of action and context is to note that "that which surrounds" specifies no simple, temporal, ordering. It occurs before, after, and simultaneously with "that which is surrounded," the "act/event" in question. On the one hand, we cannot utter a phoneme except as part of a larger unit of speech. On the other hand we cannot say sentences before we say words, nor words before synthesizing phonemes in an appropriate way. There is a complex temporal interdependence among levels of context.[1]

Another difficulty with the idea that larger units of context cause smaller ones is that it begs the question of how people assess what context they are in. Without being able to answer the question, "What is going on here," which *cannot be determined prior to knowing what script has mediated the activity,* we cannot say anything coherent about the thought processes involved. As Erikson and Schultz (1977) pointed out, "Contexts are not simply *given* in the physical setting (kitchen, living room, sidewalk in front of drug store) nor in combinations of personnel (two brothers, husband and wife, firemen). Rather, contexts are constituted by what people are doing and where and when they are doing it" (pp. 5–6). To take our example of the teacher–child exchange, it is easy to see such events as "caused" by higher levels of context: Teachers conduct lessons, that are events in classrooms, which are located in schools. The lesson is structured according to habits of the teacher, the conventions of the school, which are dictated by the board of education, which is elected by the community, and so on.

In reality, however, for the event ("a lesson") to occur the participants must actively engage in a consensual process of "lesson making." Students no less than teachers are crucial to the event called a lesson, a fact highlighted by referring to lessons as teaching/learning events. Without forgetting for a moment that the power relations among participants within events and between levels of context are often unequal, it is no less important to remember that context creation is an active, two-sided process (See McDermott & Tylbor, 1983).

The alternative idea of context suggested by these remarks fits with the meaning derived from the Latin word, *contexere,* "to weave together." This alternative metaphor of context is elaborated by Ray Birdwhistle, a sociologist who has dedicated his career to demonstrating the microgenetic organization of joint activity. When asked for his definition of *context,* Birdwhistle answered:

> I'll tell you what I like to think about: sometimes I like to think of a rope. The fibers that make up the rope are discontinuous; when you twist them together, you don't make them continuous, you make the thread continuous. . . . even though it may look in a thread as though each of those particles are going all through it, that isn't the case. That's essentially the descriptive model. . . . Obviously, I am not talking about the environment. I am not talking about inside and outside. I am talking about the conditions of the system (quoted in McDermott, 1980, pp. 14–15).

---

[1]The notion of simultaneity of levels of structuration in language is emphasized by Jackobson and Halle (1956, pp. 60–61) who wrote of de Saussure, that "despite his own insight into the phoneme as a set of concurrent distinctive features (elements différentiels des phonèmes), the scholar succumbed to the traditional linear character of language "qui exclut la possibilité de prononcer deux éléments a la fois."

A cardinal feature of the conception of context as "that which weaves together" contained in Birdwhistle's elaboration is that is problematizes the division of "the system" into two parts called "inside and outside." This aspect of context-as-weaving was highlighted by Bateson (1972) in a manner that articulates productively with my earlier elaboration of the notion of culture as medium. In his discussion of "the conditions of the system" Bateson discussed how mind is constituted through human activity involving cycles of transformations between "inside" and "outside." He wrote that obviously there are lots of message pathways outside the skin, and these and the messages that they carry must be included as a part of the mental system whenever they are relevant (p. 458). He then proposed the following thought experiment:

> Suppose I am a blind man, and I use a stick. I go tap, tap, tap. Where do I start? Is my mental system bounded at the hand of the stick? Is it bounded by my skin? Does it start halfway up the stick? Does it start at the top of the stick? (p. 459)

Bateson went on to argue that such questions are nonsensical unless one is committed to including in one's analysis not only the man and his stick, but his purposes, and the environment in which he finds himself. When the man sits down to eat his lunch, the stick's relation to mind has totally changed, and it is forks and knives that become relevant.

This way of thinking also provides the path by which it becomes possible to elaborate a cultural-historical conception of culture that includes both the level of individual mediated actions and the broader patterns of *joint* medicated activity that constitute the social order. As Wentworth (1980) noted, context is the "unifying link between the analytic categories of macrosociological and microsociological events. . . . "The context is the world as realized through interaction and the most immediate frame of reference for mutually engaged actors. The context may be thought of as a situation and time bounded arena for human activity. It is a unit of culture" (p. 92).

This notion of context recognizes the power of social institutions relative to individuals and the potential of individuals to change the environments that condition their lives. On the one hand, aspects of the "macro" level serve as constraints/resources in constituting context (and hence local activity tends to reproduce the relations in society). On the other hand, each situation is idiosyncratic in the mix of resources/constraints that are brought to bear, and hence there is no strict determination of the consequences of action that result.

SUMMARY

This chapter represents little more than a gesture at the implications of starting one's analysis of human nature by assuming that it is created in and through the medium of culture. According to my account, the fundamental constituents of that medium are artifacts, the residues of prior human activity. Artifacts exhibit a dual nature in that they are simultaneously ideal and material. Their creators and users exhibit a corresponding duality of thought, at once grounded in the material here and now, yet simultaneously capable of entertaining the far away, the long ago, and the never-has-been.

The medium of culture is more than a random assortment of artifacts, yet the principles of its structuration are so multiform and its constituent elements so unevenly distributed among its bearers that it is incapable of acting as "the cause" of human thought and action. Rather, it serves as a constraint/instrument of action that can be woven into a seemingly infinite variety of patterns of human thought and action.

When we start to treat culture as the medium of human life in this way, it becomes natural to question the longstanding Cartesian dualism between "mind" and "environment." Thought is no longer entirely an "inside the head" matter. Cognition is, to use the currently fashionable phrase, "distributed." Bateson provided one provocative image of the dynamics of thinking in such a distributed system in his thought experiment about a blind person walking to a restaurant. Mandelshtam illuminated another feature of thinking-as-mediation-through-artifacts: The thought is completed in the word, that is, after it has been mediated through the meaning system of the language/culture, and hence been transformed into a cultural artifact.

PROSPECTS

There are obvious shortcomings to my analysis in this chapter, as I warned there would be at the outset. The primary problem is that I have pursued the traditional path of the psychologist and focused on the cultural medium from the perspective of the individual. Consequently, I have slighted an analysis of cultural mediation as *joint* mediated activity. Second, I have slighted a great deal of relevant material on nature of complex forms of symbolically mediated behavior in which the artifacts involved, such as a national flag, have come to take on meanings far beyond those involved in the locally organized activities that gave birth to them.

In the space allotted I can do no more than sketch out a few of the more obvious additional directions that development of a communication theory of mind along the lines sketched here will require.

To begin with, it is necessary to expand the basic mediational triangle proposed by the Russian cultural-historical theorists to represent the fact that individuals are parts of social communities with standing rules and normative divisions of labor. Such an expanded representation of the mediational triangle has been developed by Yrjo Engeström (1987) (See Fig. 4.3). Engeström's diagram provides us with a schematic representation of the multiple ways that artifacts/culture mediate(s) the activity of individuals as members of a social group. The upper (subject–medium–object) relationship embodies the level of human action that we have focused on in this chapter. When we view these three moments in relation to those arrayed along the base of the triangle, we can see a number of lines along which individual action

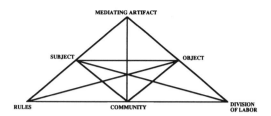

FIG. 4.3. Artifact mediation in a system of activity. The basic mediational triangle of Figure 1 is seen as part of a social system involving other people (community), social rules, and a division of labor.

is part of a larger social order. What we have been terming mediated action is seen to be constituent of, and constituted by, joint mediated activity (Lektorsky, 1984). This approach combines the individual and social levels of human life into a single unit of analysis, the activity system.

In elaborating on the way in which culture mediates between people, a number of writers have noted the strong affinity between Vygotsky and Mikhail Bakhtin (e.g., Emerson, 1981; Ivanov, 1974; Wertsch, 1991). Bakhtin (1981; 1986) focused on the utterance as the unit of speech communication, in contrast to Vygotsky's focus on the word/artifact. Speech, Bakhtin (1986) wrote, "can exist in reality only in the form of concrete utterances of individual speaking people, speech subjects. Speech is always cast in the form of an utterance belonging to a particular speaking subject, and outside this form it cannot exist" (1986, p. 71).

An equally important aspect of speech is that it is always directed at someone. Both the utterances as a whole and the words that constitute them are shaped by the fact that speech is dialogic at its core.

Pursuing these ideas, James Wertsch (1991) suggested that Bakhtin's ideas provide a natural and effective way to go beyond Vygotsky's ideas to consider the mutual relationship between sociocultural setting and mediated action.

Another set of issues that needs to be dealt with in developing a communication theory of mind is the dynamic nature of the process of mediated action itself. The standard mediational triangle, as represented in Fig. 4.1, is a static figure. So too is the representation of levels of context in Fig. 4.2 and the organization of activity in Fig. 4.3. But thinking and acting are processes that happen in time.

Those processes, to be sure, are mediated in roughly the ways that the Russian cultural-historical thinkers suggested. But as our exploration of the properties of scripts, schemas, and cultural models has highlighted, rarely is the cultural toolkit entirely adequate to the tasks at hand and even when it is adequate, there is ambiguity about which tool is appropriate and what the circumstances are.

At the "psychological level," corresponding to Fig. 4.1, one useful change is to build time into the figure by noting that there is never a perfect fit between information contained in the mediational artifacts and the information contained in the "direct" connection between person and world. The discrepancy between these two sources of structuration for thinking requires an active, ongoing, process of reconciliation/interpretation. This process is what I think of as consciousness (See Fig. 4.4).

When these same implications of the incomplete nature of cultural structuration are considered vis à vis interpersonal communication, the degree of indeterminate-

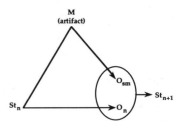

FIG. 4.4. The basic mediational relationship represented as a dynamic process in which consciousness arises from ongoing resolution of information arising from mediated and direct links between subject and object.

ness involved in the process seems overwhelming. It is considerations such as these that led Durkheim to ask how society is even possible, and to emphasize the importance of ritual and performance in making salient the cultural constraints mediating social interaction. These questions are currently being pursued by a wide range of socioculturally oriented linguists, anthropologists, and sociologists (Duranti & Goodwin, 1992).

Although there is a great deal of work to be done, I am encouraged by the evidence that a conception of culture built on a foundation of artifact mediation seems to connect many of the lines of thought needed to develop a theory of mind based in communication. Whether, and how successfully, such connections can be made remains a question for the future.

REFERENCES

Bakhtin, M. M. (1981). *The dialogic imagination: Four essays by M. M. Bakhtin.* Austin: University of Texas Press.

Bakhtin, M. M. (1986). *Speech genres and other late essays.* Austin: University of Texas Press.

Bateson, G. (1972). *Steps to an ecology of mind.* New York: Ballentine.

Bergson, H. (1983). *Creative evolution.* New York: H. Holt & Co. (Original work published 1911).

Bourdieu, P. (1977). *Outline of a theory of practice.* New York: Cambridge University Press.

Bronfenbrenner, U. (1979), *The ecology of human development.* Cambridge, MA: Harvard University Press.

Bruner, J. S. (1990). *Acts of meaning.* Cambridge, MA: Harvard University Press.

Burke, K. (1945). *A grammar of motives.* New York: Prentice-Hall.

Cazden, C. (1993, October). *Readings of Vygotsky in writing pedagogy.* Paper presented at University of Delaware, Wilmington.

Cole, M., & Griffin, P. (1987). *Contextual factors in education.* Madison: Wisconson Center for Education Research.

D'Andrade, R. (1984). Cultural meaning systems. In R. A. Shweder & R. A. LeVine (Eds.), *Culture theory: Essays on mind, self and emotion.* (pp. 88–119) New York: Cambridge University Press.

D'Andrade, R. (1974). Memory and the assessment of behavior. In T. Blalouc (Ed.), *Measurement in the social sciences* (pp. 159–186). Chicago: Aldine-Atherton.

D'Andrade, R. (1986). Three scientific world views and the covering law model. In D. Fiske & R. A. Shweder (Eds.), *Metatheory in the social sciences.* (pp. 19–42) Chicago: University of Chicago Press.

D'Andrade, R. (1990). Some propositions about the relationship between culture and human cognition. In J. W. Stigler, R. A. Shweder, & G. Herdt (Eds.), *Cultural psychology: Essays on comparative human development.* (pp. 65–129) New York: Cambridge University Press.

Duranti, S., & Goodwin, C. (Eds.). (1992). *Rethinking context: Language as an interactive phenomenon.* New York: Cambridge University Press.

Durkheim, E. (1915). *The elementary forms of religious experience.* New York: Free Press.

Emerson, C. (1981). Bakhtin and Vygotsky on internalization of language. *Quarterly Newsletter of the Laboratory of Comparative Human Cognition, 5,* 9–13.

Engeström, Y. (1987). *Learning by expanding.* Helsinki: Orienta-Konsultit Oy.

Erikson, F., & Shultz, J. (1977). When is a context? Some issues and methods in the analysis of social comparison. *Quarterly Newsletter of the Institute for Comparative Human Development, 1(2),* 5–10.

Geertz, C. (1973). *The interpretation of culture.* New York: Basic Books.

Goffman, E. (1959). *Strategic interaction.* Philadelphia: University of Pennsylvania Press.

Goodwin, C., & Duranti, A. (1992). Rethinking context: An introduction. In S. Duranti & C. Goodwin, (Eds.), *Rethinking context: Language as an interactive phenomenon.* (pp. 1–42) New York: Cambridge University Press.

Gumperz, J. (1992). Contextualism and understanding. In S. Duranti, & C. Goodwin (Eds.), *Rethinking context: Language as an interactive phenomenon* (pp. 229–252). New York: Cambridge University Press.

Holland, D., & Valsiner, J. (1988). Cognition, symbols, and Vygotsky's developmental psychology. *Ethos, 16,* 247–272.

Hutchins, E. (1986). Mediation and automation. *Quarterly Newsletter of the Laboratory of Comparative Human Cognition, 8(2),* 47–58.

Ivanov, V. V. (1974). The significance of M. M. Bakhtin's ideas on sign, utterance, and dialogue for modern semiotics. In H. Baran (Ed.), *Semiotics and structuralism: Readings from the Soviet Union* (pp. 310–367). White Plains: International Arts and Sciences Press.

Jackobson, R., & Halle, M. (1956). *Fundamentals of language.* The Hague: Mouton.

Judd, C. H. (1926). *The psychology of social institutions.* New York: Macmillan.

Kaplan, B. (1983). Genetic-dramatism: Old wine in new bottles. In S. Wapner & B. Kaplan (Eds.), *Toward a holistic developmental psychology* (pp. 53–74). Hillsdale, NJ. Laurence Erlbaum Associates.

Laboratory of Comparative Human Cognition. (1983). Culture and cognitive development. In W. Kessen (Ed.), *Mussen's handbook of child psychology* (4th Ed., Vol. 1). New York: Wiley.

Lave, J., & Wenger, E. (1992). *Situated learning: Legitimate peripheral participation.* Cambridge: Cambridge University Press.

Lektorsky, V. A. (1984). *Subject, object, cognition.* Moscow: Progress.

Leontiev, A. N. (1932). Studies in the cultural development of the child, 3: The development of voluntary attention in the child. *Journal of Genetic Psychology, 37,* 52–81.

Levina, R. E. (1981). L. S. Vygotsky's ideas about the planning function speech in children. In J. V. Wertsch (Ed.), *The concept of activity in Soviet psychology.* (pp. 17–24). Armonk, NY: M. E. Sharpe.

Luria, A. R. (1928). The problem of the cultural development of the child. *Journal of Genetic Psychology, 35,* 506.

Luria, A. R. (1932). *The nature of human conflicts.* New York: Liveright.

Luria, A. R. (1976). *Cognitive development.* Cambridge, MA: Harvard University Press.

Luria, A. R. (1979). *The making of mind.* Cambridge, MA: Harvard University Press.

Luria, A. R. (1981). *Language and cognition.* Washington: V. H. Winston & Sons.

McDermott, R. P. (1980). Profile: Ray L. Birdwhistle. *The Kinesis Report, 2,* 1–4, 15–16.

McDermott, R. P., & Tylbor, H. (1983). On the necessity of conclusion. *Text, 3,* 277–298.

Mead, G. H. (1934). *Mind, self, and society from the standpoint of a social behaviorist.* Chicago: University of Chicago Press.

Mead, G. H. (1956). *George Herbert Mead on social psychology.* Chicago: University of Chicago Press.

Nelson, K. (1981). Cognition in a script framework. In J. H. Flavell & L. Ross (Eds.), *Social cognitive development* (pp. 97–118). Cambridge: Cambridge University Press.

Ortner, S. B. (1984). Theory in anthropology since the sixties. *Comparative Studies in Society and History, 26,* 126–166.

Peckham, M. (1965). *Man's rage for chaos.* New York: Shocken.

Pepper, S. (1942). *World hypotheses.* Berkeley: University of California Press.

Rogoff, B. (1991). *Apprenticeship in thinking:* Oxford: Oxford University Press.

Sahlins, M. (1976). *Culture and practical reason.* Chicago: University of Chicago Press.

Schwartz, T. (1978). The size and shape of culture. In F. Barth (Ed.), *Scale and social organization* (pp. 215–232). Oslo: Universitetsforlaget.

Schwartz, T. (1990). The structure of national cultures. In P. Funke (Ed.), *Understanding the USA* (pp. 110–149). Tubingen: Gunter Narr Verlag.

Shweder, R. A., & D'Andrade, R. (1980). The systematic distortion hypothesis. *New Directions for Methodology in the Social Sciences, 4,* 37–58.

Shweder, R. A., & LeVine, R. A. (Eds.). (1984). *Culture theory: Essays on mind, self and emotion.* New York: Cambridge University Press.

Stern, E. (1990). Problems of cultural psychology. *Quarterly Newsletter of the Laboratory of Comparative Human Cognition, 12*(1), 12–24. (Original work published 1916)

Valsiner, J. (1987). *Culture and the development of children's actions.* Chichester: Wiley.

Valsiner, J. (1988). *Developmental psychology in the Soviet Union.* Bloomington: Indiana University Press.

Valsiner, J. (1993). Comparative-cultural research in Soviet psychology, *Journal of Russian and East European Psychology, 31*(1), 5–10.

Van der Veer, R., & Valsiner, J. (1991). *Understanding Vygotsky.* Oxford: Blackwell.

Vygotsky, L. S. (1960). *Razvitie vyschiich psikhiceskich funktsii* [The development of higher psychological functions]. Moscow: APN.

Vygotsky, L. S. (1978). *Mind in society.* Cambridge, MA: Harvard University Press.

Vygotsky, L. S. (1987). *Thinking and speech.* New York: Plenum. (Original work published 1934)

Wentworth, W. (1980). *Context and understanding: An inquiry into socialization theory.* New York: Elsevier.

Wertsch, J. V. (1985). *Vygotsky and the social formation of mind.* Cambridge, MA: Harvard University Press.

Wertsch, J. V. (1991). *Voices of the mind.* Cambridge, MA: Harvard University Press.

White, L. (1959). The concept of culture. *American Anthropologist, 61,* 227–251.

Whiting, B. B., & Edwards, C. P. (1988). *Children of different worlds: The formation of social behavior.* Cambridge, MA: Harvard University Press.

II   PRACTICAL APPLICATIONS

The phenomenon of intrapersonal communication provides an incredible plethora of research problems to be examined. It does not follow, however, that those examinations will be easy to select or to accomplish. This section reviews possible methodologies, and provides examples of various research questions currently being pursued. The applications in these chapters suggest some viable research avenues for the intrapersonal theorist to investigate.

Chapter 5.   Given the complexity and inaccessibility of intrapersonal communication, how does the theorist study it? Stacks and Sellers present various methodologies that have been used to date, and discuss the shortcomings and benefits of each together with the knowledge that has been acquired. They also provide recommendations with respect to what insights might be derived from utilizing the new technological means now available. Stacks and Sellers limit their consideration to neurophysiological methods that are particularly germane to understanding inner speech but call for a triangulation of methods in future research. Consequently, being an intrapersonal scholar requires methodological sophistication.

Chapter 6.   An important research question for the intrapersonal theorist is how intrapersonal communication develops in the individual. We are born into a world of talk, but initially can only vocalize in response. In this chapter, Yingling examines how infants acquire the interactive precursors of talk. Vocalizations, attributions of meaning, eye contact, and interaction patterns are discussed as social experiences that are essential if we are to develop inner speech and the competence it provides for talk.

Chapter 7.   The functioning of inner speech's dialogue (self-talk) in the normal adult is a rich focus for investigation for the intrapersonal theorist. The theory portion of the text argues that the norms and attitudes of one's culture are internalized during the development of self. Then, the dialectic between ego and non-ego, "I" and "Me," provides the cognitive means for adaptation by the adult in various circumstances.

Wood examines the maintenance and/or modification of gender roles as an example of the functioning of self-talk in the adult individual. We may utilize self-talk in order to persuade ourselves of the correctness of cultural values or our deviance from the same. Similarly, couples may reinforce each other's "Me" in order to continue enacting the behaviors that have become comfortable for them.

Chapter 8.   Assessing the competence of inner speech functioning constitutes another viable research focus for the intrapersonal theorist. Johnson presents vivid examples of the misunderstandings and breakdowns that can occur in *interpersonal communication* if our inner speech does not include sufficient decentering to consider the perspective of the person being addressed. He also notes that decoding (listening) as well as encoding (talking) can be an egocentric process.

5 Research: Expanding Our Knowledge of Intrapersonal Communication Processes

Don W. Stacks
University of Miami at Coral Gables

Daniel E. Sellers
University of South Alabama

Part of the process of understanding intrapersonal communication stems from an awareness of how people attempt to measure what has been labeled by some as the "black box" (Stacks, 1989b). Historically, researchers have attempted to understand the inner processes associated with intrapersonal communication through a variety of measuring techniques, some sophisticated, whereas others are rather simple. This chapter introduces you to the various ways intrapersonal communication has been measured, focusing primarily on ways we anticipate that the brain operates.

UNDERSTANDING THE BRAIN AND INTRAPERSONAL COMMUNICATION RESEARCH

Intrapersonal communication resides within the individual. Where this occurs *specifically,* however, is not totally understood. We assume that the brain—as an organ—is the repository of the communication systems that operate together to create the "mind" (Stacks & Andersen, 1989; Stacks, Hill, & Hickson, 1990). That is, the biological organ creates the mind, which in turn, reflectively yields perceptions of how people perceive themselves and others within their environments.

Physiological Models

The brain is a complex organ that processes stimuli. The brain's processing function is to make sense out of the information it receives. Until recently, contemporary theory and research has been based on a rather simple operating model (cf. Restak, 1979; Segalowitz, 1983). This model attributes to the human brain two "brains," each with specific properties; properties said to be located in either one "brain" or the other. The two brains were actually the left and right hemispheres of what is considered to be the "whole brain." This approach suggested a *dominance,* as compared to a holistic approach, for processing information—verbal (left hemisphere) and nonverbal (right hemisphere) information. Language was thought to lie primarily in two areas of the brain's left hermisphere. Broca's and Wernicke's areas of the brain (located on the posterior inferior frontal region and the postcentral region of the left hemisphere, respectively) were for many years seen as the "centers" of discourse (Broca, 1865; Wernicke, 1908). This analysis, based in part on lesions of both regions and resultant language difficulties, proved to be a major influence on later hemispheric dominance theories for language, as well as research into language processing.

Later research has suggested a more complex brain organization. MacLean (1972, 1973) argued for a *triune brain,* a brain composed of three interrelated evolutionary brains, each located around the other. This model proposes that each evolutionary brain has a specific function. The most primitive (R-complex) brain sits at the brain stem and is responsible for urges and reflex actions. Surrounding this brain is the Paleomammalian brain, comprising what we call the limbic system, which deals with impulses and qualitative (emotive) aspects of behavior. The Neomammalian brain, composed of the neocortex, is responsible for images, social laws, complex symbolic patterns, and thought.

Operationally, each brain interprets information as it is received: from the brain-stem's neural pathways into the R-complex, to the Paleomammalian, and finally to the Neomammalian. At each level, interpretation is made and a refined "message" is transmitted. Control, however, is top-down. In normal operation, the impulses and reflex actions are controlled by the Neomammalian brain's interpretation of the information it receives, as "edited" by the earlier brains. This more complex brain model provides an understanding of how the holistic brain interprets information and how the human reacts to the environment (Sellers & Stacks, 1990; Stacks, 1983).

Processing Models

Recent models (Gazzagina, 1985; Sellers & Stacks, 1990; Stacks & Andersen, 1989) argue that the brain is not as simple as the two- or the three-brain physiological models suggest. These models propose that the two major hemispheres interact with each brain level to create brain "modules." These modules form a loose federation, with some modules more "important" than others. In terms of processing, the modules form an operating hierarchy whereby control and influence is created. Different modules represent different processing capabilities and, in turn, provide input to whatever module is responsible for that particular communication function.

Each brain module has a particular processing style. The particular style may be determined by location. Modules located in the right hemisphere function differently than those in the left; modules also function differently depending on the level of brain in which they are found. Thus, the processing models suggest that as many as six brains (three levels, two hemispheres) serve to process information that may be used in overt (verbal/nonverbal) or covert (thought) communication. Stacks and Anderson (1989) argued that modular dissonance may be a by-product of information processing. Stacks (1989a), theorizing from a chaos perspective, further argued that modular interaction serves to maintain order out of the chaos of competing stimuli.

Processing Mechanisms

The brain senses stimuli (information) from the five senses. We hear verbal messages, we see some of these messages in the form of writing, but we also "see" (visually) and "hear" (paralinguistically) nonverbally in that verbal messages may create a feeling of nonverbal sensation (Hickson & Stacks, 1986). Nonverbal messages also are communicated to us through touch, smell, and possibly taste. In our experience, many people—including beginning students of intrapersonal communication—often associate communication with the auditory processing of verbal messages—or "language"—but few seem to understand the physiological processes involved in the reception and processing of those messages.

With the exception of olfaction (smell), stimuli from each sense are transmitted *contralaterally* from location to brain. What is sensed on the *left* side of the body (left ear, left hand, left foot) is received by the *right* hemisphere. What is sensed by the right side is received in the left hemisphere. Olfactory stimuli are received *ipsilaterally,* that is what the right nostral senses is communicated directly to the right hemisphere. Visual input is more complicated in that each eye has two visual "hemifields" from which information is transmitted (Andersen, Garrison, & Andersen, 1979). What we see from the right side of the eye is transmitted to the left hemisphere and visa versa.[1]

Most interpretative research uses auditory messages, both for simplicity and for the ability to cancel out one hemisphere's initial reception. Auditory reception of a verbal message occurs through the sense of hearing. This involves the reception of a message in the form of sound waves being received by the ear, transformed into mechanical, and finally, into electrochemical stimuli. Anatomically, the nerve fibers from the right cochlea (right ear) cross to the contralateral side of the brain stem and course upward through the synapse stations of the auditory brainstem. The reverse is true of the left ear. The vast majority of nerve fibers connect to the opposite side of the brain from which they are received. Some information is processed ipsilaterally, but it appears that such information merely serves an alerting function, informing the appropriate processing centers of incoming stimuli (Yost & Nielson, 1977).

---

[1]Jerison (1975) suggested that the dual transmission of visual information is rooted in survival; that because vision is so important to human survival, each eye has duplicated the other's information processing capabilities.

Linguistic Processing of Messages

Language received by the right ear is processed by the left hemisphere and its modules. Language received by the left ear is processed by the right hemisphere and its modules. Modular interpretation of the messages received occurs both within and between hemispheres. Processing within a given hemisphere occurs through interaction of the module(s) whose job is to interpret specific information and transmit it to the next module or set of modules. When information must be shared between hemispheres, it is transmitted across the corpus callosum, the only major connection between the two hemispheres at a level supportive of language processing (Stacks & Sellers, 1986).

Each module's processing is indicative of the "style" associated with the hemisphere to which it belongs. In processing an incoming message, each hemisphere receives the same information; unless there is some pathological or physical blockage of the sensory nerves, incoming stimuli (with exception of olfactory information, which is transmitted ipsilaterally) are transmitted to *each* brain hemisphere. The left hemisphere's style is highly rule governed and logical; its function is to interpret the message from the particular language structure employed. The left hemisphere can understand complex thoughts but lacks the ability to analyze emotional or highly intense or charged language. It can easily process the statement, "The girl is pretty." The right hemisphere's apparent information processing style is holistic and qualified, reserved for coarser interpretations such as emotional impact and simple rule-governed language. That is, it is required when the earlier statement is further qualified to "The girl is very beautiful." Additionally, the right hemisphere seems to have a coarse, often vulgar language associated with it, only it tends to be unconsciously produced, much on the line of Freudian "slips" (Stacks, 1983).

Although both hemispheres can process receptive language, the left's function is for decision-making regarding the total message and its intent. The right's function is to provide the necessary qualification (intensity, emotion). Because the right hemisphere is dealing with fewer rules and more "natural" information (emotional, concrete, based on sensory input as well as phonemic and semantic), the right hemisphere's processing is significantly faster than the left's (Ley, 1980; Shedletsky, 1981, 1983; Sellers & Stacks, 1985; Stacks & Sellers, 1986). Thus, the right hemisphere's interpretation of the incoming message is processed quickly and inserted into the decisional logic the left hemisphere uses to interpret the message's structure and intent. This, then, results in the "asymmetrical" activation of each hemisphere as message reception occurs.

Creating a message is more complicated, but it is assumed that language is produced through left hemispheric processing.[2] The qualification, of course, is that the right hemisphere is activated when its input is required. Compared to message reception, little research has been conducted on message production in any aca-

---

[2]This assumption holds true for people whose language is consonant dominated, such as English or French or Russian. Eastern languages, more vowel dominated, seem to indicate less clearly defined processing, with some processing occuring in both hemispheres (Tsunoda, 1978, cited in Sibatani, 1980).

demic field. This may be due to the still unknown processing pathways and mechanisms associated with *complex* messages, messages that deal with complete thoughts and arguments rather than simple words, sounds, or vowel/consonant combinations.

Summary

This section provided an overview of intrapersonal communication, the types of research employed in studying intrapersonal communication, and an understanding of how the brain operates, as well as several theoretical models of brain operation. The next section focuses on different ways to measure intrapersonal communication. The key to choosing one method or a combination of methods is the research question(s) asked. If the researcher is concerned with *cognitive aspects of intrapersonal communication,* then pencil-and-paper methods are probably best. That is, if the researcher is more concerned with the effects of intrapersonal communication processes, then mental responses equated with attitudes and beliefs are best tapped via some measuring instrument created to assess and quantify degree of attitude or belief. If the researcher is concerned with the *underlying processing involved in a communication,* psychophysiological methods are probably best. In the future, however, most questions will require that both methods be used as a way to *triangulate* (c.f. Hickson, Roebuck, & Murty, 1990) the effect as well as processing of information by the brain/mind.

MEASURING INTRAPERSONAL COMMUNICATION: STRATEGIES FOR RESEARCH

Measurement is one of the keys to understanding human behavior. We measure when we *systematically observe a phenomenon.* Measurement may be as simple as observing whether or not a behavior occurs. Measurement may be as complex as the interpretation of an EEG chart. We often create a measure to tap the underlying processes we believe (or theorize) accompany intrapersonal communication. This section focuses on the various ways researchers attempt to measure intrapersonal communication. We begin with overt, behavioral measures, move to the more complicated brain activity measures, and end with a discussion of correlating the various measures to better understand just what is intrapersonal communication.

Overt Measures of Intrapersonal Communication

Overt behavior is communication that can be directly observed (McGuigan, 1979). Because intrapersonal communication's concern is with internal states and processes, overt measures are often problematic. That is, what we "observe" hopefully is a reflection or outcome of some internal process. As with most communicative research, we are often left to rely on "intervening variables," variables that, when measured, provide an indication of the true internal processing that leads to overt communication (cf. Stacks & Hocking, 1992). Any research that hopes to understand and predict internal communication processing with overt behavior (pencil-and-paper measures for instance) may fall prey to uncertainty. Quite simply, we never really know if we have tapped the underlying process or not—and this includes the physiological measures to be discussed later in this chapter. If we widen McGuigan's (1979) definition of overt behavior to include cognitive processing *behaviors* such as behavioral indicators to some external or internal stimuli, then we have additional ways to assess intrapersonal communication. That processing, however, is still fraught with problems. Even when recording brain *activity* as representative of intrapersonal communication, do we *really* know that the activity is caused by the processing? Or, is the activity from some other source? Keep these questions in mind as you go through the rest of the chapter and see if you come to the same conclusions we do.

Observational Strategies.   When should researchers engage in observational measures? When we assume that a particular behavior is indicative of underlying intrapersonal processes, observation provides us with evidence that the process is occurring. For instance, research on emotion and nonverbal "leakage" (Ekman & Friesen, 1960) is a prime example of overt communication behavior. The assumption underlying the research is that people often betray their inner emotional feelings through micromomentary facial displays. Observation takes the form of recording incidents of facial displays. However, because these displays are extremely fast, the researcher must find a reliable way of recording the behavior. One strategy might be to film the participant's face (or body, if the research question dealt with intensity of emotion (cf. Hickson & Stacks, 1986, 1993) and examine each frame of the film for the behaviors.[3]

Some behavioral measures are rather novel. S. J. Segalowitz (personal communication, October, 1985) reported asking participants to listen to music while their heads were situated between two speakers. He was interested in finding out if there was a preference for certain types of music by one brain hemisphere. It was thought that certain music styles would be preferred by one brain hemisphere over the other. Segalowitz asked research participants to balance the sound via a balance switch, and the position was noted. Indeed, a preference was found; the right hemisphere preferred less complex musical scores, the left hemisphere more complex scores. Unpublished research by our students in determining "handedness" for playing a keyboard, however, did not find any differences between people who "play by note" and those who did not read music. It was thought that the left hemisphere—hence the right hand—would be utilized by people who could play by note when asked to replay a sequence of notes, whereas the nonreaders would use the left hand (right hemisphere, holistic, and theoretically chord oriented). Simple musical scores failed to find a difference.

---

[3]The same can be done with videotape. However, using 8mm or 16mm film provides an inexpensive and reliable measure.

Other research has correlated eye direction while responding to either emotive or cognitive tasks (Hickson & Stacks, 1993). Because lateralization would suggest that looking to the right accesses the left hemisphere, eye direction to the right would indicate processing a cognitive task; left eye direction would be found for emotive stimuli. King (1973) also suggested that the eye direction a person *displays* provides cues for observers as to the intended emotive or cognitive appeal.

Other overt behaviors include observation of stress, boredom, or tension. For instance, we might predict that tapping behavior is related to an internal state. Under certain conditions, perhaps while waiting to give a speech, we would expect that tapping is associated with nervousness. On the other hand, we might examine the synchrony of behaviors as indicative of the individual's indication of liking in an interpersonal relationship (Burgoon & Saine, 1978). If we assumed that people who like each other "sync" to the other's behaviors, then the degree of sychronism in the dyad would indicate the degree of liking. Underlying psychological conditions may be associated with overt behaviors, such as schizophrenia, which is often associated with an aversion to contact with others (Hickson & Stacks, 1986). A particularly novel measure of stress was devised by Middlemist, Knowles, and Mather (1976), who suggested that close proximity would create physiological dysfunction. The testing of this hypothesis was done in a men's restroom, where a confederate violated an unsuspecting participant's personal space by using the urinal imme-diately next to him. They then observed the time it took to urinate (measured as the time between the zip of the fly and the first splash of urine). As expected, spatial invasion increased the time it took to urinate.

The last study provides an example of the *ethical* problems often associated with overt behaviors. Is it ethical to conduct a research project without the participant's knowledge? This is something all intrapersonal researchers must consider, espe-cially when measures are used to collect data on intrapersonal processing where the participant is unaware that he or she is participating in a research project. (For a more complete treatment of this important topic, see Stacks & Hocking, 1992).

One paper-and-pencil measure used in intrapersonal research requires partici-pants to write about themselves. The *Twenty Statements* (Kuhn, 1960) self-concept measure, for instance requires that participants respond to the question "I am. . ." 20 times, each time in a complete sentence. If participants complete the test as directed, high degrees of disclosure often occur. The same is true of research that asks participants to keep journals of their daily thoughts over a period of time. What researchers are attempting to identify are the underlying cognitive and emotive thoughts—intrapersonal communications—people have regarding themselves.

Most paper-and-pencil tests are more specific, requiring that participants respond to a series of statements or questions provided in a questionnaire. This method of measurement assumes that we can assess cognitive decisions regarding some atti-tude object. Most questionnaires employ Likert-like statements, statements that require the respondent to choose from a predetermined number of responses. A typical statement might be:

SA A U D SD   I believe in intrapersonal processes.

The responses provided require participants to choose from "strongly agree" (SA), "agree" (A), "uncertain" (U), "disagree" (D), or "strongly disagree" (SD). Other potential responses might include degrees of truthfulness or agreement.[4]

Paper-and-pencil measures attempt to correlate the underlying mental processes with some form of behavior, often the only way the processes can be tapped. For instance, Zagacki, Edwards, and Honeycutt (1992) have been working with the concept of imagined interaction for a number of years. Their research requires that participants complete a questionnaire that has been demonstrated to tap into "social cognition[s] where actors imagine and therefore *indirectly* experience themselves in anticipated and/or past communicative encounters with others" [italics added] (p. 57). The 44-statement questionnaire asks participants about a "typical" imagined interaction. Each statement is responded to on a 7-point Likert-type scale ranging from "very strong agreement" to "very strong disagreement."

Paper-and-pencil and observational measures assume that a mental process has occurred and that the behaviors observed are associated with the process in question. How reliable and valid these measures are, however, is open to discussion. Researchers can test for reliability of a measure or observation, but validity is often a concern (cf. Stacks & Hocking, 1992). Then, too, as discussed earlier, the relationship between behavior and mental process is frequently difficult to determine. Just what causes which is usually open to question. Perhaps the best way to determine validity is to begin with a theory that predicts how the communication is processed, create multiple measures of that process that are linked to that theory (Stacks, Hill & Hickson, 1990), use multiple measuring instruments, and then employ both overt and covert measures of intrapersonal communication. The next section examines a second way to assess intrapersonal communication that focuses on the brain, a more covert type of measure.

Psychophysiological Measures of Intrapersonal Communication

As with the overt behaviors, there exist several levels of covert measurement. At the most observable level, researchers can tap rather gross indicators of how information is processed. In so doing they do not deal with the brain directly, but measure physiological activity within the body. At this level, researchers are concerned with general responses to underlying cognitive and affective intrapersonal processes. At other levels, researchers can tap finer indicators of information processing.

There are some general physiological measures that tap into underlying intrapersonal processes that do not deal directly with the brain. These measures include heart rate, galvanic skin response (GSR), and respiration. Although each of these measures can be measured, they require additional instrumentation to do so with any

---

[4]It is beyond the scope of this chapter to provide a detailed discussion of measurement. There are several excellent sources that discuss measurement and the issues associated with this treatment. See Emmert and Barker, 1989, and Stacks and Hocking, 1992, for treatments.

degree of accuracy, often through the use of an *electromyogram* (EMG), which measures blood pressure and heart activity.

Physiological Measures.   Physiological measures are often used to measure deception, as when someone is connected to a polygraph or "lie detector." Actually, the polygraph measures several interrerlated indicators of underlying mental processes, each associated with stress. When people lie or deceive they typically place themselves in stress (Will they be caught? Can the machine really catch them?), stress that changes their physiology.[5] These changes will be recorded across the indicators: Their hands will sweat, picked up on the GSR; they will change their rate of breathing, picked up on the respiration indicator; and the heart will beat faster, picked up through a change in blood pressure and heart rate. (See Behnke, 1989, for a discussion of the issues associated with physiological measures.)

Physiological measures have been applied in a variety of research studies, but most are found in research on communication apprehension. The typical study identifies people who are either highly or lowly communicative apprehensive recruited to participate in a research project where they are connected to the recording instruments prior to presenting a speech. Physiological changes are then associated with several paper-and-pencil as well as behavioral measures (cf. Behnke & Carlile, 1971; Behnke, Beatty, & Kitchens, 1978; Behnke, Carlile, & Lamb, 1974). Given today's miniaturization of equipment, it is fairly easy to get unobtrusive physiological recordings.

Dichotic Listening.   The assumption underlying physiological measurement is that the responses obtained represent some form of mental processing. Actually, they represent the outcome of intrapersonal communication; that is, they do not actually measure the processing of information, but the outcome of that processing. Some of the earliest measures of intrapersonal processing in the brain are found in dichotic listening and half-vision measures.

The dichotic listening measure was developed by Kimura (1961) as a way to demonstrate language processing by a particular hemisphere. When dichotic listening is employed, participants are presented two similar sounds simultaneously, one in each ear. As discussed earlier, language is normally associated with the left hemisphere, although some (rudimentary) language is associated with the right hemisphere. If the two sounds are presented at the same volume and duration, we would expect that the sound responded to by the participant would be that heard in the right ear/left hemisphere (Fig. 5.1). Although clinically used to test language processing in normal people, this procedure can be used to manipulate message reception.

---

[5]Whether or not an individual can deceive the machine is not of concern here; obviously, if someone truly believed in what they were saying or doing, then the machine would not pick up physiological differences. The assumption here is that the physiological measures *do* indicate underlying mental processes whose measurement helps test a hypothesis.

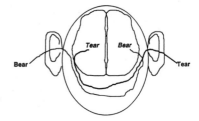

FIG. 5.1. Lateralization of language.

Two particularly relevant studies offer insight into the use of this technique. The first, by Vocate (1984) employs the traditional dichotic listening task in assessing speech lateralization in two disparate groups' language processing. The second, by Stacks and Sellers (1986), modified this technique and examined the impact of message reception by one brain hemisphere on attitude.

Vocate (1984) was interested in studying whether language processing in children was affected by bilingualism. Her theory was that bilingual children would process language more symmetrically than monolingual children, who would be lateralized toward left-hemispheric (right ear) processing, and that bilingual children would engage in more right-hemisphere language processing than monolingual children. To conduct her research, Vocate asked Native American Crow and Anglo (non-Indian) elementary students to participate in a dichotic listening study. Each child was carefully screened for hearing deficits and then carefully matched according to sex, age, grade in school, and handedness. Each student was then presented with some "new words" both aurally and visually (the same letters are used in both Crow and English languages).

The use of a dichotic listening procedure produced some interesting results. First, there were no differences between males and females for language processing by hemisphere, something previous research suggested would occur (where males are more lateralized to the left hemisphere than females for language). Second, as was hypothesized, bilinguals were found to have more right hemisphere involvement for language than monolinguals. In addition, bilinguals were significantly more accurate in their perception of speech sounds no matter which hemisphere did the processing. Clearly, the dichotic listening test provided a viable way to research how the brain processes language. As far as intrapersonal communication, the type of communication studied was rather rudimentary because language was operationalized as simple consonant/vowel combinations. However, the research questions involved with the study clearly could not involve more complex messages, as the translation and processing of a word's meaning might differ between Crow and Anglo children—then Vocate would not know if translation or processing differences accounted for her findings.

A more complex study was conducted by Stacks and Sellers (1986). We were interested in how actual *messages* were processed by the brain. No research to that date had examined complex message processing, although some had examined processing speed of simple messages (cf. Shedletsky, 1981, 1983). We hypothesized that both brain hemispheres are involved in processing and interpreting complex verbal messages, a complete persuasive message of over 3 minutes duration. We also hypothesized that brain hemisphere language processing was influenced by the language used in the messages; that highly intense messages would require right hemispheric interpretation, whereas moderate- or low-intensity messages could be processed by the left hemisphere alone. Intensity was operationalized as the substitution of words in the message that had been tested and found to be significantly different in terms of their intensity. For example, in the low language intensity condition the word "poor" was used, where the word "terrible" was used in the high language intensity condition.

The question, however, was how to isolate each brain. Obviously, a dichotic listening procedure would yield only confusion when a research participant heard two messages different for the language intensity employed during certain key arguments simultaneously. Further, what processing that might occur would not be clearly identifiable. Therefore, we opted to isolate one hemisphere from receiving the message by presenting research participants with a message in one ear, while the other was "masked" with white noise via headphones. The masking procedure is commonly used in auditory testing. The white noise (operationalized as cafeteria background noise, not speech but close to it) not only served to block the other ear from hearing the message, but also stopped any sound from the other ear due to sound vibrations from the message across the skull and sinus cavities. Thus, the message could only be processed by one hemisphere initially, and we could adequately test our hypotheses.

Our findings indicated that the way in which the message was processed—analyzed and interpreted—differed according to which hemisphere *initially* processed that message. When presented in the left ear/right hemisphere, there was "normal" reception; that is, the high intensity message was rejected as being too extreme and the moderate or low messages accepted as being appropriate for the topic—legalization of heroin.[6] When presented to the right ear/left hemisphere, however, a stronger, more emotive message was accepted. That is, when asked to respond to a series of measures that asked for attitudinal assessment on the message's topic, highly intense message reception in the right ear produced a more positive attitude toward the topic than when that same message was received by the left ear (i.e., when processed by the left hemisphere alone without the right hemisphere's initial theoretical processing of message intensity). Additionally, we noted that participants who received right-ear messages took longer to make their paper-and-pencil markings, therefore presumably the left hemisphere was having to work harder without the right's input. This was not observed in the left-ear condition. Masking, then, provided a way to provide "pure" or isolated hemisphere reception.

Other sensory inputs can be employed when conducting intrapersonal communication research. For instance, visual half-field measurement is similar to dichotic listening. Used in emotional research, participants are asked to focus on a spot in the middle of a screen where two similar figures are quickly (measured in millise-

---

[6]The message was created by a doctoral seminar in persuasion for use in several research projects. For more information, see Stacks and Burgoon (1981).

conds) presented in the far left and right visual peripheries. Using this technique, Ley and Bryden (1979) found that when asked to evaluate emotions, participants were much better at identifying emotions when the stimuli were presented in the left visual hemi-field (right hemisphere).

Measures of Brain Activity.   Actual measures of brain activity are much more complicated than dichotic or visual half-field measurement. Measures of brain activity tap into neurophysiological activity, activity defined in several ways. We can measure brain activity as brain waveforms fairly unobtrusively. Other kinds of measures require more instrumentation, and many require that participants be injected or drink radio-active isotopes. The less intrusive measures include electrical activity, as measured by the electroencephalogram (EEG), averaged EEG, evoked potentials, "brain mapping" and, more recently, magnetic resonance imaging (MRI). More intrusive measures include brain "scans," although MRI is rapidly replacing this technique as a research tool.

Research employing EEG measures is divided into three categories: ongoing EEG activity, spectral analysis, and averaged (evoked potential) activity. Ongoing EEG activity in the brain ("raw" EEG) has long been used for both medical diagnosis and for indication of changes in the state of the organism. Most research utilizing ongoing EEG activity as an indicator of the research participant's state has focused on brain waves occurring in four frequency bands. These are, *delta*, 0.05 to 4.0 Hertz (Hz); *theta*, 4.0 to 8.0 Hz; *alpha*, 8.0 to 13.0 Hz; and *beta*, 14.0 to 40.0 Hz. The most attention in intrapersonal communication research has been given to the *alpha* and *beta* brain waves.

Measures of changes in mental activity that utilize these waves have concentrated on changes in the amplitude and shifts in frequency of the alpha wave. The alpha is used as an index of the level of attention, with higher levels of alpha recorded in the resting state. As mental activity increases, the alpha wave decreases or is "suppressed" and the frequency shifts to a higher level.

The beta wave is associated with increased mental activity and the shift from alpha to beta is most noted in the initial change of the research participant from "resting" to "attention." Using the technique of "spectral analysis" or "compressed spectral array," Giannitrapani (1966, 1969, 1975) investigated the effect of "task changes" on changes in EEG activity. Compressed spectral array (CSA) procedures provide a way to analyze otherwise complex and long EEG data. By using a computer and a program that employs Fast Fourier Transform (FFT), CSA displays the processed EEG data as a function of frequency and power over time. Data trends or dramatic shifts in the EEG data may be seen using CSA.

Giannitrapani (1985) cautioned potential researchers as to the pitfalls of this technique. He stated that changes in the spectral displays might be due to factors in the Fournier algorithms used to interpret the activity rather than intrinsic changes in EEG activity. Observations of this technique in the author's laboratory suggest that there may be an initial change in the alpha/beta activity when a research participant is given a task change, but there appears to be a fairly rapid return to the pretask state.

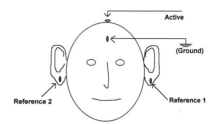

FIG. 5.2. Electrode montage for two-channel recording of P300.

By using an array of electrodes placed on the scalp, electrical potentials gener-ated by neural activity in parts of the brain can be "mapped" and thereby indicate regions of the brain that have been activated by some task (Fig. 5.2). The Interna-tional 10–20 system for the electrode montage is the standard for electrode place-ment in EEG studies (Jasper, 1958). A common application of the procedure has been the study of hemispheric specialization, particularly in the area of language processing. It is generally assumed that for the vast majority of individuals (esti-mates range from 97% to 99% of the population), the left hemisphere is predisposed for language processing, regardless of the person's handedness. If a participant is given an auditory task followed by a visual task, the resulting shift in electrical activity will be indicated by a shift in the electrical potentials recorded from differ-ent locations on the scalp. If an auditory language task is introduced following a resting state, the alpha wave for the left hemisphere should decrease with a resulting increase in beta activity (cf. Riccillo, 1989).

In a study that used the suppressed alpha wave as evidence for verbal versus nonverbal hemispheric processing, Moore (1979) asked right-handed research par-ticipants to listen to either a message or to Mozart's *Concerto in E Flat* while attached to an electroencehalograph. In the verbal condition, participants were asked to silently count the number of times they heard the words "a" and "the" while listening to the message. For the nonverbal task, they simply listened to the melody of the Mozart concerto. Before participants heard the stimuli, they were asked to close their eyes, sit in a comfortable position, and not to move. This assured a base-line recording of EEG activity at rest.

Moore found that there was significantly less suppressed alpha in the linguistic condition in the left hemisphere than in the right hemisphere. There were no differ-ences in suppressed alpha between the right and left hemispheres for the nonverbal stimulus. Moore's finding supports the theory that linguistic processing is evidenced by suppressed alpha and that the left hemisphere's style is to process linguistic information. He also reported no differences between male and female processing of verbal or nonverbal stimuli, something analogous to Vocate's (1984) and our (Stacks & Sellers, 1986) earlier findings.

The difficulty in interpreting the use of spectral analysis of EEG activity relates to the fact that it only indicates a possible *shift* in the location of brain activity; however, it does provide a more precise location for neurological processing than the more general measures discussed earlier. The researcher interested in determin-ing whether a communicative task is processed in the right or hemisphere—frontal, temporal, parietal, or occipital areas of the brain—would utilize techniques of spectral analysis and brain mapping. Brain mapping refers to a technique of computerized-evoked response topography. Multiple electrode sites are used to gather simultaneous evoked potentials. Differences in neural activity in the various brain locations are then "mapped" out to show the location of this neural activity. Thus, both shift and location provide an idea of what processing has occurred and where that processing took place.

Moore (1979) amplified this methodological concern about *what type of processing* was occurring in discussing his findings, especially regarding the nonverbal findings:

> Interestingly, it was not unusual for some subjects to report that they were analyzing the music rather than attending to the melody which may well suggest left hemispheric, segmental processing. . . . Other subjects reported "thinking about the event of the day," again, suggesting linguistic rather than non-linguistic processing. The importance of these observations underscores the need for attentional controls in the hemispheric research, particularly when overt responses during ongoing processing tasks are not required of the subject. (p. 324)

With the development of high-speed, averaging computers, an additional technique utilizing EEG became possible. The evoked-response technique involves the use of EEG activity in a different way. The background electrical activity of the ongoing EEG and electrical activity from muscular action can be removed in order to "see" specific neural activation. In the auditory evoked response, the specific neural activity is a result of a sound being presented to the ear, resulting in a series of "wave peaks" indicating a concentration of nerve firings at a specific time interval in milliseconds (ms) from the onset of the auditory signal. These wave peaks are measured in such a way that a peak occurring 300 ms after hearing the stimulus is labeled *P300* and is thought to occur as the third peak wave (identified as P3). Intrapersonal communication processing usually occurs at and after the P300 peak; thus, the P300 or P3 wave can be used for intrapersonal research dealing with language processing (Meador et al., 1987).

In a study conducted by Sellers, Brown, and Sick (1989), normal hearing participants between the ages of 18 and 22 years were presented a number of different types of sounds to elicit the P3 wave. The first condition required the discrimination of simple tones. The second condition involved discrimination based on linguistic differences in speech stimuli. The third condition required discrimination of phonetic differences between speech stimuli. The results indicated that the P3 elicited by both speech stimuli exhibited longer latencies than those for tones. There were no significant differences between males and females on any of the conditions. The linguistic condition yielded longer latencies than the phonetic conditions, suggesting again that speech processing occurs much "further" in the brain and takes longer (in terms of milliseconds) than simple tones or phonetics.

Meador et al. (1987) recorded event-related potentials using phonemic and semantic word tasks. In the phonemic tasks, participants were asked to count words that rhymed with "book" in the first condition and words that rhymed with "hat" in the second. In the semantic tasks, they were required to count words that were the names of foods and words that were the names of animals. Meador et al. found that the participants required to process semantic tasks exhibited longer P3s, concluding that the increased latencies were due to the increased levels of neural processing required for more difficult language tasks. That is, as complexity of communication processing increased, the amount of processing increased proportionally.

These studies indicate that measures of brain activity may be useful for determining processing times required for different types of stimuli and may be sensitive to differences between the discrimination of speech and nonspeech stimuli. When coupled with behavioral assessment techniques, more may be learned about the process of intrapersonal communication. Consider, for example, these findings with those of Stacks and Sellers (1986). They theorized that hemispheres isolated from the other's information processing input would produce different interpretations of messages. Further, they suggested that the left hemisphere, when isolated from initial input from the right hemisphere, would have to transfer information across the corpus callosum to the right hemisphere for interpretation. This process, they suggested, occurred in the right ear/left hemisphere conditions, noting that it was taking participants in this condition longer to decide how to respond to the attitudinal measures. If participants' brain activity was simultaneously being recorded as they heard and processed the message, both location and processing shifts may *possibly* be identified.

The event-related potential may represent a short-term memory upgrade rather than a level of linguistic processing. However, it is still unclear exactly what neural processes are responsible for these potentials. When these are correlated with brain mapping, we may begin to get a better picture of not only where in the brain certain neural processes take place, but also possible levels of processing. We still do not have the instrumentation necessary to determine exactly *what* or *what types* of intrapersonal processes take place during this stage of communication. It is certain that as technology continues to develop we will begin to have the methodology for probing farther into covert, physiological process.

PROBLEMS WITH ASSESSING
AND INTERPRETING
INTRAPERSONAL COMMUNICATION

As with any approach to studying human communication, there are problems associated with intrapersonal communication assessment. However, the problems associated with intrapersonal communication are less easily worked out than in other areas. For instance, we begin with the concept, "intrapersonal communication." Almost by definition, researchers delving into this area of communication are working with something they never will *see*. We can infer what occurs within the "black box," but all we actually have are good guesses. Research conducted with physiological measures must make two critical assumptions: (a) that what is measured represents what is actually going on within the individual, and (b) that when measured the individual is actually engaged in intrapersonal communication. Researchers cannot guarantee that what they are studying is actually what they are measuring.

A second problem is associated with *accessing the language centers* thought responsible for intrapersonal communication. Most of our most sophisticated measuring instruments are still primitive, forcing researchers to rely on patterns of behavior. We are still relatively uncertain exactly *when* language is understood and processed, how far in time information must go before it takes on the characteristics of a "message" and becomes true intrapersonal communication. EEG measures activity across a broad region of the brain; dichotic listening and visual hemi-field measures assess even grosser neurological information. Physiological measures lie yet somewhere between and are, at best, one step removed from the actual processes they relate to. Overt measures are at least another step removed from the physiological processes and may or may not actually represent what the individual believes or thinks at the time of the measurement.

Third, there is the problem of correlating the measures obtained to actual language processing. In terms of overt measures, we assume that language, communication—verbal and nonverbal—is related to the processes under study, but the actual correlation between behavior and *attitude* is low. We are beginning to understand how a message is decoded and processed, but we have little knowledge of how messages are created, from inception to actual utterance. We assume the lateralization process tells us something about how the normal brain operates, but we have precious little evidence of how it actually works in a variety of different settings, or with different messages. What we do know provides us with some message strategies, but more is needed. Future research must find ways of triangulating overt and covert measures in such a way that we gain understanding not only of brain processing, but also how that processing alters communication at both intrapersonal *and* interpersonal levels. That is, we must find ways of interpreting covert behaviors and relating them to conscious communication.

FUTURE
OF INTRAPERSONAL COMMUNICATION
RESEARCH

Of all the areas of study in communication, intrapersonal communication research may be the most exciting. As we gain an understanding of how we communicate within ourselves, we begin to open a window to understanding what makes us act as we do. Intrapersonal communication focuses on the cognitions of importance to us: attitudes, emotions, beliefs, and values. These we represent through verbal and nonverbal communication. After all, we are what we believe we are, and we create our expectations from the language we employ and the behaviors we exhibit. Future intrapersonal research should cast more knowledge our way as to why we do what we do. In the same light, new methods for analyzing both overt and covert behavior will provide the necessary data to test our theories of intrapersonal communication.

How will this come about? First, as noted earlier, intrapersonal research must begin to *triangulate* its methods. No other research area has the potential for this type of multiple methodology. But to do so means that we must learn how to conduct physiological research; we must begin to cross-train with researchers of other areas. In the case of this chapter, Stacks is a communication theorist and researcher, Sellers is an audiologist. Although both are well researched in the area of the brain, only one of us is really well versed in the advanced physiological research and language processing (Sellers), whereas the other's contribution is more along the line of attitudinal and intrapersonal theory, methodology, and analysis (Stacks). As individuals, we could not answer the research questions posed; as a team, however, we were able to conduct the research and advance our theory. Thus, through a triangulation not only of method, but also of approach to research we are closer to understanding the brain–mind relationship in the processing of intrapersonal communication.

The future of intrapersonal research should follow this team approach. As computers become smaller and yet more powerful, as techniques for accessing the brain's activity are improved, and as people begin to cross-train in their research areas, more will be known about intrapersonal communication. Today, it is possible to acquire *and* analyze EEG activity with a personal computer, an electrode array, and statistical programming, things that required more equipment and mainframe computers less than 15 years ago. We have just begun to tap the potential for intrapersonal communication research; to understand intrapersonal processes at a much deeper depth, we need both advanced theory and methodological sophistication. When we have arrived at that state, how the brain/mind operates may come into better focus.

SUMMARY

This chapter focused on the role of research in expanding our knowledge of intrapersonal communication. It began by focusing on an understanding of what intrapersonal communication is and the general types of research conducted by intrapersonal researchers. We then explored the various research methods employed with an eye toward new research techniques and a better understanding of how intrapersonal communication research can be conducted. A large focus was on psychophysiological approaches. Finally, we explored some of the problems associated with intrapersonal communication research and the potentials it provides.

REFERENCES

Andersen, P. A., Garrison, J. P., & Andersen, J. F. (1979). Implications of a neurophysiological approach for the study of nonverbal communication. *Human Communication Research, 6,* 74–89.

Behnke, R. R. (1989). Issues of measurement, instrumentation, and analysis of physiological variables. In C. V. Roberts & K. W. Watson (Eds.), *Intrapersonal communication processes: Original essays* (pp. 203–216). New Orleans, LA: SPECTRA Publishers.

Behnke, R. R., Beatty, M. J., & Kitchens, J. T. (1978). Cognitively-experienced speech anxiety as a predictor of trembling. *Western Journal of Speech Communication, 42,* 270–275.

Behnke, R. R., & Carlile, L. W. (1971). Heart rate as an index to speech anxiety. *Speech Monographs, 38,* 65–69.

Behnke, R. R., Carlile, L. W., & Lamb, D. H. (1974). A psychophysiological study of state and trait anxiety in public speaking. *Central States Speech Journal, 25,* 249–253.

Broca, P. (1865). Sur la faculte du language articule. *Bulletin Societe Anthropologia, 6,* 493–494.

Burgoon, J. K., & Saine, T. J. (1978). *The unspoken dialogue: An introduction to nonverbal communication.* Boston: Houghton-Mifflin.

Ekman, P., & Friesen, W. V. (1960). Nonverbal leakage and clues to deception. *Psychiatry, 32,* 88–106.

Emmert, P. J., & Barker, L. L. (Eds.). (1989). *Measurement of communication behavior.* White Plains, NY: Longman.

Gazzagina, M. (1985). *The social brain: Discovering the networks of the mind.* New York: Basic Books.

Giannitrapani, D. (1966). EEG differences between resting and mental multiplication. *Perceptual and Motor Skills, 22,* 339–405.

Giannitrapani, D. (1969). EEG activity frequency and intelligence. *Electroenceph and Clinical Neurophysiology, 27,* 480–486.

Giannitrapani, D. (1975). Spectral analysis of the EEG. In K. Dolce (Ed.), *Computerized EEG analysis* (pp. 384–402). Stuttgard: Fischer.

Giannitrapani, D. (1985). *The electrophysiology of intellectual functions.* New York: Karger.

Hickson, M. L., Roebuck, J. B., & Murty, K. S. (1990). Creative triangulation: Toward a methodology for studying social types. In N. K. Denzin (Ed.), *Studies in symbolic interaction* (Vol. 2, pp. 103–127). Greenwich, CT: JAI Press.

Hickson, M. L., & Stacks, D. W. (1986). *NVC: Nonverbal communication studies and applications* (2nd Ed.). Dubuque, IA: Wm. C. Brown.

Hickson, M. L., & Stacks, D. W. (1993). *NVC: Nonverbal communication studies and applications* (3rd ed.). Dubuque, IA: Wm. C. Brown.

Jasper, H. (1958). The ten-twenty electrode system of the International Federation. *Electroencephalorary and Clinical Neurophysiology, 10,* 371–375.

Jerison, H. J. (1975). Evolution of the brain. In M. C. Wittrock (Ed.), *The human brain,* (pp. 39–62). Englewood Cliffs, NJ: Prentice-Hall.

Kimura, D. (1961). Some effects of temporal-lobe damage on auditory perception. *Canadian Journal of Psychology, 15,* 156–165.

King, A. (1973). The Eye in Advertising. *Journal of Applied Communications Research, 1,* 1–12.

Kuhn, M. H. (1960). Sex-attitudes by age, sex, and professional training. *Sociological Quarterly, 9,* 39–55.

Ley, R. (1980). *Emotion in the right hemisphere.* Unpublished doctoral dissertation, University of Waterloo, Ontario.

Ley, R., &Bryden, M. (1979)|Hemispheric differences in recognizing faces and emotions. *Brain and Language, 7,* 127–138.

MacLean, P. (1972). Cerebral evolution and emotional processes: New findings on the strietal complex. *Annals of the New York Academme of Sciences, 193,* 137–140.

MacLean, P. (1973). The brain's generation gap: Some human implications. *Zygon/Journal of Religion and Science, 8,* 123–127.

McGuigan, F. (1979). *Psychophysiological measurement of covert behavior: A guide for the laboratory.* Hillsdale, NJ: Lawrence Erlbaum Associates.

Meador, K., Hammond, E., Loring, D., Feldman, D., Bowers, D., & Heilman, K. (1987). Auditory P3 correlates of phonemic and semantic processing. *International Journal of Neuroscience, 35,* 175–179.

Middlemist, R. D., Knowles, E. S., & Mather, C. F. (1976). Personal space invasions in the lavatory: Suggestive evidence for arousal. *Journal of Personality and Social Psychology, 33,* 541–546.

Moore, W. R. (1979). Alpha hemispheric asymmetry of males and females on verbal and non-verbal tasks. *Cortex, 15,* 321–327.

Restak, R. (1979). *The brain: The last frontier.* New York: Doubleday.

Riccillo, S. (1989). Physiological measurement. In P. J. Emmert & L. L. Barker (Eds.), *Measurement of communication behavior,* (pp. 267–295) White Plains, NY: Longman.

Segalowitz, S. J. (1983). *Two sides of the brain: Brain lateralization explored.* Englewood Cliffs, NJ: Prentice-Hall.

Sellers, D. E., Brown, C., & Sick, S. (1989). A comparison of event-related auditory potentials elicited by tones and speech. *ARO Abstracts, 32.*

Sellers, D. E., & Stacks, D. W. (1985). Brain processing and therapy. *Journal of Communication Therapy, 3,* 30–50.

Sellers, D. E., & Stacks, D. W. (1990). Toward a hemispheric processing approach to communication competence. *Journal of Social Behavior and Personality, 5,* 45–59.

Shedletsky, L. J. (1981). Cerebral asymmetry for aspects of sentence processing. *Communication Quarterly, 29,* 3–11.

Shedletsky, L. J. (1983). Cerebral asymmetry for aspects of sentence processing: A replication and extension. *Communication Quarterly, 31,* 78–84.

Sibatani, A. (1980). It may well turn out that the language we learn alters the physical operation of our brains. *Science, 210,* 24–46.

Stacks, D. W. (1983). Toward a preverbal stage of communication. *Journal of Communication Therapy, 3,* 39–60.

Stacks, D. W. (1989a, November). *The modular mind and intrapersonal communication processes.* Paper presented to the Speech Communication Association, San Francisco.

Stacks, D. W. (1989b, November). *What's inside the black box?* Paper presented to the Speech Communication Association, San Francisco.

Stacks, D. W., & Andersen, P. A. (1989). The modular mind: Implications for intrapersonal communication. *The Southern Communication Journal, 54,* 273–293.

Stacks, D. W., & Burgoon, J. K. (1981). The role of nonverbal behaviors as distractors in resistance to persuasion in interpersonal contexts. *Central States Speech Journal, 32,* 61–73.

Stacks, D. W., Hill, S. J., & Hickson, M. (1990). *An introduction to communication theory.* Dallas, TX: Holt, Rinehart and Winston.

Stacks, D. W., & Hocking, J. E. (1992). *Essentials of communication research.* New York: Harper-Collins.

Stacks, D. W., & Sellers, D. E. (1986). Toward a holistic approach to communication: The effect of "pure" hemispheric reception on message acceptance. *Communication Quarterly, 34,* 266–285.

Vocate, D. R. (1984). Differential cerebral speech lateralization in bilingual Crow Indian and monolingual Anglo children. *Neuropsychologia, 22,* 487–494.

Wernicke, C. (1908). The symptom-complex of aphasia. In A. Church (Ed.), *Diseases of the Nervous System.* New York: Appleton.

Yost, W. A., & Nielsen, D. W. (1977). *Fundamentals of hearing: An introduction.* New York: Holt, Rinehart and Winston.

Zagacki, K. S., Edwards, R., & Honeycutt, J. M. (1992). The role of mental imagery and emotion in imagined interaction. *Communication Quarterly, 40,* 56–68.

6 Childhood: Talking the Mind Into Existence

Julie Yingling
Humboldt State University

A student recently expressed to me her surprise and delight with the material on early communicative and cognitive development we were covering in class. She had been told and subsequently believed that language development was simply an unexplained "miracle." Miraculous as human development may appear, our knowledge about the process, although far from complete, is light-years from what we knew only 20 years ago. Scholars from a variety of disciplines—psychology, linguistics, cognitive science, social psychology and speech communication, to name a few—have come to recognize that human behavior is extraordinary largely because its communicative mode is speech, *and* that we must know more about the development of that mode before we can understand and adequately explain human behavior and cognition.

How is it that we become human communicators? How is it that we develop thought processes unique to humans? And what does one have to do with the other? *I contend that specifically human thought, the mind, emerges from an active process of internalizing experience with the tool of speech; this process requires interaction with others who occupy various positions on the same path of lifelong development.* To bolster this thesis I will give a brief history of the major schools of thought regarding developmental processes, integrate the theoretical and empirical literature to illustrate the process in early development, examine a few contexts—play, friendships, and classroom interaction—in which the process has been observed, and discuss the implications of talking the mind into existence.

PERSPECTIVES ON DEVELOPMENT

What follows is the cook's tour of the history of developmental theory: behaviorism, a stage theory of individual cognition, and interactional theory linking speech and thought. Each theory has influenced the way we think about development; however, we will focus on the failures of behaviorism and stage theory and on the successes of the interactional perspective in explaining and predicting communicative and cognitive development.

Behaviorism: Language as Learned Associations

One of the earlier scientific perspectives of development assumed the infant to be "tabula rasa" or a blank slate upon which to chalk the structure and content of experience. This behavioral view assumes that social behaviors are entirely the consequences of reinforcement. That is, stimulus–response bonds could as adequately account for a child's language behavior as they accounted for the training of Ivan Pavlov's famous salivating dogs. If one substitutes a new conditioned stimulus (a bell) for an old unconditioned stimulus (food), the new stimulus would produce the same response (salivation) as the old.

Although B. F. Skinner made a valiant attempt to explain language learning in terms of operant conditioning (a speaker is reinforced by a listener for producing a verbal operant), there were too many gaps in the theory to account for what the human communicator does. The kinds of voluntary, rational, and logical thought processes we daily employ and especially those that produce creative and novel utterances cannot be adequately explained by stimulus–response associations. Behaviorism has long since fallen from the favor of scholars interested in human development.

Pavlov's reputation in America was founded on the influence his work with classical conditioning had on the behaviorists, yet his true interest was in the human cerebral processes, which indeed are based on conditional reflexes but go well beyond them. Jerome Bruner (1986) reported that American psychologists exposed to the earlier works assumed "the *real* Pavlov was about conditioned reflexes." Rumors of his "gaga theories of personality" or "neo-Pavlovian" ideas appeared later "in the form of justification for other Russian work" especially the work of Vygotsky (p. 70). We shall return to the Pavlovian theory that provided a stepping-stone for his Russian colleagues, but we will first consider the contributions of the next great influence on developmental theory: Jean Piaget.

A Stage Theory of Individual Cognitive Development

The Piagetian tradition certainly differs from behaviorism, and indeed from the scientific reductionist tradition as a whole. Piaget was interested in the individual development of logical thought and recognized that development involves qualitative transformations. Although he used a traditional scientific framework to describe cognitive development, he was indeed a naive dialectician (Tolman, 1983). That is, he developed a spontaneous dialectical method in order to focus on the study of interrelationship and change (Bidell, 1988). In contrast to reductionism, which "artificially separates processes into elements for temporary study out of context," the dialectical approach attempts to "grasp processes in the full complexity of their interrelationship" (pp. 331–332). Piaget, despite his immersion in the Western scientific tradition, managed to convey the notion of holistic process in his theory. We will examine only the highlights of his views on thought and language.

Piaget's most well-known work is that which delineates stages of thought and associates each stage with a structure or cluster of concepts (Ginsburg & Opper, 1969). Scholars, especially psychologists, found stage theory extremely useful and proceeded to use the four stages as a framework for too many studies to recount here. Useful as the stages have been, they have not successfully predicted further development (Gelman & Baillargeon, 1983), therefore many scholars have moved to a more organic or orthogenetic approach that describes development in terms of gradual shifts from globality to increasing differentiation (Werner, 1957). So, although many of Piaget's basic ideas about development are still useful, the notion of distinct stages receives less acclaim than it originally did.

Piaget articulated a fresh perspective on cognitive development, but his stance implies that communication is secondary to cognition. He took the position that cognition is primary—that the child possesses incipient thought processes that remain egocentric until communication draws the child's attention to the needs of others and then he or she becomes socialized. That is, cognition comes first, then speech arises to serve it; to express it. In Piaget's first major work, *The language and thought of the child* (1926), he identified the phenomenon of egocentric speech, which is characterized by "remarks that are not addressed to anyone . . . and that . . . evoke no reaction adapted to them on the part of anyone to whom they may chance to be addressed" (p. 55). It is the kind of talk children use that does *not* serve the purpose of communicating to another. Piaget's conclusion is that egocentric speech serves no purpose for the child except that it may make the child uncomfortable enough to move to a more socialized world view. The final perspective to be considered comes from a scholar who disagreed with Piaget about the function of egocentric speech and about the role of social interaction in development.

An Interactional Theory of Speech and Thought

The story of Vygotsky's work begins where Pavlov's ends. Early in this century, Pavlov used Descartes' notion of the conditioned reflex to study nervous processes. Later in his career he developed the notion of the Second Signal System to explain the role of speech in cognition. Built upon the bases of two simpler cognitive systems, the Second Signal System went beyond sheer reflex responses to link multiple stimuli by a unitary verbal symbol (Dance & Larson, 1976, p. 95). "Speech . . . is connected up with all the internal and external stimuli which can reach the cortex, signaling all of them and replacing all of them, and therefore it can call forth all those reactions . . . normally determined by the actual stimuli themselves." (Pavlov, 1960, p. 407).

Beginning in the 1920s, Lev Semyonovich Vygotsky was the new voice in Soviet psychology and very much a critic of orthodox behaviorism but he was also repelled by the method of subjective introspection. His solution to this dilemma confronting Soviet psychology was to use Pavlov's notion of the Second Signal System: the "world as processed through language" (Bruner, 1986, p. 70). Pavlov had done little with the idea, but it gave Vygotsky the perfect vehicle for successfully introducing his concepts to the proper Marxists for whom Pavlov was an icon (Bruner, p. 71). Vygotsky's *Thought and Language* (or to be accurate, *Thinking and Speech*—more on this later) was first published in 1934, shortly after his death at the age of 38. In Vygotsky's brief career, his ideas attracted brilliant and productive colleagues such as Luria and Leont'ev in the Soviet Union. The same book was translated to English in 1962 and has since influenced western scholars as well. Let us now examine his contributions.

Because everything to follow is influenced to some degree by Vygotsky's theory, we should begin by clarifying his ideas about speech, language, and cognition. *Myshlenie i Rech* is most accurately translated as *Thinking and Speech* rather than the well known title *Thought and Language* (Wertsch, 1979). True to his dialectical perspective, Vygotsky was interested in the dynamics of human activity, not static representations. He was "mainly concerned with emphasizing the social activity of speech or speaking rather than the structure of the language system" (p. 4). Furthermore, Soviet psychology typically uses a broader interpretation of speech than do we in the West. According to Leont'ev, they studied social interaction, or speech activity, rather than reducing communication to the simple transfer of messages (cited in Wertsch, 1979, p. 4).

Vygotsky also viewed thinking as a dynamic process. One of his tenets, crucial for our purposes, is that the child uses speech to alter the power of thought. To explain how the child does this, Vygotsky undertook a critique of Piaget's analysis of egocentric speech. Recall Piaget's claim that egocentric speech served no purpose but was just a way station on the path to socialized speech, or speech planned for and directed to another. Vygotsky claimed that indeed egocentric speech did have a purpose: to serve the child in regulating his or her own behavior. "Egocentric speech is inner speech in its functions; it is speech on its way inward, intimately tied up with the ordering of the child's behavior" (Vygotsky, 1962, p. 46). That is, egocentric speech is speech for one's own purposes, spoken externally at first, then internalized to be used silently to direct behavior, to sort out one's thoughts. Egocentric speech does not merely accompany actions, but "transforms" them; "the child begins to use speech to guide, organize and plan them" (Hickman, 1985, p. 238). Vygotsky (1962) gave an example:

> A child of five and a half was drawing a streetcar when the point of his pencil broke. He tried, nevertheless, to finish the circle of a wheel, pressing down on the pencil very hard, but nothing showed on the paper but a deep colorless line. The child muttered to himself, "It's broken," put aside the pencil, took watercolors instead, and began drawing a *broken* streetcar after an accident, continuing to talk to himself from time to time about the change in his picture. (p. 17)

Vygotsky continued to experiment with the notion that egocentric speech becomes an internal mental function by examining how children reflect on word meanings and thus build concepts. In addition, he examined the learning process in children and in 1934 hypothesized a "zone of proximal development" as the difference between "actual development as determined by independent problem solving" and "potential development as determined through problem solving under adult guidance or in collaboration with more capable peers" (Vygotsky, 1978, p. 86). This conceptualization of a learning window for children has been used by many interested in the educational process.[1] Countless scholars, from Bruner, Cazden, and Cole to Wertsch and Zinchenko have been influenced by his views. The speech communication discipline was introduced to Vygotsky through Frank Dance and Larry Wilder, among others. As we explore the developmental process of talking the mind into existence, we will encounter these names again, as well as others.

Although all of the evidence in support of our thesis—that the mind emerges from internalizing interactive speech experience—may not be drawn from scholars who identify themselves with Vygotsky, most subscribe to the interactionist perspective no matter whom they credit. Now our questions become more specific. What is mind? How is it distinct from brain? What role does speech play in developing the mind? What does the process look like in infants, toddlers, school-age children? And how might we use our knowledge of the process to improve the outcome?

METATHEORETICAL CONSIDERATIONS

Genetic Foundations

Critical to Vygotsky's theory is a genetic explanation of development. He and Luria called attention to a turning point in the behavior of the child when the lines of development bifurcate "into natural-psychological and cultural-psychological development" (cited in Wertsch, 1991, p. 25). Vygotsky believed that higher mental functions such as voluntary attention, logical memory, and the formation of concepts appear twice in development, first on the social plane, between people, and then on the psychological plane, forming a mind (Vygotsky, 1978, p. 57). Mind is intrapersonally constructed on the basis of interpersonal problem-solving. Although Vygotsky did not specify the origins of the "natural-psychological" line of development, interactionists since have attempted to clarify these sources of the human early propensity to interaction. We will examine two competing explanations: behaviorism and nativism.

Theories about the origins of human communicative behavior at one time consisted of two contrasting positions: behaviorism, which assumes that we bring only very general capacities into the world and then learn everything we need to be

---

[1]Forman and Cazden (1985) provided support for learning within the zone of proximal development; some of that work is reported in the later section of this chapter on classroom interaction.

human communicators, and nativism, which assumes that we are genetically endowed with specific capacities for languaged communication. We concluded earlier that behaviorism was inadequate to explain human communicative behavior, so we now turn to the contributions of two proponents of nativism: Lenneberg and Chomsky.

Nativism.   For Lenneberg (1967), language is a product of a species-specific cognitive function, that in turn, is a consequence of human biological peculiarities (p. 374). The peculiarities that distinguish humans from other primates include increased brain volume and a change to upright posture that resulted in a bend in the vocal tract. This bent-tube structure brought with it a wider range of human sounds—articulated and phonated sounds we know as speech.[2] The maturation of both brain and speech structures brings the developing individual to a language-ready state. So, for Lenneberg, we have the genetic endowment to prepare us to receive language. To summarize the effect of these physiological endowments on human cognition: A brain ready to use speech input may be augmented *by* that input to produce higher psychological processes found only in humans—alternatively, the mind, or Pavlov's Second Signal System.

For Chomsky, however, the important genetic endowment is a specific brain structure for grammar, or the ordering of language elements. For example, the very general rule for word order in English is SVO, or subject-verb-object; and of course there are many other more complicated rules that native speakers seem to know unconsciously. Linguists, however, have not been able to satisfactorily describe all the rules of even one language. So, Chomsky posited an innate "language acquisition device" (LAD) or universal grammar. He has been both lauded and criticized for this theory. One reasonable criticism is that it overlooks a key biological principle: genetic variation (Lieberman, 1991, p. 131). That is, simply because it is genetically transmitted "some children would lack one or more of the genetically coded components of the language faculty" (p. 131)....

> A biologically plausible Universal Grammar cannot have rules and parameters that are so tightly interlocked that the absence of any single bit of putative innate knowledge makes it impossible for the child to acquire a particular language. (p. 132)

So, we have a bigger brain, the emergent capacity for speech, but perhaps no innate language acquisition device imposing grammar. If, as Vygotsky claimed, interactive behaviors are the "natural-psychological" first line of development toward integrating brain and speech to form a mind, where do these behaviors come from and how do they emerge? Some would say that we need not only peculiarly human physiology, but also an environment of willing and capable interacting others to become human. They are the interactionists.

---

[2]See Philip Lieberman (1991) for a recent explanation of the speech structures and how they may have evolved.

Interactionism. Jerome Bruner (1986), an American admirer of Vygotsky, concluded:

> Any innate Language Acquisition Device, LAD, that helps members of our species to penetrate language could not possibly succeed but for the presence of a Language Acquisition Support System, LASS, provided by the social world, that is matched to LAD in some regular way. It is LASS that helps the child navigate across the Zone of Proximal Development to full and conscious control of language use. (p. 77)

Bruner is one of a group of scholars who believe in the importance of very early social communication but wish to specify more clearly than did Vygotsky the structure of that early interaction. He observed that very early parent–child exchanges provide the framework or "scaffolding" on which the child can build a working knowledge of language and the world. As we explore the evidence for very early capacities for speech and thought and later transformations, we will hear much more from the interactionists.

THE PROCESS OF MIND-BUILDING

Infancy: The Cognitive Function of Speech Sounds

We have often thought of infants as incompetent humans—they cannot speak, think or even locomote as adults do. However, as we have observed them with increased specificity and improved technology we find they indeed have some surprising propensities for interaction that distinguish them from even the brightest of other primates.

We are all familiar with some of the signals infants send to gain adult attention; usually crying is the first. Although the cry is certainly informative to the adult about the state of the infant (Wolff, 1966), other early communicative behaviors are perceived as more prosocial by adults and are soon learned by infants to be reliable initiators of interaction. We will examine two: gaze and vocalization.

The infant's most successful method of regulating interaction in the first four months of life is the use of gaze to initiate or terminate contact. However, the infant is limited to regulating the amount of input by gaze avoidance—most gaze shifts observed in the first 4 months are disassociated from interactive events (Stern, 1974) and related to neither the dyadic partner's behavior nor to an internal representation of external behavior. Such a representation, if it occurred, could be the beginning of expectations for interaction that are part of social cognition; however, it just doesn't happen with gaze alone.

The general capacity for cognitive representation requires "the coordination of at least two sensorimotor systems into a higher-order skill" (Fischer & Corrigan, 1981, p. 269). One combination that appears to be critical to normal human development is speech plus any other system. Speech provides a sensory-motor system well suited for coordination with other systems. The two activities of audition (sensory) and vocal production (motor) are naturally coordinated in the speaker. The contrast between two actions in one system fosters self-regulating feedback and ultimately the recognition of self as a regulator, first of one's own speech productions and behavior, then of others'. Dance (1979) called this the acoustic trigger to conceptualization and suggests that the quality of the infant's sound-making/acoustic behavior that accounts for this trigger "is the simultaneity of subjectivity and objectivity provided by the infant's oral/aural behavior, resulting in the perception of contrast" (p. 205). That is, the infant now may recognize the difference between an internal state (the experience of creating the sound) and an external one (hearing one's sound that has existed outside of self). The long term effects, he suggested, eventuate in symbolic conceptualization. First, we will explore the immediate results.

What kind of aural/oral experience fosters this conceptualizing effect? Berry (1969) claimed that audition alone has a "tonic influence" on the level of spontaneous activity in the brain (pp. 38–39). Audition is an available and useful sense even before birth, whereas vocalization begins with purely vocalic (vowel) sounds at birth and later shifts to articulated speech (consonantal) at approximately 6 months. However, interactive behaviors in this 6-month period apparently serve to integrate the two senses communicatively.

In the first 4 months, the infant appears to match or synchronize behaviors with the caregiver quite predictably (Condon & Sander, 1974; Stern, 1974) but apparently reflexively; by the 9th month, the infant is only minimally influenced to match behaviors (Thomas & Martin, 1976). That is, the infant begins life predisposed to automatically match interactive behaviors (smiling, vocalizing), then shifts to fewer matching behaviors, and later returns to matching interaction voluntarily. Sander (1977) described this change as a shift from a biosocial level of interaction to a psychosocial level. Perhaps Sander's levels correspond conceptually to Vygotsky's two lines of development—natural-psychological and cultural-psychological. As I interpret this shift, the infant is involved in a process of self-differentiation by transforming adaptive schemata to self-regulative structures to truly interactive processes. Because we know that the speech system is uniquely suited to making self–other distinctions, once the infant can speak, the nature and patterns of interactions change to reflect a recognition of his or her own interactive influence: the infant exerts more control.

The effects of the move to voluntary control of one's own speech behavior are observed first in the expansion of vocalic types (4 to 6 months), then in a shift to reduplicated speech syllables including consonants (7 to 10 months) in which the infant will use one type of syllable in long strings of repetitions (Oller, 1980). We might then reason that a cognitive correlate accompanies this vocal shift. Bever (1961) claimed that the discontinuity in vocalic versus consonantal output can be mapped onto a neurological discontinuity in subcortical reflex control versus more voluntary cortical control. He offered two possible explanations: one, that the shift in vocal output is "caused" by the shift from reflex to cortical organization of behavior; or two, that "analytic phonetic differentiation" (elaborating components of syllables—consonants as well as vowels) must follow the "syncretic syllabic stage" (producing largely syllabic vowels) rending cortical activity more important (Bever, 1982, pp. 155–157). In the first syncretic stage, the infant uses global schemata for producing vowels, but must then move to the analytic phase of focusing on the component processes of a skill like producing phones consisting of consonants as well as vowels (p. 154). Whether this quiescent period of cortical inhibition of lower brain systems in the absence of structures to replace them reflects a neurological cause, a developmental one, or both, Bever argued that the "regression" is a function of "maturationally progressive analytic processes." (p. 155)

Further evidence of developing control of speech and thought comes from Elbers (1982), who suggested that infants cognitively grasp articulatory contrasts and vary them purposefully in babbling. I found that when infants babble alone, they decrease and stabilize the length of their speech sounds from 22 to 34 weeks of age. They repeat sounds increasingly for practice and variety, then decrease the repetitions as they develop sound preferences (Yingling, 1984). Ferguson (1978) suggested that these preferred speech sounds are used by the infant to link meaning with sound; they use particular sounds in particular experiential contexts. Now, so far, it may seem that the infant alone is doing the hard work of linking speech and cognition. What is happening interactively?

Proto-Conversation: Interactive and Cognitive Shifts

Even neonates show some predisposition to act in accord with other humans. Newborns will move their bodies in synchrony to adult speech patterns; their movements are timed to change direction, for example, as a pause occurs in adult speech (Condon, 1977). Do the infants anticipate adult speech patterns? Undoubtedly not. In the first 6 months of life, infants apparently cannot retrieve a cognitively stored standard for comparison with an observed stimulus (Kagan, Kearsley, & Zelazo, 1978, p. 100). Rhythmic habituation based on subcortical neural processes is a simpler explanation for this behavior than the kinds of expectations adult humans use to mutually influence interaction (Cappella & Greene, 1982).

At this point, we might find it useful to distinguish an infant's "schema" from an "expectation." Schemata are the result of subcortical rhythms set to repeated stimuli, whereas expectations are cognitive standards established by regulating one's mental representations. The latter is voluntary; the former is not. When the infant notices a discrepancy between her established schema and her observation and can adjust her behavior accordingly, true expectations may begin. Let's say that she has a schema for her mother's vocal pattern to which her own body movement is entrained. If the pattern changes (a new person speaks, or mother is in a bad mood) she will probably be upset and react globally (cry, close her eyes) *unless* the discrepancy is noted as a higher cognitive level as varying from a cognitive standard. Then her reaction may be different—perhaps interested gaze at first, followed by some behavior that demands an adult response such as noncry vocalization.

Stern and his colleagues (Stern, Jaffe, Beebe, & Bennett, 1975) claimed that noncoactive vocal patterns (one speaker at a time or turn-taking) transform to later dialogic exchanges, whereas coactive vocal patterns (simultaneous sounds) transform to emotional exchanges (such as chants or cheers). Dialogue is voluntary, therefore speech must become voluntary to be dialogic.

In a longitudinal study (Yingling, 1985) of four infant–caregiver pairs from the infants' 5th to 9th month, noncoactive speech or turn-taking increased, whereas gaze remained coactive. Furthermore, infants began to interrupt caregiver speech at about the utterance duration that caregivers had established in previous sessions; infants adjusted their behavior and influenced their partner's behavior on the basis of expectations stored in long-term memory. Over time, caregiver's utterance durations decrease as infant's utterance durations increase; the infant appears to exert increasing influence over the interactive process. These proto-conversations are the preverbal child's milieu. The interactive behaviors that begin to appear before the first word such as turn-taking, attention-getting, and goal-directed action are necessary elements of the true conversations that appear later.

In further observations of infant–caregiver pairs (Yingling, 1990/1991), adults used repetitions of requests, questions, and formulating the gist of events to engage infants. If the infant resisted giving appropriate responses, adults repeated formulations and even physically manipulated the infant's behavior (e.g., adjusting infant grip on a rattle). However, infants between 22 and 36 weeks were beginning to form their own agenda for interaction, so parents often yielded to infant resistance, with apologies, requests for repairs, accounts, and reformulations to give expression to the infant's agenda. Infants increased their interactive strategies over the 3-month period. They would at first comply with the interactive games set by the adult (peek-a-boo, etc.), but as games extended beyond their expected time and behavior limits, they began to use simple escape methods such as gaze avoidance and fussy vocalizations. As their sophistication increased, more complex combinations of strategies appeared.

For example, at $7\frac{1}{2}$ months, Sara began to respond appropriately to her mother's game of "yeay, Sara" by responding with an approximation of the word "yeay," then she tired and changed not only the sound but its timing. At 8 months, she used direct gaze, increased proximity, and vocalization to obtain the return of a block from her mother who had been trying to get it away from her. From this kind of cooperative interaction, infants appear to build interpretive procedures for handling conversations; they adapt simple acts for escape and gradually build their repertoire toward complexes of acts for influencing interactive goals.

Toward Language: Intentions, First Words and New Ideas

The preverbal child, in order to signal communicative goals, must realize first that events occur in ordered sequences with "one event (the infant's gestures and vocalizations) occurring prior to and capable of causing later events," and then that people are capable of serving as a means to an end (Golinkoff & Gordon, 1988, p. 104). Both realizations are precursors to the use of intentional communication behaviors (Harding & Golinkoff, 1979). Although infants begin to use single words late in their first year, we consider them preverbal or prelinguistic until they begin to demonstrate that they understand the symbolic function of words: The symbol can be substituted for its referent but is not the same thing as its referent (Bates, 1979, p. 144). Ordinarily the child does not begin to use words in the absence of their referents until 18 months or later. We will now look at how intention emerges in that transition stage from 9 to 18 months.

As we already have seen, infants can certainly communicate their desires with gestures, vocalizing, eye gaze, and combinations of these. Some scholars claim that caregivers pull intention from their infants; that they treat infant behavior as intentional, thus infants learn the possibility to intend (Newson, 1978, pp. 36–37). Scholars also have assumed typically that mothers interpret infants' acts and their goals pretty well; however, about half of the time mothers initially fail to understand their infants' signals (Golinkoff, 1986). So, how does intention emerge?

The preverbal child indeed may indicate by nonverbal expression *that* they prefer or do not prefer, but will have a great deal of trouble indicating *what* it is that they do or do not prefer. When the infant-initiated communication is immediately understood by the caregiver, it is usually because the child has gazed at the preferred object, pointed, and/or vocalized (Golinkoff & Gordon, 1988, p. 112). Successes increase from 9 to 18 months, as do combinations of vocalizations plus gestures. When caregivers fail to understand they will often ask questions to reformulate the interaction, that is, negotiate the episode. The child may appear to want a particular object but fail to signal *which* object in a visual field of many. As the caregiver persists in negotiating the episode, the infant increases the chance of successfully obtaining the desired object by using communicative chains: consecutive episodes in which the infant's signals refer to the same object or event (p. 120). When children persist in referencing topics, they gain "much insight into what does and does not work for creating joint attention and shared focus." (p. 122). For example, the infant may point in the direction of a number of objects and simultaneously vocalize; mother then responds with an offer of a grape and, "Oh, you want a grape." In the next turn, the infant may either accept the grape (success) or push it away and continue to signal (p. 107). When motivation to attain a goal is high, the child may focus more intently on the caregiver's use of a word or two to reformulate intent (p. 122). By chaining discourse, even preverbally, the child prepares to acquire the shared meanings necessary for human communication. The child needs the deictic function of words and soon begins to use it.

Moving yet closer to language, children begin to use conventional words late in the first year. Soon after, they begin to figure out that objects continue to have an existence even if they can't see them, and that processes are related to products. Gopnik and Meltzoff (1986) guessed that these linguistic developments (using words meaningfully) are quite specifically related to cognitive developments such as object permanence and means–ends relations. They found strong correlations between the ability to solve a difficult object-permanence task [3] and the appearance of

---

[3]This test requires finding an object following a series of hidden displacements. An object is hidden in the hand; the hand is placed under A, then B, then C. The object is left under C. The child may then search under A, then B, then C, or directly under C.

disappearance words (e.g., "gone"); as well as between the ability to solve means–ends tasks[4] and the appearance of success/failure words (e.g., "there" and "uh-oh"). They conclude that certain problem-solving abilities appear with certain specific meanings, and that conceptual and semantic developments are closely inter-twined—they influence and facilitate each other (pp. 1051–1052). Further evidence from language-delayed children demonstrates that they perform significantly poorer on means–ends relationships than do normally developing children (Snyder, 1975). Language acquisition is apparently intimately connected with certain kinds of cognitive developments. So far, though, the language developments are entirely semantic; children are developing meanings for sounds. What of syntactic development? When children begin to use several words, how do they know how to combine them and what do they need to know to do so?

Combining Words: Syntax and Sense-Making

Now we can assume that the child has started to use a few words, but we cannot assume that the child uses language. Language consists not only of phonological (speech sounds), semantic (meaning), and pragmatic (getting things done) functions that we've demonstrated the child can use very early in life, but also a syntactic function that has to do with the rules for combining words in a language or "the grammar of arrangement" (Bolinger, 1975, p. 23). Grammar is the broader term for a formal description of linguistic behavior (Lieberman, 1975, p. 90). Grammatical processes, suggested Mattingly (1972), may serve as an interface between the innate structures for brain and speech; grammar matches "the potentialities of an intellect to the limitations of our devices for producing and perceiving sounds" (Liberman, 1975, p. 4). We need grammar to link sounds to meanings.

There are two competing positions on the acquisition of grammar. Recall that Chomsky assumed that children must "bring to the language acquisition task certain innate clues about the range of possible human grammars" (Bates & MacWhinney, 1979, p. 168); that is, grammar works from the inside out to language specifics. The second position, a functionalist approach, claims that grammar is a system derived from the constraints of the communicative task. This grammar is guided by "the pragmatic and semantic structure of communications interacting with the performance constraints of the speech channel" (p. 168). The semantic and pragmatic functions we mentioned earlier are competing for access to the speech channel; we can resolve that competition in different ways, all of which involve only four kinds of signals: (a) lexical items (words), (b) word order, (c) morphological markers (e.g., adding an "s" to "pen" to change its meaning), and (d) intonational contours (speech inflections) (p. 169). We will examine a case of word order that is related to the young child's social knowledge.

Generally, children under 2 years of age do not know the syntactic rules for putting together words into sentences (Bloom, 1973, p. 55) thus they simply use one

---

[4]Means–ends tasks included using a stick to obtain an object, placing a necklace in a bottle, and stacking a set of rings on a post. See Gopnik and Meltzoff (1986), p. 1043, for a complete list of tasks.

word at a time—but still manage to convey a fairly complete idea. One fortuitous result of being able to use intonational contours and lexical items very early in development is that the child can express both topic and comment in one word and perhaps an accompanying gesture. The child who knows the word "more" may make a request by raising the intonation or a command by emphasizing a falling inflection. In each case the comment is expressing desire, "I want more" or "May I have more?" but the topic is unclear from speech alone. Usually the item is physically present and may be indicated by pointing or by gaze. In the one-word period, children are likely to encode the element that attracts their attention. Now, how is the child likely to order words when they begin to combine several?

Functionalists suggest that the first word order is likely to be comment-topic ("gimme ball") because the comment is the important information from the *child's* perspective (Bates & MacWhinney, 1979, p. 190). Of course, the listener needs to hear what this is all about—the topic first. So they predict that, although the earliest ordering is comment-topic, it then changes to topic-comment ordering (recall that English is a subject-verb-object language). The shift from comment fronting to topic fronting may well be related to a shift from egocentric perspective to a socialized perspective that takes into account the listener's information needs (p. 211). Now, we take a closer look at this critical shift toward social knowledge.

Inner Speech: Internalizing the Means to a Mind

Both Piaget and Vygotsky studied "collective monologues" in children under 7 years of age. Both observed that children do not think as adults do, but the gradual movement to more socialized speech was interpreted by Piaget as an adaptation to the pressures for considering the listener. On the other hand, Vygotsky saw in this shift a "transition between two quite different functions of language" (Wood, 1988, p. 27). At first, speech serves to regulate the behavior of the speaker, later as speech is internalized it becomes an instrument of thought and transforms the way the speaker thinks. "The physical activity of speaking . . . becomes internalized to create verbal thinking" (p. 27).

A. R. Luria (1961), a student of Vygotsky, proposed three stages of regulative development based on his experiments with young children. In the first, from $1\frac{1}{2}$ to 3 years old, adults control the child's behavior verbally. Commands can initiate actions but not inhibit them; once the child is told to put on his shoes, he will treat any countercommand as encouragement. In the second stage, between 3 and 4 or 5 years, control still resides with the adult but that speech is now able to inhibit as well as to initiate action. The beginnings of verbal self-regulation may be observed in this stage. Finally, between $4\frac{1}{2}$ and 5 years, control is transferred from the "impulsive aspect" of speech to the meanings of words, and verbal self-control is internalized.

Luria's experiments consisted of presenting a sequence of light signals to the child and instructing him to press a small rubber bulb when the signals occur. Two-year-olds begin to press the bulb as soon as they are instructed—they can't wait for the lights. Later they wait for the lights but tend to perseverate—that is to repeat squeezing the bulb. If the child is given a clear feedback signal when he or she presses the bulb (i.e., a bell), they can coordinate their responses better. Luria believed that the verbal system must achieve a greater degree of organization than the motor system for the child to take over control from the external source. One way to bring verbal and motor systems into contact is to ask children to press the bulb at the same time as they say "go." Motor performance improves for 3-to 4-year olds with this instruction. But at this age, the verbal response is the source of motor excitation rather than the meaning of the word. The result will be the same whether you tell the child to say "press" or "don't press"—they will press the bulb. But in the final stage it is the word per se that apparently has the effect. The red button is pressed because the child says "press red."

Several Americans have attempted to replicate Luria's experiments (Jarvis, 1963; Miller, Shelton, & Flavell, 1970; Wilder, 1969), with varying degrees of success. Bloor (1977) and Wozniak (1972) attributed the replication difficulties to misunderstandings about Luria's theory and the Americans' experimental norms, which differ from the Soviets'. Bloor contended that inhibition effects were the main problem in interpreting the various sets of results; the role of language in initiating responses remains reliable (p. 96).

Vygotsky envisioned two separate streams of development—a stream of thought and a stream of language—that began to flow together, each informing the other and creating new forms of both thought and language. What does the child now do with the self-regulation that inner speech provides? She can sort out her thoughts about the world—solve problems, recode messages for effective interaction, and begin to build concepts on the basis of symbols.

Concept Formation: Sophistication in Meaning

When an adult and a child agree on a referent for a word (e.g., "ball" refers to that round rubbery object), it is tempting to assume that they share meaning. In fact, although their meanings may coincide, they do not match. The child's meaning does not reside in a ready-made concept, but is just beginning to develop. Vygotsky (1962) proposed a progression in this development from "unorganized heaps" to "complexes" and finally to "concepts." He explained concept formation as a complex activity

> in which all the basic intellectual functions take part. The process cannot, however, be reduced to association, attention, imagery, inference, or determining tendencies. They are all indispensable, but they are insufficient without the use of the sign, or word, as the means by which we direct our mental operations, control their course, and channel them toward the solution of the problem confronting us. (p. 58)

The *"heap"* emerges when the child groups together a number of referents—the objects are linked by a chance impression alone (for example, my friend's 1-year-old now uses the word "duck" to refer not only to ducks, but goats, squirrels, and even his Dad).

"Complexes" are of several types, gradually paving the way to genuine concepts. Now the bonds between referents are concrete and factual, not simply subjective.

The *chain complex* has no nucleus of meaning but is based on consecutive individual links between one referent and another. In Vygotsky's experiments, children were given blocks in a variety of colors, shapes, and sizes. Suppose we give a child a yellow triangle and ask him to form a group of "Tuesday" blocks like this one. The child may pick out a few triangular blocks until his attention is caught by the blue color of the block he just added so he switches to blue blocks of any shape until a rounded block catches his fancy and he's off again in pursuit of rounded blocks (Vygotsky, 1963, p. 64). The attribute that links these "Tuesday" blocks keeps changing during the process. Another example is the child who says "wawa" for the water splashing in her tub, then again for the water splashing from the garden hose, then on a trip to fill the car with gas she uses "wawa" when she sees the hose from the pump. We would consider such usage erroneous and hasten to provide a new word for the gas station experience.

Another type of complex is *associative;* it is based on any bond the child notices. The first block the child is given is named again, but this time forms the nucleus of the group to be built by the child. Any bond between the nucleus block and another block suffices for inclusion in the family of objects—it could be a contrast, a proximity in space, or a common trait like color. So, if we start with a yellow triangle, the child may then pick a yellow oblong, then a blue rod because it is next to the yellow triangle, then a blue triangle and so forth—but she ultimately calls them all by the name given, for example, "Tuesday" blocks. The word becomes the family name of a group of objects all related to one element—the nucleus—in many kinds of ways (p. 62).

"Pseudoconcepts" form the bridge between complexes and concepts. In this experiment, the child with the yellow triangle picks out all the triangles. Now, we might assume that this set has been assembled on the basis of an abstract concept of a triangle, but the child is guided by concrete, visible likenesses among blocks (p. 66). "Although the child agrees with the concept in its outward form, he/she in no way agrees with the adult in the mode of thinking or in the type of intellectual operations that he/she brings to the pseudoconcept" (cited in Wertsch & Stone, 1985, p. 170). The child does not freely construct complexes, claimed Vygotsky, but "finds them already constructed in the process of understanding others' speech" (p. 171). The concepts used in constructing mental processes are provided by one's speech community—the word provides an already prepared form of generalization (p. 171).

We have now followed the humanizing process from physiological endowments, through speech and interaction as they shift from biological developments to psychological constructions, on to the now interconnected speech and thought giving rise to language, and finally to the internalization of speech to serve thought in coding socialized speech, in the development of concepts, in the development of consciousness. Consciousness is the "awareness of the activity of the mind" (Vygotsky, 1962, p. 91) and emerges along with scientific concepts. School instruction apparently provides the sorts of hierarchical systems of concepts necessary for mastery of generalization. When the concept "flower" becomes generalized, the subordinate relationship of "rose" to "flower" allows a conceptual system to form (p. 93). The schoolchild however is not aware of his own conceptual operations; introspection begins to develop during the school years and gradually moves toward consciousness of the intellect itself. In the next section, we examine what the child is doing with inner speech in several childhood contexts—preschool play, classroom interaction and friendship.

INTERACTIVE CONTEXTS
FOR DEVELOPING A MIND

The development of inner speech, although an active creative process, must have its origins in social interaction. Interpsychological functioning in social contexts progresses to the intrapsychological functioning of the mind.

Play and the Preschooler

In the preschool years, play is the leading source of the kinds of development we have considered. Play, far from being a simple source of pleasure (which it often is *not*), has everything to do with unmet needs and desires. Very young children tend to gratify their needs immediately. Ultimately, however, if the child is to interact with others, gratification must be delayed. Children play to realize unrealizable desires through the use of imagination (Vygotsky, 1967, pp. 7–8). If play is essentially wish fulfillment, how does it serve development? The answer, in part, has to do with the acquisition of rules for behavior. Imaginary situations contain rules of behavior even if only implied. If you ask children to play a real situation, they seem easily able to do so. Vygotsky's example concerned two sisters who played at being sisters. In life, they behave as sisters without thinking, but in play these behaviors becomes rules for the play and thus bring the rules to awareness—they become conscious of what characterizes being a sister (e.g., they hold hands as well as verbally emphasize their connectedness in contrast with others: "that is theirs, not ours" p. 9).

A game with rules "immediately turns into an imaginary situation in the sense that as soon as the game is regulated by certain rules, a number of actual possibilities for action are ruled out" (p. 10). Games generally evolve from those with an overt imaginary situation and covert rules (e.g., the sisters) to those with overt rules and a covert imaginary situation (e.g., chess). In play, the child can begin to act independently of the immediate perception; she can recognize a concrete use of an object but act differently toward it (e.g., put a wooden spoon to her ear and say "hello?"). Thus the meaning rather than the object dominates behavior.

By the time the child begins school, play is "converted to internal processes . . . going over into internal speech, logical memory, and abstract thought" (p. 13). It is the first effect of "emancipation from situational constraints" and the beginning of the child's will (p. 14). Following the rules of the game requires self-restraint, which the child learns because observing the rules promises greater pleasure from the game than the immediate gratification of an impulse (e.g., counting to 10 before "seeking" in hide-and-seek rather than simply rushing off in pursuit of the hiders).

Not only does play develop the ability to choose, or will, but it allows the child to behave beyond his daily capacities. "Play creates the zone of proximal development" (p. 16) in its focus on subordinating behavior to rules. Children could not keep up this sort of controlled behavior all the time, but play provides a time-bound opportunity to practice capacities above the level of their average behavior.

At school age, play does not disappear but now permeates the child's attitude to reality (p. 17). In schoolchildren, play without action becomes imagination (p. 8).

Classroom Interaction

Schoolchildren are faced with multiple tasks. They not only must master scientific concepts in formal education, but must also successfully interact with their peers. If learning consists of internalizing social interaction processes, then interaction in the classroom is critical. Yet, the traditional model for education has focused on individual work in a fairly silent classroom. What is the effect? We will first examine a series of studies on the effects of private speech (egocentric speech as it becomes intrapersonal communication) on task performance, and then look to recent considerations of the "zone of proximal development" in classroom practices.

The notion of private speech, or speech-to-and-for-self, has captured the attention of developmental psychologists. Private or egocentric speech becomes more task relevant from 4 to 7 years (Istomina, 1975). Initial private speech is characterized by overt vocalization (kindergarten and first grade) but becomes more covert with age (second to fourth grade) and gradually becomes less intelligible to an outside listener (Manning & White, 1990). Even in adults, the nerves of the tongue and lips are activated during difficult or novel mental tasks (Cacioppo & Petty, 1979; Sokolov, 1972). This suggests that private speech, even as it becomes silent, facilitates complex thought; the older children are adapting private speech for cognitive purposes as they internalize it. That process describes the development of intrapersonal communication.

Vygotsky characterized inner speech as disconnected and incomplete; syntax is simplified, meaning is condensed and fewer words are used (1962, p. 141). As egocentric speech is internalized. It begins to go through these transformations toward inner speech, thus would certainly be unintelligible—as would the inner speech of an adult to a would-be mind-reader. In contrast to the largely social function of external speech, inner speech facilitates the development of one's own thoughts, "as preliminary drafts of social speech, as a private voice for self-regulation, and as a workspace for formulating overt actions." (Cacioppo & Petty, 1983, p. 717)

In several well-designed studies, Berk (1986) and later Berk with Bivens (Bivens & Berk, 1990), tested the relationship of egocentric speech to task, attention, and task performance. Although Berk and Bivens study what Piaget called egocentric speech, they termed it "private speech" because these children, from first to third grades, were already capable of socialized speech, thus the term egocentric is misleading. We might then consider this "speech for self" the early stage of true intrapersonal communication as defined earlier in this volume. When children used task-relevant speech intrapersonally, they demonstrated greater attentional focus to the task and reduced extraneous, tension-reducing behaviors (rhythmic movements, self-manipulation). IQ was positively related to task-driven "private speech" at grade one, but negatively related at grade three (Berk, 1986, p. 676). In a longitudinal study following children through first, second, and third grades, Bivens and Berk (1990) found that "individual trajectories of private (intrapersonal) speech development were paralleled by similar changes in behavioral self-control and attentiveness to seatwork tasks (in this case, individual math practice) over the early elementary years" (p. 443). They tested the use of such speech during individuals' work on arithmetic problems and found that although the task-relevant speech was unrelated to concurrent math achievement, it was positively related to math achievement in the year following the observations. That is, it takes some time for the cognitive effects of intrapersonal communication to accumulate. Developing in tandem with the internalization of speech are the abilities to inhibit distracting body movements and to sustain attentional focus (p. 459), necessary capacities for the schoolchild in a learning environment.

Now, the child is obviously doing some serious work internalizing speech for self—developing intrapersonal communication—but what is going on interactively? The zone of proximal development describes the discrepancy between solitary and social problem-solving. Recall that the "level of potential development (is) determined through problem-solving under adult guidance or in collaboration with more capable peers" (Vygotsky, 1978, p. 86). Cazden (1988) examined the nature of classroom discourse in depth and was particularly convinced that peer interactions are much more important to cognitive development than we have acknowledged. "A series of investigators including Inagaki, Lomov, and Kol'tsova (cited in Forman & Cazden, 1985) have concluded that 'peer interaction helps individuals acknowledge . . . and integrate a variety of perspectives on a problem" *and* that this process produces "superior intellectual results" (p. 330).

Collaborative problem-solving that requires managerial skills and planning leads to achievements that neither child can perform alone. A peer observer provides "some of the same kinds of 'scaffolding' assistance that others have attributed to the adult in the teaching context" (p. 343). An example of two fifth-grade boys given a chemistry problem reported that they first used deductive reasoning as a social activity—they guided, prompted and corrected each other. Months later both were able to generate all possible solutions by themselves—they both internalized the deductive process (p. 343). Considering the powerful effect of peer interactions, "they may be especially important in school because of limitations and rigidities characteristic of adult–child interactions in that institutional setting" (p. 344).

Friendships

Children are not only learning scientific concepts and reasoning processes, they are learning relationships—what to expect and what is expected. Much of the research conducted on children's concepts of friendship has used a person-centered cognitive framework that ignores the role of speech processes in relationships (Yingling, 1992). The few interactionists involved in this kind of research include Youniss (1978, 1980), who assumed that children's friendships are constituted interpersonally, and Rizzo and Corsaro (1988) who took the Vygotskian view that children) internalize the experiences of peer relationships to develop a concept of friendship.

Child–child and child–adult relationships are not only different but lead to two types of understanding: Peer relations lead to mutuality; adult-child relations lead to self-constructions that take into account social expectations for interaction (Youniss, 1978). In other words, peer friendships help the child realize friendship rules involving collaboration and reciprocity, whereas adult–child relationships help the child to see self in terms of broader rules for appropriate behavior.

As early as the first grade, children appear to have an internalized concept of friendship and their interactions display many behaviors (helping, sharing, loyalty) mentioned by adults as characteristic of friendship (Rizzo & Corsaro, 1988). Though they have internalized a concept of friendship, it is rather idealized and resistant to change. When a first-grade partner failed to live up to his friend's expectations for friendship (e.g., did not share) the injured party was reluctant to alter his ideas about friendship but instead engaged in disputes in which he insisted on adjustments in his friend's behavior (p. 232). In the process of these negotiations the child discovers and invents novel uses for the concept, thus refining notions of friendship. Earlier research found that children's self-reports of friendship consisted of fairly superficial characteristics, such as proximity, common activities, and propinquity (Bigelow, 1977; Selman, 1981); however the child's practical knowledge is apparently much more complex than they are able to report. Recall that the process of internalization involves a lag between the demonstrated ability to act according to a principle and the ability to consciously reflect on that principle. Again, knowledge begins in interaction and only later becomes reflective. This human process of building a mind by internalizing experience is one that seems to occur in a "series of cyclical movements from the interpersonal to the intrapersonal with the contribution of cognitive reflection . . . increasing in importance and complexity with successive cycles" (Rizzo & Corsaro, 1988, p. 236). What are the broad implications of this sort of process for development?

CONCLUSION

One of the very clear implications of an interactional theory of speech-and-thought's internalization process is that communication, both interpersonal and intrapersonal, continues to develop throughout the lifespan. Contrary to the implications of stage theories of cognitive development that end with a final stage in adolescence, social participants continue to internalize experience and thus refine the mind as long as they interact.

Consider the concept of egocentrism, not egocentric speech, which occurs at an early stage in development before speech "goes underground," but egocentric thought, which is an inability to decenter or view the situation from a perspective other than one's own. Several scholars have postulated that egocentrism returns after very early thought, but in different forms with different effects. An adolescent who has reached the supposed final stage of thought is able to understand that others have differing views but "fails to differentiate between what others are thinking and his own mental preoccupations" and thus believes that "others are preoccupied with his appearance and behavior" (Elkind, 1967, pp. 1029–1030). Although Elkind used a Piagetian perspective and thus assumed that all mental structures were in place, he then reported that "gradually" the adolescent comes to recognize the difference between own and others' concerns. Apparently, this is another cycle of internalization.

Other scholars have reported a deterioration of cognitive abilities in old age (Sanders, Laurendeau, & Bergeron, 1966), along with a tendency to reduced frequency of social interaction. Looft and Charles (1971) tested young (average 18 years) and old (average 77 years) adults for cognitive egocentrism, or the inability to decenter, and found a significant difference between the two groups. In addition to their superior abilities for decentering, more of the young adults talked more about the social-interaction task (they discussed how they would approach the task) than did older adults. One explanation for these results is that we need continued spoken interaction to retain not only our social skills but related cognitive capacities as well. That is, we must keep internalizing experience via spoken language.

As the child constructs the mind, moving toward a consciousness of intellect, the adult too may continue to construct consciousness moving toward an awareness of an individual purpose or role in the larger human network. In any case, the "talk" or symbol-use with which we engage interacting others, whether in formal classroom and therapeutic settings or informal intimate contexts, is the raw material that constitutes the seemingly miraculous process of building and maintaining a mind.

REFERENCES

Bates, E. (1979). The emergence of symbols: Ontogeny and phylogeny. In W. A. Collins (Ed.), *Children's language and communication: Symposia on child psychology* (Vol. 12). Hillsdale, NJ: Lawrence Erlbaum Associates.

Bates, E., & MacWhinney, B. (1979). A functionalist approach to the acquisition of grammar. In E. Ochs & B. B.Schieffelin (Eds.), *Developmental pragmatics* (pp. 167–211). New York: Academic Press.

Berk, L. E. (1986). Relationship of elementary school children's private speech to behavioral accompaniment to task, attention, and task performance. *Developmental Psychology, 22,* 671–680.

Berry, M. F. (1969). *Language disorders of children.* New York: Appleton-Century-Crofts.

Bever, T. G. (1961). *Development from vocal to verbal behavior in children.* Unpublished master's thesis, Harvard, Cambridge, MA.

Bever, T. G. (1982). Regression in the service of development. In T. G. Bever (Ed.), *Regressions in mental development: Basic phenomena and theories* (pp. 153–188). Hillsdale, NJ: Lawrence Erlbaum Associates.

Bidell, T. (1988). Vygotsky, Piaget and the Dialectic of Development. *Human Development, 31,* 329–348.

Bigelow, B. (1977). Children's friendship expectations: A cognitive-developmental study. *Child Development, 48,* 246–253.

Bivens, J. A., & Berk, L. E. (1990). A longitudinal study of the development of elementary school children's private speech. *Merrill-Palmer Quarterly, 36,* 443–463.

Bloom, L. (1973). *One word at a time.* The Hague: Mouton.

Bloor, D. (1977). The regulatory function of language. In J. Morton & J. C. Marshall (Eds.), *Psycholinguistics: Developmental and pathological* (pp. 73–97). Ithaca, New York: Cornell University Press.

Bolinger, D. (1975). *Aspects of language* (2nd ed.). New York: Harcourt Brace Jovanovich.

Bruner, J. (1986). *Actual minds, possible worlds.* Cambridge, MA: Harvard University Press.

Cacioppo, J. T., & Petty, R. E. (1979). Attitudes and cognitive responses: An electrophysiological approach. *Journal of Personality and Social Psychology, 37,* 281–299.

Cacioppo, J. T., & Petty, R. E. (1983). *Social psychophysiology: A sourcebook.* New York: The Guilford Press.

Cappella, J. N., & Greene, J. O. (1982). A discrepancy-arousal explanation of mutual influence in expressive behavior for adult and infant–adult interaction. *Communication Monographs, 49,* 89–114.

Cazden, C. B. (1988). *Classroom discourse: The language of teaching and learning.* Portsmouth, NH: Heinemann.

Condon, W. (1977). A primary phase in the organization of infant responding. In H. R. Schaffer (Ed.), *Studies in mother-infant interaction* (pp. 153–176). New York: Academic Press.

Condon, W. S., & Sander, L. W. (1974). Neonate movement is synchronized with adult speech. *Science, 183,* 99–101.

Dance, F. E. X. (1979). Acoustic trigger to concepualization: A hypothesis concerning the role of the spoken word in the development of higher mental processes. *Health Communications and Informatics, 5,* 203–213.

Dance, F. E. X., & Larson, C. E. (1976). *The functions of human communication.* New York: Holt, Rinehart and Winston.

Elbert, L. (1982). Operating principles in repetitive babbling: A cognitive continuity approach. *Cognition, 12,* 45–63.

Elkind, D. (1967). Egocentrism in adolescence. *Child Development, 38,* 1025–1034.

Ferguson, C. A. (1978). Learning to pronounce: The earliest stages of phonological development in the child. In F. D. Minifie & L. L. Lloyd (Eds.), *Communicative and cognitive abilities—Early behavioral assessment* (pp. 273–297). Baltimore, MD: University Park Press.

Fischer, K. W., & Corrigan, R. (1981). A skill approach to language development. In R. Stark (Ed.), *Language behavior in infancy and early childhood* (pp. 245–273). Amsterdam: Elsevier North Holland.

Forman, E. A., & Cazden, C. B. (1985). Exploring Vygotskian perspectives in education: The cognitive value of peer interaction. In J. V. Wertsch (Ed.), *Culture, communication and cognition: Vygotskian perspectives* (pp. 323–347). Cambridge, England: Cambridge University Press.

Gelman, R., & Baillargeon, R. (1983). A review of some Piagetian concepts. In P. H. Mussen (Ed.), *Handbook of child psychology: Volume III. Cognitive Development* (4th ed., pp. 167–230) New York: Wiley.

Ginsburg, H., & Opper, S. (1969). *Piaget's theory of intellectual development: An introduction.* Englewood Cliffs, NJ: Prentice-Hall.

Golinkoff, R. M. (1986). I beg your pardon? The preverbal negotiation of failed messages. *Journal of Child Language, 13,* 455–476.

Golinkoff, R. M., & Gordon, L. (1988). What makes communication run? Characteristics of immediate successes. *First Language, 8,* 103–124.

Gopnik, A., & Meltzoff, A. N. (1986). Relations between semantic and cognitive development in the one-word stage: The specificity hypothesis. *Child Development, 57,* 1040–1053.

Harding, C. G., & Golinkoff, R. M. (1979). The origins of intentional vocalizations in prelinguistic infants. *Child Development, 50,* 33–40.

Hickman, M. E. (1985). The implications of discourse skills in Vygotsky's developmental theory. In J. V. Wertsch (Ed.), *Culture, communication and cognition; Vygotskian perspectives* (pp. 236–252). Cambridge, England: Cambridge University Press.

Istomina, Z. M. (1975). The development of voluntary memory in pre-school age children. *Soviet Psychology, 13,* 5–64.

Jarvis, P. E. (1963). *The effect of self-administered verbal instructions on simple sensory-motor performance in children.* Unpublished doctoral dissertation, University of Rochester, New York.

Kagan, J., Kearsley, R. B., & Zelazo, P. R. (1978). *Infancy: Its place in human development.* Cambridge, MA: Harvard University Press.

Lenneberg, E. H. (1967). *Biological foundations of language.* New York: Wiley.

Liberman, A. M. (1975). Introduction to the conference. In J. F. Kavanagh & J. E. Cutting (Eds.), *The role of speech in language* (pp. 3–7). Cambridge, MA: The MIT Press.

Lieberman, P. (1975). The evolution of speech and language. In J. F. Kavanagh & J. E. Cutting (Eds.), *The role of speech in language* (pp. 83–106). Cambridge, MA: The MIT Press.

Lieberman, P. (1991). *Uniquely human: The evolution of speech, thought, and selfless behavior.* Cambridge, MA: Harvard University Press.

Looft, W. R., & Charles, D. C. (1971). Egocentrism and social interaction in young and old adults. *Aging and Human development, 2,* 21–28.

Luria, A. R. (1961). *The role of speech in the regulation of normal and abnormal behavior.* New York: Liveright.

Manning, B. H., & White, C. S. (1990). Task-relevant private speech as a function of age and sociability. *Psychology in the Schools, 27,*365–372.

Mattingly, I. G. (1972). Speech cues and sign stimuli. *American Scientist, 60,* 327–337.

Miller, S., Shelton, J., & Flavell, J. (1970). A test of Luria's hypothesis concerning the development of verbal self-regulation. *Child development, 41,* 651–665.

Newson, J. (1978). Dialogue and development. In A. Lock (Ed.), *Action, gesture, and symbol* (pp. 31–42). London: Academic Press.

Oller, D. K. (1980). The emergence of the sounds of speech in infancy. In G. H. Yeni-Komshian, J. F. Kavanagh, & C. A. Ferguson (Eds.), *Child phonology Vol. I: Production* (pp. 73–112). New York: Academic Press.

Pavlov, I. P. (1960). *Conditioned reflexes: An investigation of physiological activity of the cerebral cortex.* (G. V. Anrep, Trans. & Ed.) New York: Dover. (Original work published 1927)

Piaget, J. (1926). *The language and thought of the child.* (M. Gabain, Trans.) New York: World Publishing.

Rizzo, T. A., & Corsaro, W. A. (1988). Toward a better understanding of Vygotsky's process of internalization: Its role in the development of the concept of friendship. *Developmental Review 8,* 219–237.

Sander, L. W. (1977). The regulation of exchange in the infant–caregiver system and some aspects of the context–content relationship. In M. Lewis & L. Rosenblum (Eds.), *Interaction, conversation and the development of language* (pp. 133–156). New York: Wiley.

Sanders, S., Laurendeau, M., & Bergeron, J. (1966). Aging and the concept of space: The conservation of surfaces. *Journal of Gerontology, 21,* 281–286.

Selman, R. (1981). The child as a friendship philosopher. In S. Asher & J. M. Gottman (eds.), *The development of children's friendships* (pp. 242–272). New York: Cambridge University Press.

Snyder, L. (1975). *Pragmatics in language-deficient children: Prelinguistic and early verbal performatives and presuppositions.* Unpublished doctoral dissertation, University of Colorado.

Sokolov, A. N. (1972). *Inner speech and thought.* New York: Plenum.

Stern, D. N. (1974). Mother and infant at play: The dyadic interaction involving facial, vocal and gaze behaviors. In M. Lewis & L. Rosenblum (Eds.), *The effect of the infant on its caregiver* (pp. 187–214). New York: Wiley.

Stern, D. N., Jaffe, J., Beebe, B. & Bennett, S. L. (1975). Vocalizing in unison and in alteration: Two modes of communication within the mother–infant dyad. *Annals of the New York Academy of Sciences, 264,* 89–100.

Thomas, E. A. C., & Martin, J. A. (1976). Analysis of parent–infant interaction. *Psychological Review, 83,* 141–56.

Tolman, C. (1983). Categories, logic, and the problem of necessity in theories of mental development. *Studia Psychologica, 25,* 179–190.

Vygotsky, L. S. (1962). *Thought and language.* (E. Hanfmann & G. Vakar, Trans.). Cambridge, MA: The MIT Press.

Vygotsky, L. S. (1967). Play and its role in the mental development of the child. *Soviet Psychology,* *5*(3), 6–18.

Vygotsky, L. S. (1978). *Mind in society: The development of higher psychological processes.* Cambridge, MA: Harvard University Press.

Werner, H. (1957). The concept of development from a comparative and organismic point of view. In D. B. Harris (Ed.), *The concept of development* (pp. 125–148). Minneapolis: University of Minnesota Press.

Wertsch, J. V. (1979). From social interaction to higher psychological processes: A clarification and application of Vygotksy's theory. *Human Development, 22,* 1-22.

Wertsch, J. V. (1991). *Voices of the mind: A sociocultural approach to mediated action.* Cambridge, MA: Harvard University Press.

Wertsch, J. V., & Stone, C. A. (1985). The concept of internalization in Vygotksy's account of the genesis of higher mental functions. In J. V. Wertsch (Ed.), *Culture, communication and cognition: Vygotskian perspectives* (pp. 162–179). Cambridge, England: Cambridge University Press.

Wilder, L. (1969). The role of speech and other extra-signal feedback in the regulation of the child's sensory motor behaviour. *Speech Monographs, 36,* 425–34.

Wolff, P. H. (1966). The natural history of crying and other vocalizations in early infancy. In B. M. Foss (Ed.), *Determinants of infant behavior* (vol. 4, pp. 81–109). New York: Wiley.

Wood, D. (1988). *How children think and learn.* Great Britain: Basil Blackwell.

Wozniak, R. H. (1972). Verbal regulation of motor behavior: Soviet research and non-Soviet replications. *Human Development, 15,* 13–57.

Yingling, J. (1984, May). *Infant speech timing: The development of individual control.* Paper presented at the International Communication Association convention, San Francisco, CA.

Yingling, J. (1985, February). *Mutual influence in infant–caregiver dyads.* Paper presented at the Western Speech Communication Association convention, Fresno, CA.

Yingling, J. (1990/1991). "Does that mean 'no'?": Negotiating proto-conversation in infant–caregiver pairs. *Research on Language and Social Interaction, 24,* 71–108.

Yingling, J. (1992, February). *Children's talk as constitutive of friendships.* Paper presented at the Western States Communication Association convention, Boise, ID.

Youniss, J. (1978). The nature of social development: A conceptual discussion of cognition. In H. McGurk, (Ed.), *Issues in childhood social development* (pp. 203–227). London: Methuen.

Youniss, J. (1980). *Parents and peers in social development: A Sullivan-Piaget perspective.* Chicago: University of Chicago Press.

7 Engendered Identities: Shaping Voice and Mind Through Gender

Julia T. Wood
University of North Carolina at Chapel Hill

> *To be an "I" at all means to be gendered.*
> —Fox-Genovese (1991, p. 120)

Fox-Genovese's statement underlines the inevitable connection between gender and individual identify. To be a human self is to be inescapably, incessantly gendered. In recent decades substantial interdisciplinary research has enlarged our understanding of the nature of gender and the ways in which it is ascribed to individuals. Less effort, however, has focused on ways in which individuals incorporate, sustain, and sometimes resist socially prescribed gender. In this chapter I probe intrapersonal processes that influence how individuals import gender, as well as how they uphold or contest the gendered identities that culture urges upon them. To pursue these issues I draw on the conceptual framework of symbolic interactionism as originally and most richly articulated by Mead (1934). His unwavering intellectual quest was to understand how society "gets into" a person, enabling him or her to participate in the collective life that antedates any and all individuals.

Unlike his contemporaries, Mead did not view self and mind as substances and did not believe either exists at birth; rather, he conceived both as processes acquired in and through symbolic interactions with others. Mind, which the preceding chapter discusses, is the ability to use significant symbols—those that have relatively common meanings among members of a society. Concurrent with learning to use significant symbols, individuals gain access to culturally assigned meanings and values that saturate language. Only with the emergence of mind is an individual able to understand the social world, to interact within it, and, thus, to acquire the reflective intelligence definitive of selfhood.

Self, too, within symbolic interactionism is acquired as one is talked into membership in the human community. Mead defined self as the ability to reflect on oneself—to be simultaneously the subject and object of one's thinking. This is possible only as the individual learns to engage in the symbolic process of taking the roles of others. In taking the self as an object, Mead noted, individuals reflect on themselves not from some idiosyncratic or acultural viewpoint, but specifically from the perspective of particular others or the generalized other, that is, the community as a whole. Understandings of social meanings, rules, and roles are imported from interaction with others and invoked in self-talk to conceive, judge, and direct one's self. Thus, the self is necessarily, inevitably social: It is known from the perspectives of others, which reflect the values, meanings, and understandings resident in the broad society. For Mead the reflexive self begins outside of the individual in the community of others with whom she or he engages and whose perspectives inform one's own; in fact, Mead (1934) was unequivocal in his insistence that the individual must experience others *before it is possible to experience self.*

Within Western culture, gender is a primary aspect of selfhood, intricately tied as it is to the social order (Cancian, 1987, 1989; Fox-Genovese, 1991; Janeway, 1971; Miller, 1986; Riessman, 1990; Wood, 1993b). Abundant evidence indicates that conceptions of gender figure prominently in how others, especially parents, respond to infants and children (Maltz & Borker, 1982; Safilios-Rothschild, 1979; Wood & Lenze, 1991). The extent to which gender expectations inhere in humans' incipient interactions may explain why gender is one of the first aspects of identity to crystallize. From birth on, infants confront others who respond to them as gendered beings; thus, as they internalize the perspectives of others, they unavoidably see themselves significantly in terms of gender. For this reason, a full understanding of gender traces the intermingling of individual experience and cultural practices to reveal the intricate dialect between personal identity and social life.

Drawing on Mead's germinal ideas, this chapter inquires, first, into how individuals acquire culturally constructed understandings of gender and, second, into how intrapersonal processes sustain or revise prescribed gendered identities. Three sections comprise my essay. I begin by elaborating the nature of gender as a social-symbolic category central to both cultural life and selfhood. Next, I summarize what is known and believed about personal and social processes that construct masculinity and femininity. I then focus on how individuals use self-talk to construct feelings, attitudes, and behaviors that sustain or resist culturally legitimated gender identities.

GENDER AS A FUNDAMENTAL
SOCIAL-SYMBOLIC CATEGORY

Whereas sex and gender were once used interchangeably, increasingly scholars and clinicians find it important to distinguish the two (Epstein, 1988; Fox-Genovese, 1991; Scott, 1986; West & Zimmerman, 1987; Wood, 1993a, 1993c). Sex refers to biological, genetic, and/or physiological qualities characteristic of males and females. For example, females have an XX sex chromosome, whereas most males have an XY sex chromosome; males generally are more adept at left-brain usage, whereas females tend to have right-brain specialization and greater development of the corpus callosum, which allows crossover from one lobe to the other; females have ovaries and clitorises, whereas males have testes and penises. Sex, then, is a biological given that is permanent unless altered through extraordinary medical procedures.

Gender,[1] on the other hand, is a social-symbolic category. Though often defined as what individuals learn to associate with sex, this depiction obscures systemic cultural processes and structures that compose and sustain arbitrary understandings of gender (Epstein, 1982, 1988; Oakley, 1972; Scott, 1986) as well as the preeminence of gender in constituting individual identity (Dyk & Adams, 1990; West & Zimmerman, 1987; Wood & Lenze, 1991; Wood, 1993b). Although societies vary in the extensiveness with which they draw gender distinctions, all known societies rely on gender as a primary mode of organizing collective life. Epstein (1988) noted that "gender distinctions are basic to the social order in all societies. . . . gender orders society and is ordered by it" (p. 6). Culturally constructed gender ideologies enable societies to specify relations between women and men as well as roles, rights, and activities available to, required of, and denied to each.

Gender distinctions cannot be explained by biological (i.e., sexual) differences. Biological reasons for assigning women to caretaking in the home and men to hunting away from home, which may have been functional historically, are no longer necessary and are frequently dysfunctional. They cannot account for persisting associations of women with personal life and men with public activity. Further, such distinctions, even if historically defensible, do not authenticate a number of other gender injunctions (e.g., abridged legal rights for women, inequitable educational opportunities, belief that women have smaller brains, differential salaries for women and men who do the same or comparable work) that persevere bereft of any relation to biological characteristics. Reflecting on this, Epstein (1988) insisted that "the overwhelming evidence created by the past decade of research on gender supports the theory that gender differentiation—as distinct, of course, from sexual differentiation—is best explained as a social construction rooted in hierarchy" (p. 15).

Gender is thoroughly ensconced in social structures that reflect and perpetuate particular social orders (Goldner, Penn, Sheinberg, & Walker, 1990; Janeway, 1971; Okin, 1989; Wood, 1993b). Institutions such as jurisprudential system, education, religion, the military, and civic life are organized in ways that delineate masculinity and femininity and stipulate relationships between women and men. In turn, these institutions are structured and upheld by discursive activities that continually rein-

---

[1]Inconsistent terminology characterizes scholarship on gender. What I label gender some researchers refer to as gender role, sex role, or psychological sex role. Following West and Zimmerman (1987), I prefer to avoid the term *role* because a role is something people engage in only in particular contexts, moments, and/or relationships. In contrast, we "do gender" all the time and cannot avoid "doing gender." Like race and class, gender is a primary and enduring aspect of individual identity that is misrepresented by the term role.

scribe the particular gendered arrangements favored by a culture at a given point in history (Weeden, 1987). Gender and the systems of relations it specifies, then, are basic to social orders and serve to legitimate the arbitrary arrangements, opportunities, and exclusions on which they depend.

Because gender is constituted to support particular forms of social life, it is historically and culturally contingent: The meanings of masculinity and femininity, as well as attendant relations between women and men, vary dramatically over time and across cultures. Within Western culture, for example, the transformation from agricultural to industrial economies was accompanied by reconfigurations of masculinity and femininity and, more broadly, of cultural life itself. Historians such as Cancian (1987, 1989), Degler (1980), and Douglas (1977) have demonstrated that gender distinctions were less rigidly dichotomous in the agrarian lifestyle than in the industrial one that followed. In the former, both women and men assumed major responsibilities for family life and economic survival, which were intimately intertwined. With the emergence of factories and mass paid labor, work was reformulated as something that took place outside of the home, and the ideology of separate spheres was born: Men's place was in the impersonal, immoral, public sphere, whereas women were situated in the personal, pure, private sphere (Cancian, 1987, 1989; Ryan, 1979; Welter, 1966).

By the middle of the 19th century both the social world and gender were sharply bifurcated, creating distinct realms and placements for men and women: Men did work away from home and women nurtured personal relationships within the home. Expunged from social understandings of femininity were a number of qualities such as ambition, strength, and decisiveness, all of which had been vital to women's roles in agrarian life; eradicated from masculinity were many qualities including emotionality, interdependence, and nurturance, all of which had been essential to men's participation in family life. Confined to the private domain, femininity was redefined as nutritiveness, purity, feelings, and caring for others. In parallel manner, masculinity was refashioned to hinge on independence, aggressiveness, self-control, achievement, and emotional reserve (Cancian, 1989; Douglas, 1977).

The reformulation of genders that accompanied industrialization remains largely intact. Despite the fact that a majority of American women now work outside of the home and participate actively in legal, political, religious, and educational institutions in public life, the ideology of separate spheres and gendered placement within them survives. In a recent report Riessman (1990) observed that "the institutionalized roles of husband and wife continue to provide a general blueprint for marriage, situating men's work primarily in the public sphere and women's in the private sphere" (p. 51). As this century winds to an end, femininity remains linked with home, family, and qualities such as deference, emotional expressiveness, affiliation, caring for others, and reproductivity. Masculinity, in contradistinction, continues to be located in the public arena of work and civic life and is prescriptively associated with power, independence, rationality, emotional reserve, and productivity.

The foregoing discussion demonstrates that gender, unlike sex, is not innate, invariant, or a property of individuals. Rather, gender is an historically and culturally contingent social-symbolic category by which relatively minor biological differences are inscribed with major social significance. Like other axes of social order, the gender system is buttressed by cultural structures and practices, and it circumscribes the options open to individuals, making certain choices more likely and more comfortable than others. Inevitably, then, a culture's gender ideology assigns identities for women and men and delimits the opportunities available to each.

BECOMING GENDERED: DEVELOPING VOICE AND SELF

So far I have argued that gender is a social-symbolic and analytic category that reflects and sustains a culture's preferred hierarchy and associated identities for women and men. Yet gender is also profoundly personal in meaning and implication. As Fox-Genovese (1991) reminded,

> In practice, gender exists not as an abstraction but as a system of relations—the specific relations between women and men. Societies ground prescriptions and practices in the specific roles that they assign to women and to men. . . . Culture encourages women and men, neither of whose biology unconditionally dictates their acquiescence, to internalize those prescriptions and practices as gender identity. (p. 120)

Subjective selfhood and the entire range of activities comprising individual lives, then, are intricately entangled with social structure and ideology.

Humans are transformed from initially sexed beings into culturally gendered persons quite quickly because gender constancy is generally believed to develop at least by the age of 5 (and many argue much earlier). Three intellectual traditions have particularly advanced knowledge of how infants acquire social understandings of gender in constructing their identities. Social scientific research empirically demonstrates a range of ways in which external influences from parents, peers, and others teach and reinforce gendered identities in infants and young children; psychoanalytic theories illuminate formative, intrapsychic processes implicated in becoming gendered; and life-span developmental research reveals how individuals use later experiences to elaborate and revise initially conferred gendered identities. I wish now to clarify how each of these traditions contributes to understandings of gender.

Social Scientific Research

Scholars in psychology, sociology, education, women's studies, communication, and political science have generated substantial knowledge about ways in which interaction with others, especially parents and peers, influences children's emerging senses of themselves, including their gender. Even before a child is born, parents generally have distinctive expectations for sons and daughters that largely reflect their own inculcated gender ideologies. From the moment of birth, parents tend to treat male and female children in generalizably different ways. Typically they urge sons to be independent, active, staunch, and emotionally restrained, and they encourage daughters to form relationships, and to be dependent, emotionally expressive, deferential, and self effacing (Goldner et al., 1990; Jones & Dembo, 1989; Safilios-Rothschild, 1979; Thompson & Walker, 1989; Thorbecke & Grotevant, 1982; Wood & Lenze, 1991).

Compounding parental engendering practices are those that punctuate interaction with peers, who are themselves engendered. A particularly illuminating study of how peer activity fortifies cultural prescriptions for gender was Maltz and Borker's 1982 analysis of the understandings tacitly taught through children's games. Reporting that boys and girls play distinctive kinds of games, Maltz and Borker identified interaction rules that inhere in games typical of each sex. They concluded that standard boys' games (e.g., soccer, baseball) tend to be structured by rules, competitive, and played in large groups; and they teach boys to use communication to assert self, to gain and hold attention, and to vie for status within an interpersonal hierarchy. Girls' games (e.g., house, school, jump rope), on the other hand, are emergently and processually structured, cooperative, and typically involve few players; and these teach girls to use communication to build relationships of equality, to include and support others, to attend to process of interaction at least as much as its outcomes, and to share the "talk stage." In directing boys toward power, self-reliance, and assertion and girls toward affiliation, interdependence, and responsiveness to others, these gendered communication patterns echo and reinforce gender differentiated parental socialization that researchers have repeatedly documented (Maltz & Borker, 1982; Safilios-Rothschild, 1979; Tannen, 1990; Thorbecke & Grotevant, 1982).

From sociologists and political scientists in particular we have gained insight into intricate ways in which cultural beliefs about gender are inscribed on individuals. Writing of this, Fox-Genovese (1991) noted that a child is

> born into a society that has its own view of the proper or normative relations between women and men. . . . All societies and cultures, through education in the broad sense, encourage women and men to identify with the roles available to them. When the process is successful, gender appears to both women and men as the seamless wrapping of the self. (p. 120)

Yet, Fox-Genovese's language must be qualified by recognizing that although socialization strongly attempts to feminize girls and to masculinize boys, sex and gender are not invariantly correlated: Females can be masculine, and males can be feminine in their behaviors, attitudes, goals, and ways of perceiving and interacting. Research from social scientists has substantially enlarged knowledge of how influences external to individuals promote development of genderized self definitions. Valuable as this information is, however, it does not elucidate how internal psychological processes interact with external influences to create gendered identities. This process has been the focus of work within the psychoanalytic tradition.

Psychoanalytic Theory

Supplementing empirical research are rich insights from psychoanalytic theorists such as Chodorow (1978, 1989), Miller (1986), and Eichenbaum and Orbach (1983). Among clinicians there is widespread consensus regarding the existence, etiology, and nature of gender-differentiated identity development. Their explanations provide a convincing account of how internal psychological processes contribute to engendering women and men.

Within the past 20 years a number of psychoanalytic theorists have argued that development typically does not occur in the same way and does not yield equivalent outcomes for males and females. The developmental pattern that seems characteristic of masculine individuals proceeds increasingly toward autonomy and self assertion, generating a highly independent self (Erikson, 1958; Kohlberg, 1958; Piaget, 1932/1965). More typical of feminine individuals is a progressive orientation toward relationships and interdependence, fostering a self deeply connected with others (Belenky, Clinchy, Goldberger, & Tarule, 1986; Gilligan, 1982; Miller, 1986; Rubin, 1985; Wood & Lenze, 1991).

Psychoanalytic theorists locate the etiology of gender-differentiated developmental paths in the family psychodynamics, particularly in the pivotal, primary relationship between mother and child, which is believed to establish basic themes and relational stances that reverberate throughout life.[2] According to Chodorow (1989), perhaps the most widely respected feminist psychoanalytic theorist, "that we are all mothered by women, that in all societies women rather than men have primary parenting responsibilities, is an important social and cultural fact that still bears remarking and analyzing" (p. 6). The constancy of women as primary caregivers for both male and female infants instigates disparate rather than similar developmental processes and outcomes. Tracing these distinctive paths to whether mother and child are similar or different, Chodorow (1978, 1989) argued that between a mother and daughter there is a fundamental likeness that leads daughters to define themselves through a primary identification with their mothers. A young girl imports her mother into herself in so fundamental a manner that the mother becomes quite literally a part of the daughter, not some external point of reference.[3] Because this

---

[2]Chodorow (1978) and many other clinicians who have attempted to delineate feminine developmental paths draw upon the object-relations tradition within psychoanalytic thought. This choice is not uncontroversial and has occasioned substantial criticism. A key point of contention is whether the small structure of family, central to Chodorow's object-relations account, can adequately address the broad gender system as socially constituted and promoted. In her more recent work (1989, pp. 6–8) Chodorow has attenuated her earlier emphasis on family dynamics, particularly mother–child relationships, by recognizing explicitly that relations of gender and power are also insinuated in the community, economy, and state.

[3]Chodorow and others describing this process decisively are not referring to role identification or role modeling, both of which are more externally located and superficial processes than what concerns Chodorow. Importing mother refers to what is formally called psychic introjection, whereby another becomes part of the core self such that the other cannot be extricated from oneself. This affects identity and the relationship to another in ways far more profound and enduring than role modeling or identification.

process transpires before mind or self is fully acquired, a girl's initial efforts to define her own identity occur within and are infused by her relationship to her mother. Thus, her earliest sense of selfhood is entwined with relatedness: The two occur concurrently so that being connected to others is inseparable from being, which has led Surrey to refer to feminine identity as a "relational self."[4]

Intense identification between a mother and son seldom occurs, because the two are basically dissimilar. Theorists suggest that boys recognize in a rudimentary way that they differ from their mothers and, more importantly, mothers realize the difference and reflect this awareness in how they interact with sons. Because the option of defining himself through identification with his mother is foreclosed, a boy must pursue a different developmental path in which he differentiates from his mother by separating and declaring himself to be "not mother." This basic maneuver, essential if the boy is to delineate a masculine identity for himself, establishes independence and distance from others as central to his self definition. Boys' initial interdependence with another must be denied and forsaken, rendering separation a cornerstone of masculine identity.

Psychoanalytic accounts reveal gender to be central to self-definition and illuminate a fundamental divergence in developmental routes to masculine and feminine identities. For feminine individuals, identity can be (arguably, must be) charted within relationship to another; for masculine children, identity requires separation from others. Underlining this, Chodorow (1989) insisted that "through relation to their mother, women develop a self-in-relation, men a self that denies relatedness" (p. 15). This basic difference resonates throughout life, affecting identities, goals, and patterns of interaction in other, later relationships. It is also fully consistent with findings of social science that certify men's independent and women's affiliative tendencies.

Two caveats should accompany consideration of psychoanalytic accounts of gendered development. First, it is prudent to identify what is included and excluded within their scope of interest and to hold the theories accountable for only that which they claim as their purview. Psychodynamic explanations have been interpreted to imply that at least the most formative influences on identity occur during

---

[4]Psychoanalytic theory has been criticized for essentializing men and women. Chodorow (1989) herself acknowledged that psychoanalytic feminism "can be read. . .to imply that there is a psychological commonality among all women and among all men" (p. 4) and went on to advocate psychoanalytic accounts of men and women of color and nondominant classes to reduce this tendency toward essentializing gender. Later Chodorow quite directly denied an essentialist view: "Gender difference is not absolute, abstract, or irreducible; it does not involve an essence of gender," (p. 100). My own writing in this essay and elsewhere runs the risk of appearing essentializing because it is impossible not to rely on abstractions such as "men," "women," "femininity," and "masculinity." I assume, however, that each of these categories encompasses a range of particular individuals whose sociopolitical-economic-personal-historical situations render them unique in numerous ways. Individuality and diversity notwithstanding, this essay reflects my conviction that because gender is a system of social relationships that are reflected in the perspective of the generalized other, it has some highly consistent, though not universal, consequences for women and men as groups.

infancy, fixing it as a structure that simply unfolds, relatively impervious to subsequent experience.[5] Yet, clearly, much happens after age 5 that directly effects how people conceive themselves, including their gender. The tendency within psychoanalytic theories to stress the impact of early influences on identity should be read not as a comprehensive claim of what creates selfhood, but rather as an argument for the importance of processes that occur within early years that are the particular focus of psychoanalytic theory.

A second cautionary note is that psychoanalytic accounts of development are not amenable to testing. Responding to this criticism, Chodorow (1989) advised that "until we have another theory which can tell us about unconscious mental processes, conflict, and relations of gender, sexuality, and self, we had best take psychoanalysis for what it does include and can tell us rather than dismissing it out of hand" (p. 4). Unquestionably, considerably more study and observation are needed to cultivate the promise and reveal possible limitations in psychoanalytic accounts of engendering and related processes such as moral development (Gilligan, 1982; Surrey, 1983).

These qualifications notwithstanding, existing psychodynamic explanations offer coherent descriptions of gender differentiated developmental processes that are compelling in their capacity to explain and predict values, attitudes, and actions empirically associated with women and men. At this juncture, then, it seems reasonable to accord credence to psychoanalytic representations of intrapsychic processes that enjoy both face validity and congruence with findings from other intellectual traditions.

Because psychoanalytic theory defines as its purview psychodynamics within families during the years of infancy, its explanations of how individuals become gendered stop around age 5 or 6. One consequence of this is that psychodynamic explanations of engendering, along with empirical evidence of ways in which society shapes gender, can mislead us to think that gender is a "done deed" by the time a child enters elementary school. Given this, it is unsurprising that conceptions of gender prevalent in scholarship have tended to be decidedly static in their (usually tacit) assumption that gender is established early and persists as a relatively stable, enduring quality of individuals. Operating out of this conceptual perspective, researchers have studied gender as a personality trait while neglecting longitudinal investigations that might disclose ways in which genders change in response to maturation, social interaction, and self-talk. Recently this view has been criticized for misrepresenting gender as a basically standard component inserted into individuals during infancy that then remains essentially constant throughout life (Risman &

---

[5]This criticism may be inappropriate in its assumption that psychoanalytic theory actually posits such a limit on identity development. Emphasis on the substantial influence of family psychodynamics is the avowed focus of psychoanalytic work—the field's purview. Whatever occurs later is outside of the scope of a framework designed to account for how identities initially arise. Thus, psychoanalytic theory's inattention to later influences on selfhood and gender identity is an appropriate delimitation of conceptual concerns.

Schwartz, 1989; Scott, 1986). Critics have urged scholars and clinicians to develop more dynamic views that recognize gender changes as a result of lifetime experiences as well as the continuous self-talk in which individuals engage.

Understandings of Gender Development Beyond Infancy

Calls for more processual understandings of gender reflect a growing awareness that gender is historically and culturally contingent. Common to a myriad of emergent efforts to reconceptualize gender as dynamic are widely embraced inclinations to decenter knowledge and to recognize the situatedness and diversity of social experience and intrapersonal communication. Standpoint theory offers a broad conceptual framework that informs a host of more specific approaches to studying how gendered identities and incumbent attitudes and feelings arise responsively to situations and roles one enters throughout life. Resisting the monolithic, positivistic perspectives characteristic of modernist thinking, standpoint theory holds that humans are shaped by diverse material, social, and historical circumstances within which their lives are embedded. Thus, argue standpoint theorists, the particular circumstances—or stand-point—of a person's or group's location in cultural life have profound ontological and epistemological consequences.

Collins (1986) relied on standpoint theory to show that Black women scholars possess specialized knowledge resulting from their dual situation as "outsiders within" (i.e., as minorities who hold membership in majority institutions). In a particularly well-known application of standpoint theory, Ruddick (1989) examined how the role of mother and the activities involved in mothering evoke "maternal thinking—an intrapersonal process that centers on values, attentions, priorities, and understandings of relationships specifically promoted by the process of mothering. Quite recently, Harding (1991) extended existing work on relationships between situated experience and ways of knowing into a fairly coherent and promising theoretical stance that argues that an individual's position in a culture shapes not only *what* she or he knows, but also *how* she or he knows (i.e., self-talk). Recognition that diverse situations cultivate particularized identities and knowledge underlies a range of specific projects that reveal that gender, like other constituents of identity, reflects its social-historical location. In what follows I highlight two specific approaches that reflect standpoint logic.

Articulated by Risman and Schwartz (1989), a microstructural perspective is rooted in the assumption that "men and women are not created all at once—at birth or during early socialization—but are continually re-created during the life cycle by the opportunities available to them and their interactions with others" (p. 1). Illustrative of this approach is Risman's (1989) study of how being primary parents affected men's behaviors. She reported that "men who mother" are more nurturing, attentive to others' needs, and emotionally expressive than men in general, findings she interpreted as reflecting the fathers' development of skills and attitudes necessary in their situations as caretakers. Cancian's (1987, 1989) program of research, associated with a microstructural approach, demonstrates that men and women developed quite different skills and attitudes as changing social definitions of the sexes altered the situations women and men occupied and the sorts of activities they were called upon to perform.[6] Highlighting the situated character of gender, the microstructural approach directs our attention to how individuals' interpretations of experiences throughout life reconfigure their understandings of gender.

A second promising approach is Hochschild's (1975, 1979, 1983, 1989) sociology of emotions, or sociology of feelings. Although I discuss this in detail later, I note it here as an illustration of emergent conceptualizations of gender as developmental. Starting from the assumption that emotions are not merely personal, but are learned through symbolic interactions with others that form what Mead termed the "Me," Hochschild argued that a culture designates particular emotions as appropriate for specific roles as those are defined at any particular historical moment. Demonstrating this through a series of empirical studies Hochschild (1979, 1983, 1989), advanced three important premises: (a) Societies' institutional structures and discursive practices specify "feeling rules" that define what feelings ought to accompany what roles; (b) members of a culture, presumably because they have been socialized into its common understandings through learning to use significant symbols, are aware of these "feeling rules;" and (c) individuals engage in "emotion work" through self-talk to generate feelings they recognize as appropriate and to squelch those deemed inappropriate for the roles they occupy.[7]

Corroboration for Hochschild's ideas is found in several investigations, some of which predated her articulation of the theory yet nonetheless support it. In a particularly impressive program of research, Kohn and Schooler (1973, 1978, 1982) employed a sophisticated design that allowed them to determine the causal relationship between job activities and men's personalities. They concluded unequivocally that work affects a man's personality more than the converse, and they demonstrated that jobs significantly influence self-esteem, psychological well-being, anxiety levels, moral perspectives, and cognitive flexibility. Recently Belenky and her colleagues (1986) theorized that women's ways of learning and knowing differ from those of men as a result of the sexes' distinctive positions in private and public life. Researchers have also shown that the disparate lessons boys and girls internalize in early socialization lead to a number of gender-differentiated behaviors such as parental involvement with children (Thompson & Walker, 1989), styles of friendship (Wright, 1982, 1988), responses to dissatisfaction in close relationships

---

[6]Cancian produced convincing historical evidence that during the early, agrarian phase of America's existence men and women were much more similar in their activities and prescribed natures than they were following the industrial revolution. Specifically, she demonstrated that men were substantially involved with families and women were active participants in work. In separating work life from home life and placing one sex in each realm, Cancian argued that the ideology of separate spheres was born and, with it, redefinitions of men as independent, impersonal, and emotionally controlled and women as relational, highly personal, and emotionally expressive.

[7]Hochschild distinguished between "surface acting" in which one works to appear to others to be feeling a particular emotion that is socially and situationally expected, and "deep acting," in which one works to bring forth within self an emotion believed to be expected or required. The former has to do with persuading others one is feeling what one "should," the latter with producing that feeling that assures oneself one is responding appropriately. (See Hochschild, 1983, chapter 3).

(Rusbult, 1987), ways of expressing love (Bergner & Bergner, 1990; Napier, 1977; Schaef, 1985; Swain, 1989; Tavris, 1992; Thompson & Walker, 1989; Wood, 1993b), orientations toward interpersonal power (Belk & Snell, 1988; Christensen & Heavey, 1990; Lerner, 1980; Paul & White, 1990; Peplau & Gordon, 1985; Schneider & Gould, 1987; Thompson, 1991; White, 1989), and predispositions toward violence and abuse of intimates (Dobash & Dobash, 1979; Goldner, Penn, Sheinberg, & Walker, 1990; Gordon, 1988; Ptacek, 1988; Thompson, 1991). In a range of ways, then, it seems clear that how individual men and women conceive their genders depends in large measure on the particular locations in which they are situated and the perspectives held by others who inhabit those situations. By extension, how individuals conceive themselves interacts with self-talk to guide how they define and enact gender.

This line of inquiry suggests that the impact of early socialization is mitigated—perhaps substantially—by experiences over the course of a lifetime and, especially, by the symbolic and physical environments in which people are enmeshed and the understandings and identities those contexts invite and impede. Emergent scholarship that acknowledges the situatedness of ongoing experience and traces its influence on identities importantly attenuates conventional views of gender as largely fixed during infancy. Recognizing that gender on both social and individual levels is processual, not static, prompts us to appreciate more fully that, within definite limits of personal history and capacities and cultural pressures, individuals can and do engage in self-talk to edit prescribed meanings of genders.

By focusing on internal, psychological processes through which individuals are initially engendered, as well as ways in which social and interpersonal experiences modulate self conceptions, this discussion compliments the preceding summary of external influences on gender. In tandem, the two disclose an intricate, ongoing interaction between personal and social processes through which individuals acquire and continually revise their embodiments of gender. This dialectic between the individual and society echoes Mead's insistence that just as the social world constitutes individuals (the Me), so do individuals (the I) edit the generalized other's dicta to personalize their identities and revise understandings resident in the social order.

Thus far I have argued that gender is both a social-symbolic category, which is established and sustained through cultural structures and processes, and a linchpin of individual identity. My survey of interdisciplinary findings disclosed that existing academic scholarship demonstrates that a variety of external influences contribute to initial gender identities, whereas psychoanalytic theory illuminates internal, psychic processes by which individuals interpret external events in ways that bear on their senses of themselves as gendered beings. Finally, I have suggested that conceptions of gender generally have been overly static and will benefit from standpoint theory, as well as more specific approaches reflecting standpoint logic. Microstructural approaches and the sociology of emotions are examples of dynamic conceptualizations that promise to invigorate thinking about changes in individual and cultural meanings of gender. With this background, I turn now to the question of how individuals sustain and alter the gender identities society inscribes upon them.

SUSTAINING AND RESISTING
CULTURAL VIEWS OF GENDER:
SELF-TALK AND ITS SOCIAL CONSEQUENCES

Symbolic interaction theory is particularly heuristic in framing thinking about this issue. Mead recognized that individuals not only interact with others, they also interact with themselves, relying on symbols imported from social interaction with others. Mead's answer to this central inquiry—how does society get into the individual?—points quite directly to internal dialogues in which individuals engage. These internal dialogues, also called self-talk, frame the world we believe to exist, define our identities and positions within that world, and suggest guidelines for our attitudes and actions. Yet this self-talk is necessarily social talk, for in learning language individuals acquire social values, which then permeate and inform the ways in which they communicate with themselves. Mead's theories, then, form a foundation for exploring ways in which individuals use self-talk both to sustain and to resist culturally legitimated definitions of femininity and masculinity.

Sustaining Culturally Validated Gender Identity

Explicitly acknowledging symbolic interactionism as a primary intellectual foundation, Hochschild, along with others, developed a sociology of emotions, which I previewed in the preceding section.[8] Her pioneering work in this area contends that feelings are structured by and embedded in normative social life. Emotions, then, like values and understandings, are learned, interpreted, and enacted within socially constructed frameworks of significance. Further, and particularly important for my considerations here, Hochschild argued that people do what she terms "emotion work" to bring forth in themselves the feelings they believe they should experience and to suppress those they think they should not feel in various situations and roles. In so doing, individuals sustain not just for others, but also for themselves, the integrity of their identities.

The rapidly growing scholarship on sociology of emotions (Franks, 1985) offers intriguing hints about ways that "emotion work" functions as self-talk to help men and women maintain gendered identities. Within the limits of this essay I cannot elaborate fully the scholarship on sociology of emotions, nor can I trace multiple,

---

[8]The extent to which Mead actually dealt with emotions and, more to the point, framed them within symbolic interactionist understandings is a matter of some disagreement. Clearly the nature of emotions and their role in social-symbolic life were not primary concerns to Mead. Nonetheless, although Mead's early thinking dealt with emotions only very peripherally and apart from symbolic interaction, his more mature theorizing, especially as reflected in *Mind, Self, and Society,* suggests he recognized emotion as part of symbolic interactions. In this later thinking Mead located emotions in the impulse to act (i.e., the prepatory stage of behavior) and suggested they contributed to how an individual anticipated and, thus, evaluated and directed his or her action. Mead (1932) can be interpreted to have foreshadowed Hochschild's conception of "emotion work" in his reference to the necessity of "checking the response that is responsible for the emotion" (p. 396).

complex intersections among emotion work, gendered identities, and cultural ideologies. I will, however, suggest the promise of this approach by highlighting several specific investigations that illuminate relations among gender, self-talk, and emotion work.

In her detailed analysis of the training of flight attendants for Delta Airlines, Hochschild (1983) called attention to the different kinds of feelings and activities allowed and expected of male and female personnel. The assumption of male authority permeated working conditions for attendants, both in their interactions with passengers and among each other. "Because her gender is accorded lower status, a woman's shield against abuse is weaker" (p. 175), which suggests why women flight attendants "tend to be more exposed than men to rude or surly speech, to tirades against the service, the airline, and airplanes in general" (p. 174) and are "expected to 'take it' better, it being more their role to absorb an expression of displeasure and less their role to put a stop to it" (p. 178).

Even more telling were the hierarchical relations between male and female attendants themselves, who were formally peers. Because airline passengers accorded stewards greater respect than stewardesses, the stewards came to feel they were entitled to such regard even from their female colleagues. Thus, reported Hochschild, this "increased the amount of deference that male workers felt their female co-workers owed them, ... One young male attendant said that certain conditions had to be met—and deference offered—before he would obey a woman's orders" (p. 177). Only by enacting "the woman as subordinate role," could women be successful in their jobs as flight attendants; males similarly enacted "the man as authority who deserves deference role" to be successful in their equivalent jobs. Perhaps most interesting is Hochschild's finding that the women and men seemed not just to be engaging in role enactment to meet others' expectations of how they should be and feel, but actually did the deep emotion work to bring forth what they accepted as appropriate feelings: deference for women and superiority for men. In this way the men and women seemed to accept and perpetuate differential treatment and feelings prescribed for their respective genders. Thus, "female workers often went to their male co-workers to get them to cast a heavier glance" at a disruptive passenger because "a look from a male carries more weight" (p. 179). Hochschild's observations suggest clear links between social interaction and self definition: As passengers and co-workers indicated what was expected, male and female flight attendants responded "appropriately" by staying within their gender roles. Thus, feeling rules, as well as action rules, can be precipitated by how we see ourselves reflected in others and by our socialized tendencies to take the perspectives of those others to define to ourselves who we are.

Consider, next, Hochschild's (1989) investigation of how couples deal with discrepancies between cultural views of manhood and womanhood and the realities in their particular marriages. In one couple Hochschild studied, Peter's dream of owning a bookstore was realized only because Nina, to whom he had been married for 12 years, was a high powered and highly paid business executive. Because Nina and Peter entered their marriage with traditional expectations that the man would provide the income and the woman would care for the home, they both found her salary shameful, something they kept scrupulously secret from family and friends and assiduously avoided discussing between themselves. His gender ideology prevented him from recognizing, much less appreciating her financial contributions to their lives; her gender ideology precluded her feeling she was entitled to substantial "help" from Peter in homemaking chores. To preserve their individual and couple identities, Nina and Peter colluded to define their marriage such that "both felt Nina was lucky to be married to such an unusually understanding man" (p. 105). To obscure their deviation in *content* from conventional genders, they preserved the *form* of prescribed genders by agreeing that Nina depended on Peter. This collaboratively constructed view obligated Nina to feel grateful to Peter and justified his feeling he was taking care of Nina by accepting her salary, thus sustaining the orthodox hierarchy between men and women.

Exploring feelings of gratitude and obligation among the people she studied, Hochschild probed how people who depart from standard gender arrangements nonetheless often maintain the essential gendered relation of female subordination. In Nina and Peter's case, for example, she "made up for out-earning her husband (and breaking the cultural rule) by working a double day" (p. 105) that ensconced her in the conventional service role within the home. In enacting this role Nina also demonstrated acceptance of a related cultural rule by showing she was grateful to her husband for what he allowed her to do—in this instance, all of it! Hochschild observed, "We have here the emotional underbelly of gender ideology—not . . . anger and resentment, but . . . apology and gratitude" (p. 105).

Like many women chronicled in Hochschild's widely read *The Second Shift* (1989), Nina sustained the subordinate status and caregiver role prescribed for females by talking herself into feeling grateful for minor contributions from Peter to homemaking responsibilities and feeling lucky that he "allowed" her to both work and be married. For their parts, Peter and other husbands studied sustained the superior status and provider role prescribed for men by resisting gratitude for what their wives' salaries provided them and by refusing to share equally in "women's work." Thus, spouses rely on self-talk to do the emotion work of bringing forth feelings they believe they should have as wives and husbands. In turn, self-talk buttresses spouses' conceptions of themselves as adhering to conventional gendered identities in the face of unconventional gender behaviors.

A range of other work supports and extends Hochschild's sociology of emotions. In a study of women who care for their elderly mothers, Aronson (1992) explored how daughters felt about caregiving, how they persuaded themselves to accommodate their work and family lives to meet their mothers' needs, and how they justified lack of equivalent help from brothers. Intensive interviews with daughters led Aronson to conclude that women engage in self-persuasive strategies informed by three facets of cultural views of femininity: (a) They reminded themselves that caring for others is part of their role as women/daughters; (b) they told themselves it is more appropriate to interrupt or constrain their personal and career lives than to interfere with their brothers' "important responsibilities"; and (c) they fortified their motivation by saying to others and themselves it would be irresponsible, cold, or otherwise bad (i.e., unwomanly) not to care for their mothers.

Importantly, Aronson identified guilt as a primary means by which daughters kept themselves embedded in caregiving, and she asserted that it results from women's socialization into prioritizing relationships over autonomy (Aronson, 1992, p. 23; also see Chodorow, 1989, p. 58). A woman who pursues her own interests when someone else needs or wants her energies is selfish, and selfish is bad. Relatedly, Chodorow (1989, p. 6) argued that Western women's characteristic inclination toward guilt stems from a sense of self as interwoven with others, whereas Shott (1979, p. 1324) explained guilt as a consequence of reflexive role-taking in which a person assumes the perspective of the generalized other and from that vantage point judges it to be abnormal and wrong for a woman not to show care. Aronson was able to identify specific examples of self-talk, particularly self-censorship, by which daughters persuaded themselves they should/had to continue caring for their mothers, regardless of costs to them personally. They told themselves things such as "I shouldn't mind taking care of mother," "I have no right to complain about the difficulties of balancing a career and taking care of mother," and "I should feel guilty about complaining." Through such self talk, daughters kept themselves in line with prescriptions for femininity and also persuaded themselves to persevere in caregiving activities.

Research in a quite different area sheds additional light on ways people use self-talk to bring forth emotions that conform to cultural gender ideologies. Several studies suggest that how women and men express sadness, or depression, may reflect efforts to comply with prevailing images of masculinity and femininity. Prepubescent males have higher rates of depression than same-aged females; after puberty, however, this switches so that from ages 18 to 64 more women than men are diagnosed as depressed in all groups except Old Order Amish, college students, and recent widows (Hoeksema, 1990). It seems reasonable to suspect that the greater number of women diagnosed as depressed after puberty reflects intensified gender socialization during that period: Young men are pushed increasingly toward being strong, self-reliant, confident, and taking initiatives, whereas young women are urged to be dependent, passive, and self-effacing, qualities that clearly put one at risk for low self-esteem and contentment and that hinder material achievements.

Two other less obvious issues shed further light on the disproportionate number of women diagnosed as depressed. There may be a feminine bias in assessing depression, and masculine and feminine individuals may engage in distinctive kinds of self-talk that differentially affects how they feel. Turning to the first issue, it is important to reflect on the method of diagnosing depression. It is assessed by the presence of particular symptoms, yet the symptoms consistently reflect feelings and behaviors that women, but not men, are socialized to display. Criteria for diagnosis include crying, feeling powerless, talking about unhappiness, eating disorders, expressing misery, feeling sad, and being inactive or passive (Riessman, 1990). These virtually comprise a description of the feminine gender as culturally defined! In her impressive study of depression Hoeksema (1990, p. 42) remarked that "perhaps men are unwilling to show the classic symptoms of depression because these symptoms are considered unmanly, and instead exhibit depression through other symptoms." Riessman (1990) concurred, reporting that women report crying, talking with others about their problems, and seeking help, whereas men more typically say they respond to sadness by taking some kind of direct action, either constructive (e.g., burying himself in his work) or destructive (e.g., drinking). Prescriptions for manhood disallow crying, being emotionally expressive with others, seeking help, or acting passively. If, as Riessman argued, mental health professionals have "set up women's modes of expressing distress as the standard" (p. 159), then what is being measured may not be depression, but rather what is defined as an appropriate way for women to express unhappiness. Given that feminine ways of dealing with sadness comprise clinical criteria for diagnosing depression, it's predetermined that more women than men will be judged to be depressed!

Also related to the disproportionate number of women diagnosed as depressed may be engendered means of coping with feelings of unhappiness. Hoeksema (160 ff.) claimed that men respond to depression by distracting themselves with other activities that draw their attention away from their problems. In contrast, women tend to respond introspectively by making their unhappiness the primary focus of their thinking: They ruminate about their feelings, elaborately go over the reasons they feel so bad, and otherwise bring into heightened consciousness just how unhappy they are. In essence, Hoeksema suggested that women may tend to enhance, rather than diminish their distress by engaging in self-talk that enhances awareness of just how bad they feel. Tavris (1992) advanced a similar conclusion, noting that "women's expressive style carries a price tag. It leads many women to rehearse their problems and constantly brood about them, rather than learning to distract themselves or take action to solve them" (p. 268). The kind of self-talk Tavris, Riessman, and Hoeksema described is, of course, entirely consistent with femininity because women are allowed to feel sad, passive, and needy and to express all of those feelings. More masculine ways of coping with sadness—silent anguish, taking action, distraction—are discounted as indicators of depression.

The allowances and disallowances for emotional expression inherent in cultural prescriptions for genders make it likely that many individuals will become conflicted. A masculine woman who feels sad might find it uncomfortable either to express her feeling in ways prescribed for femininity (which she has not internalized) or to express it in ways appropriate for masculinity (which will not be recognized by others as legitimate for her). Similarly, a feminine male might face the same double bind in having to choose between emotional expression consistent with his self identity, for example, crying, talking with others, or expression that conforms to social expectations of how men act. Cases of such conflicted individuals raise the issue of how persons contest cultural prescriptions of masculinity and femininity.

Contesting Culturally Legitimated Views of Gender

Realizing that self-talk is used to sustain culturally validated gender identity should not blind us to its potential to enable individuals to resist inculcated views of women and men. Individuals contest—and sometimes change—unconventional images of men and women that have been inculcated into them. For instance, Kaye and Applegate's (1990) observations of men who took care of elderly people revealed that placement in those roles led men to develop capabilities and feelings they had not previously shown and ones more generally associated with cultural views of femininity than masculinity. Similar findings were advanced by Risman (1987, 1989) from her studies of single fathers, whom she reported were notably more empathic, attentive, and expressive of intimacy than is typical of contemporary masculinity. Summarizing her findings, Risman (1989) noted that "situational demands of role requirements influence adult behavior and lead men to mother" (p. 163), exhibiting the kinds of feelings and behaviors widely ascribed to women. Implicit in these findings is understanding that the impact of situations on outward action is mediated by self-talk through which individuals revise self-definitions to evoke feelings and behaviors they judge appropriate in particular situations.

Additional evidence that individuals change their gendered identities comes from a series of studies (Miller, Schooler, Kohn, & Miller, 1979) focused on the relationship between work and women's personality. Consistently the authors found that the structural characteristics of women's jobs better predicted personality than the converse, demonstrating convincingly that people are deeply affected by ongoing experiences. Epstein (1968, 1981) further illuminated the relationship between women's resistance of culturally sanctioned femininity and their enmeshment in professional life. In a longitudinal study of female attorneys, Epstein showed that initially these professionals defined limited ambitions that deferred to prevailing cultural views of women. Yet, they progressively enlarged their ambitions and willingness to state these over a 10 year period when they were engaged in the work of lawyering. In a subsequent study, Epstein (1982) reported that women who occupied business and professional roles developed senses of personal power, entitlement, and ambition that they had not possessed at the outset of careers and that could not be predicted by early socialization experiences. Related work (Hochschild, 1975; McGowen & Hart, 1990; Wood & Conrad, 1983) corroborates the finding that work environments influence how individuals conceive and display gender and documents paradoxes that arise between simultaneously adhering to social definitions of femininity and professionalism.

Research reviewed here builds a compelling case that individuals sometimes reform understandings of what it means to be masculine or feminine. Just as social situations are crucial to understanding how and why individuals sustain culturally prescribed gender identities, so are they central to realizing how individuals contest those. As individuals participate in new environments, they rely on self-talk to refashion their identities in ways that cohere with or resist normative expectations inherent in the contexts they inhabit and the perspectives of others with whom they interact. What it means to be a woman or man is reconfigured through symbolic interactions and internal dialogues with new others whose perspectives individuals import, as well as through individuals' self reflections on who they have been and wish to become.

SUMMARY

Woven throughout this chapter are two central arguments: First, that a gendered society fosters gendered individuals; and, second, that gendered individuals engage in self-talk to reproduce and, sometimes, to alter socially constructed prescriptions for gender. By organizing individuals' understanding of gender from the perspective of culture (Mead's Me), existing social orders encourage individuals to act in ways that reinforce and perpetuate agreed-on arrangements and the ideology underlying them. Equally important, though until now less remarked upon, are ways in which experiences in varied situations and the self-talk used to interpret them transform how men and women conceive themselves. By entering new locations and engaging in new kinds of activities, individuals acquire new grist for their intrapersonal communication; in turn, they may use self-talk to develop cognitive, affective, and behavioral tendencies that alter their gender identities and "speak back" to the culture about what women and men may be and do.

Through interactions with others, including especially families, boys and girls acquire selfhood and, with it, their initial senses of what it means to be male or female. Risman and Schwartz (1989) insisted that "how people are embedded in social networks helps create gendered behavior. . . . Men and women [are] differentially embedded in social networks" (p. 6). Building on this, I have argued that because males and females from birth on are situated in systematically and generalizably distinct physical and symbolic worlds, the selves they typically construct differ in fundamental ways. The divergencies arise out of both experiences in the world and internal self-talk through which individuals indicate to themselves what those experiences mean and imply for their identities as women and men.

Gendered selves arise from our internalization and editing of views and voices of others who tell us what it means to be masculine and feminine. By importing these perspectives and using self-talk to mediate them, men and women often persuade themselves to act and feel in ways that sustain the gendered identities that they have been assigned and that the culture expects and rewards. Yet, society, no more than anatomy, is destiny: Not all individuals invariably and completely accept social prescriptions for gender; on occasion they contest cultural dicta; when they do so, self-talk is a primary process through which they convince themselves of the viability of not-yet socially legitimated identities and how they might enact those in interactions with the world. Self-talk, I have argued, is not unrelated to social talk. How women and men represent gender to themselves inevitably reflects wider discourses that saturate the entire culture. Thus, individuals may rely on feeling rules, emotion work, and, more primarily, self-talk reflective of social views to keep themselves in conformity with conventional images of their genders.

Yet, in the face of pervasive and powerful socializing forces that impel conformity, a point made recurrently in my analysis bears reiteration here. Neither culture nor individuals is static; both evolve. As they do, personal and social understandings of gender are transformed, sometimes gradually, sometimes abruptly. In pushing beyond pervasive analyses of ways in which gender is inscribed on members of a society, I have explored how it is that people sometimes instigate change both in themselves and in broader social meanings. Here too, self-talk seems primary as a process by which individuals rewrite gender. Internal dialogues through which people question prevailing views of masculinity and femininity and incumbent prerogatives empower them to resist encrusted gender ideologies and to craft and enact alternative ones. Self-talk that foments change, although different in content from that which sustains the status quo, is equally informed by social experiences within particular physical and symbolic communities. Thus, as women and men increasingly locate themselves in environments divergent from those traditionally open to them, and as they participate in the discourses of those environments, they contribute to and acquire new vocabularies of meaning and identity. In turn, this pries open possibilities for innovative constructions of themselves, gender, and the kinds of relationships possible between women and men.

ACKNOWLEDGEMENT

I am indebted to Michelle Violanti and Chris Inman whose research added to the substance of this chapter. I also benefited from Donna Vocate's and Jerry Phillips' responses to an earlier draft of this essay.

REFERENCES

Aronson, J. (1992). Women's sense of responsibility for the care of old people: "But who else is going to do it?" *Gender and Society, 6,* 8–29

Belenky, M., Clinchy, B., Goldberger, N., & Tarule, J. (1986). *Women's ways of knowing.* New York: Basic Books.

Belk, S. S., & Snell, W. E., Jr. (1988). Avoidance strategy use in intimate relationships. *Journal of Social and Clinical Psychology, 7,* 80–96.

Bergner, R. M., & Bergner, L. L. (1990). Sexual misunderstanding: A descriptive and pragmatic formulation. *Psychotherapy, 27,* 464–467.

Cancian, F. (1987). *Love in America: Gender & self development.* Cambridge, England: Cambridge University Press.

Cancian, F. (1989). Love and the rise of capitalism. In B. Risman & P. Schwartz (Eds.), *Gender in intimate relationships* (pp. 12–25). Belmont, CA: Wadsworth.

Chodorow, N. (1978). *The reproduction of mothering: Psychoanalysis and the sociology of gender.* Berkeley, CA: University of California Press.

Chodorow, N. (1989). *Feminism and psychoanalytic theory.* New Haven, CT: Yale University Press.

Christensen, A., & Heavey, C. (1990). Gender and social structure in the demand/withdraw pattern in marital conflict. *Journal of Personality and Social Psychology, 59,* 73–81.

Collins, P. H. (1986). Learning from the outsider within: The sociological significance of Black feminist thought. *Social Problems, 33,* 514–532.

Degler, C. N. (1980). *At odds: Women and the family in America from the revolution to the present.* New York: Oxford University Press.

Dobash, R. E., & Dobash, R. P. (1979). *Violence against wives: A case against patriarchy.* New York: Free Press.

Douglas, A. (1977). *The feminization of American culture.* New York: Knopf.

Dyk, P. H., & Adams, G. R. (1990). Identity and intimacy: An initial investigation of three theoretical models using cross-lag panel correlations. *Journal of Youth and Adolescence, 19,* 91–110.

Eichenbaum, L., & Orbach, S. (1983). *Understanding women: A feminist psychoanalytic approach.* New York: Basic Books.

Epstein, C. F. (1968, November). Women in professional life. *Psychiatric Spectator,* n.p.

Epstein, C. F. (1981). *Women in law.* New York: Basic Books.

Epstein, C. F. (1982, November). *Changing perspectives and opportunities and their impact on careers and aspirations: The case of women lawyers.* Paper presented at the Annual Scientific Meeting of the Gerontological Society of America, Boston.

Epstein, C. F. (1988). *Deceptive distinctions: Sex, gender, and the social order.* New Haven, CT; Yale University Press.

Erikson, E. (1958). *Young man Luther.* New York: Norton.

Fox-Genovese, E. (1991). *Feminism without illusions.* Chapel Hill, NC: University of North Carolina Press.

Franks, D. D. (1985). Introduction to the special issue on the sociology of emotions. *Symbolic Interaction, 8,* 161–170.

Gilligan, C. (1982). *In a different voice: Psychological theory and women's development.* Cambridge, MA: Harvard University Press.

Goldner, V., Penn, P., Sheinberg, M., & Walker, G. (1990). Love and violence: Gender paradoxes in volatile attachments. *Family Process, 29,* 343–364.

Gordon, L. (1988). *Heroes of their own lives.* New York: Viking.

Harding, S. (1991). *Whose science? Whose knowledge? Thinking from women's lives.* Ithaca: Cornell University Press.

Hochschild, A. (1975). The sociology of feeling and emotion: Selected possibilities. In M. Millman & R. M. Kanter (Eds.), *Another voice* (pp. 280–307). New York: Doubleday/Anchor.

Hochschild, A. (1979). Emotion work, feeling rules, and social structure. *American Journal of Sociology, 85,* 551–595.

Hochschild, A. (1983). *The managed heart: Commercialization of human feeling.* Berkeley: University of California Press.

Hochschild, A. (1989). The economy of gratitude. In. D. Franks & E. D. McCarthy (Eds.), *The sociology of emotions: Original essays and research papers* (pp. 95–113). Greenwich, CT: JAI Press.

Hochschild, A., with Machung, A. (1989). *The second shift: Working parents and the revolution at home.* New York: Viking/Penguin.

Hoeksema, S. N. (1990). *Sex differences in depression.* Stanford, CA: Stanford University Press.

Janeway, E. (1971). *Man's world, woman's place: A study in social mythology.* New York: Dell.

Jones, G. P., & Dembo, M. H. (1989). Age and sex role differences in intimate friendships during childhood and adolescence. *Merrill-Palmer Quarterly, 35,* 445–462.

Kaye, L. W., & Applegate, J. S. (1990). Men as elder caregivers: A response to changing families. *American Journal of Orthopsychiatry, 60,* 86–95.

Kohn, M., & Schooler, C. (1973). Occupational experience and psychological functioning: An assessment of reciprocal effects. *American Sociological Review, 38,* 97–118.

Kohn, M., & Schooler, C. (1978). The reciprocal effects of the substantive complexity of work and intellectual flexibility: A longitudinal assessment. *American Journal of Sociology, 84,* 24–52.

Kohn, M., & Schooler, C. (1982). Job conditions and personality: A longitudinal assessment of their reciprocal effects. *American Journal of Sociology, 87,* 1257–1286.

Kohlberg, L. (1958). *The development of modes of thinking and choices in years 10 to 16.* Unpublished doctoral dissertation, University of Chicago.

Lerner, G. (1980). Internal prohibitions against female anger. *American Journal of Psychoanalysis, 40,* 137–148.

Maltz, D. N., & Borker, R. (1982). A cultural approach to male–female miscommunication. In J. J. Gumpertz (Ed.), *Language and social identity* (pp. 196–216). Cambridge, England: Cambridge University Press.

McGowen, K. R., & Hart, L. E. (1990). Still different after all these years: Gender differences in professional identity formation. *Professional Psychology: Research and Practice, 21,* 118–123.

Mead, G. H. (1932). *The philosophy of the present.* Chicago: Open Court Press.

Mead, G. H. (1934). *Mind, self, and society.* Chicago: University of Chicago Press.

Miller, J. B. (1986). *Toward a new psychology of women* (2nd. ed.). Boston: Beacon.

Miller, J., Schooler, C., Kohn, M., & Miller, K. (1979). Women and work: The psychological effects of occupational conditions. *American Journal of Sociology, 85,* 66–94.

Napier, A. Y. (1977). *The rejection–intrusion pattern: A central family dynamic.* Unpublished manuscript. University of Wisconsin-Madison, School of Family Resources.

Oakley, A. (1972). *Sex, gender, and society.* London: Temple Smith.

Okin, S. M. (1989). *Justice, gender, and the family.* New York: Basic Books.

Paul, E., & White, K. (1990). The development of intimate relationships in late adolescence. *Adolescence, 25,* 375–400.

Peplau, L. A., & Gordon, S. L. (1985). Women and men in love: Gender differences in close heterosexual relationships. In V. E. O'Leary, R. K. Unger, & B. S. Wallston Eds.), *Women, gender, and social psychology* (pp. 257–291). Hillsdale, NJ: Lawrence Erlbaum Associates.

Piaget, J. (1965). *The moral judgment of the child.* New York: The Free Press. (Original work published 1932)

Ptacek, J. (1988). Why do men batter their wives? In K. Yilo & M. Bograd (Eds.), *Feminist perspectives on wife abuse* (pp. 133–157). Newbury Park, CA: Sage.

Riessman, C. (1990). *Divorce talk: Women and men make sense of personal relationships.* New Brunswick: NJ: Rutgers University Press.

Risman, B. J. (1987). Intimate relationship from a microstructural perspective: Men who mother. *Gender and Society, 1,* 6–32.

Risman, B. J. (1989). Can men mother: Life as a single father. In B. Risman & P. Schwartz (Eds.), *Gender in intimate relationships* (pp. 155–164). Belmont, CA: Wadsworth.

Risman, B., & Schwartz, P. (Eds.). (1989). *Gender in intimate relationships.* Belmont, CA: Wadsworth.

Rubin, L. (1985). *Just friends: The role of friendship in our lives.* New York: Harper and Row.

Ruddick, S. (1989). *Maternal thinking.* New York: Ballentine.

Rusbult, C. A. (1987). Responses to dissatisfaction in close relationships: The exit-voice-loyalty-neglect model. In D. Perlman & S. W. Duck (Eds.), *Intimate relationships: Development, dynamics, and deterioration* (pp. 209–238). Newbury Park, CA: Sage.

Ryan, M. (1979). *Womanhood in America: From colonial times to the present* (2nd. ed.). New York: New Viewpoints.

Safilios-Rothschild, C. (1979). *Sex role socialization and sex discrimination: A synthesis and critique of the literature.* Washington, DC: National Institute of Education.

Schaef, A. W. (1985). *Women's reality.* New York: Random House.

Schneider, B. E., & Gould, M. (1987). Female sexuality: Looking back into the future. In B. B. Hess & M. M. Ferree (Eds.), *Analyzing gender: A handbook of social science research* (pp. 120–153). Newbury Park, CA: Sage.

Scott, J. (1986). Gender: A useful category for historical analysis. *American Historical Review, 91,* 1053–1075.

Shott, S. (1979). Emotion and social life: A symbolic interaction analysis. *American Journal of Sociology, 84,* 1317–1334.

Surrey, J. L. (1983). The relational self in women: Clinical implications. In J. V. Jordan, J. L. Surrey, & A. G. Kaplan (Speakers), *Women and empathy: Implications for psychological development and psychotherapy* (pp. 6–11). Wellesley, MA: Stone Center for Developmental Services and Studies.

Swain, S. (1989). Covert intimacy: Closeness in men's friendships. In B. J. Risman & P. Schwartz (Eds.), *Gender in intimate relationshps* (pp. 71–86). Belmont, CA: Wadsworth.

Tannen, D. (1990). *You just don't understand: Women and men in conversation.* New York: Morrow.

Tavris, C. (1992). *The mismeasure of woman.* New York: Simon and Schuster.

Thompson, E. H., Jr. (1991). The maleness of violence in dating relationships: An appraisal of stereotypes. *Sex Roles, 24,* 261–278.

Thompson, L., & Walker, A. J. (1989). Gender in families: Women and men in marriage, work, and parenthood. *Journal of Marriage and the Family, 51,* 845–871.

Thorbecke, W., & Grotevant, H. D. (1982). Gender differences in adolescent interpersonal identity formation. *Journal of Youth and Adolescence, 11,* 479–492.

Weeden, C. (1987). *Feminist practice and poststructuralist theory.* Oxford, England: Basil Blackwood, Ltd.

Welter, B. (1966). The cult of true womanhood: 1820–1860. *American Quarterly, 18,* 151–174.

West, C., & Zimmerman, D. H. (1987). "Doing gender." *Gender and Society, 1,* 125–151.

White, B. (1989). Gender differences in marital communication patterns. *Family Process, 28,* 89–106.

Wood, J. T., & Conrad, C. R. (1983). Paradox in the experience of professional women. *Western Journal of Speech Communication, 47,* 305–322.

Wood, J. T. (1993a). Engendered relations: Interaction, caring, power, and responsibility in intimacy. In S. W. Duck (Ed.), *Relational processes, Volume 3: The contexts of close relationships* (pp. 26–54). London: Sage.

Wood, J. T. (1993b). Enlarging conceptual boundaries: A critique of research on interpersonal communication. In S. Bowen & N. Wyatt (Eds.), *Transforming visions: Feminist critiques of speech communication* (pp. 19–49). Cresskill, NJ: Hampton Press.

Wood, J. T., & Lenze, L. F. (1991). Gender and the development of self: Inclusive pedagogy in interpersonal communication. *Women's Studies in Communication, 14,* 1–23.

Wood, J. T. (1993c). *Who cares: Women, care, and culture.* Carbondale, IL: Southern Illinois University Press.

Wright, P. H. (1982). Men's friendships, women's friendships, and the alleged inferiority of the latter. *Sex Roles, 8,* 1–20.

Wright, P. H. (1988). Interpreting research on gender differences in friendship: A case for moderation and a plea for caution. *Journal of Social and Personal Relationships, 5,* 367–373.

8 Intrapersonal Spoken Language: An Attribute of Extrapersonal Competency

John R. Johnson
University of Wisconsin—Milwaukee

My 3-month-old daughter rocks back and forth in her swing and begins to cry at a feverish pitch. My son of 21 months pounds his fists on his highchair and says in a loud and repetitive manner, "GUP" "GUP." My 11-year-old daughter sighs loudly and says, "Nothin," when I ask her what she did in school today. My wife, who is opening the mail, utters a depressing and fearful "Ohhhhhhhhhhhhhhh." These are the everyday behaviors that test our sanity and cause us to consider monastic lives of talking only to ourselves. The good news is that somewhere along the way the baby's cry becomes meaningful and "Gup" "Gup" becomes "Please may I have something to eat." The adolescent "Nothin" is replaced with a more sophisticated statement of at least two words and the "Ohhhhhhhhhhhh" turns out not to be a letter from the Internal Revenue Service. Instead of taking a vow of silence we launch ourselves forward with the optimistic attitude that all is well, and, if not, we can "talk about it."

Our lives are dependent on communication, and this makes it such a pervasive phenomenon that we tend to take it for granted. Yet, if we step back and carefully examine the process, we are left in a state of awe. How is it that the human infant, hours after birth, is interacting with and regulating the behavior of its caregivers? How is it that we move from an inarticulate state to being able to speak our ideas to others? And how is it that friends, lovers, and even strangers are able to make sense out of each other's utterances. Equally interesting is why there are wide variations in our abilities to do all of these communicative acts.

Although our understanding of human communication has significantly increased during this century, our understanding of it is admittedly limited. I will assert in this chapter that one of the reasons for our limited understanding of human communication is that we have failed to account for the central role intrapersonal spoken language plays in symbolic communication. Among the reasons for this failure is our lack of formal and sustained effort at defining the major levels and forms of symbolic communication. Intrapersonal communication has been defined as being practically everything, including thinking aloud to oneself, daydreaming, fantasizing, self-concept, and silent thought. By being everything, intrapersonal has ended up being nothing. It is no wonder we have a difficult time trying to understand its role in the larger process of symbolic communication.

Another reason for our limited understanding is that we have avoided seriously looking at how the various levels and forms (e.g., intrapersonal, interpersonal, public) of human communication interface with each other. At issue, for example, is how and to what degree does self-talk affect the talk we have with others? Similarly, how does the talk we have with others affect how we talk to ourselves? We have typically treated human communication as a phenomenon occurring on separate and independent levels. We have professional interest groups dedicated, for the most part, to the exclusive study of interpersonal, group, public, mass, intrapersonal, and other types of communication. Rather than seeing the whole of human communication we have chosen to divide it into small areas of academic and political interest.

In this chapter I address both of the above limitations. First, I provide a taxonomy of terms and definitions useful in describing the various levels of human communication. Second, I describe how intrapersonal spoken language interfaces with, is affected by, and affects the other levels and forms of symbolic communication. Particular attention is paid to how the intrapersonal level influences extrapersonal spoken language competency.

ATTRIBUTES
OF INTRAPERSONAL SPOKEN LANGUAGE

The task of defining the nature of intrapersonal is a difficult one. The process involves ascertaining the attributes, or those things that must be present for a phenomenon to be said to be present, and then developing a logical system or taxonomy that illustrates how various terms and concepts are related. Regardless of its difficulty, it is a task that must be undertaken. Without a definition of intrapersonal and its accompanying levels (e.g., interpersonal and public) of human communication, theoretical and empirical research will be fragmented and inconsistent. As Delia (1977) stated: "If concepts are fuzzy, research will yield fuzzy results. Data have meaning only within a system of concepts, rendering them meaningful. If one's concepts do not provide a way of understanding a range of data, it will be meaningless. Conceptual clarity, hence, is the minimum necessary ground for any productive research effort" (p. 83).

The act of proposing a definition of anything automatically opens one to being accused of being a reductionist, of drawing conceptual lines too narrow or too wide, of limiting or expanding too far the nature of a phenomenon. However, if terms are not defined or are done so in a global or nonspecific manner, we are placed in the position of either not knowing what to study or having to study everything. This tension causes some researchers to assume an "Alice in Wonderland" approach and declare that the terms they use can mean whatever they choose them to mean.

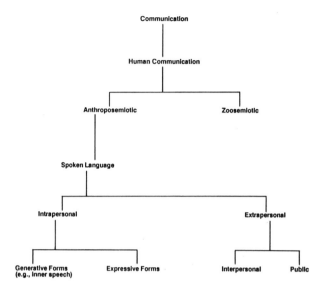

FIG. 8.1.   A taxonomic model of communication and spoken language.

Although correct in the strictest sense, this type of reasoning does little to develop and expand formal theory. Defining anything is serious business and ought not to be done in haste, for poorly constructed definitions inevitably lead to illogical conclusions.

In this chapter I provide a series of terms and definitions useful in the study of human communication. In so doing, I do not mean to imply that my definitions represent the correct or final answers. The process of defining phenomena is best described as evolutionary rather than absolute. It is not that one sets out to find the answer, rather one sets out, with each generation of research, to find a better answer.

Figure 8.1 presents the major terms used in this chapter. They are ordered deductively, with the most general term listed first, followed by increasingly more specific terms. Thus spoken language is understood to be a form of human communication, which in turn is a form of communication. The genesis of this taxonomy of terms primarily rests on the theoretical work of Dance (1970, 1980, 1982), Dance and Larson (1972, 1976), Sokolov (1972), and Vygotsky (1986, 1987).

Communication

The term *communication* has historically, and across a variety of academic disciplines, been used to refer to a wide range of activities, including ants burying their dead, honey bees flying to particular locations, intra- and extracellular and biological information activities, mating calls, and, of course, humans talking and writing to one another (Altman, 1967; Hinde 1972, 1974; Sebeok, 1968, 1972, 1977; Smith, 1977).

The diversity of meanings associated with the term *communication* necessitates that its definition be general enough to identify the common attributes of all of these various types of communication (Dance, 1970, 1980). One definition proposed by Dance is well suited to meet this objective. "Acting upon information. Limited to organisms. The act may take place within an organism or between or among organisms (the organism may or may not be human). At this level neither intent nor success is implicit in the concept of communication" (Dance, 1982, p. 125).

Academicians associated with departments of communication, speech communication, speech, and so on, may object to this broad definition because they use the term *communication* in an extremely parochial fashion. However, whether these academics admit it or not, the vast majority of their colleagues from other disciplines, as well as the general population, do not use the term *communication* as a synonym for human or symbolic forms of communication.

Human Communication

As a result of the very general nature of "communication," it is essential that we differentiate its various levels and forms. This differentiation can be made using several different criteria. For example, Johnson and Dance (1980) differentiated communication on the basis of the biological classification of the organism communicating (monera or one-celled organisms, plants, animals). Because this chapter is concerned with the phenomenon of intra*personal*, my discussion will focus on human forms of communication. Borrowing from the work of Dance (1982), the concept of human communication can be defined as "acting upon information by humans" (p. 126).

Although the term *human communication* is a more precise label than is "communication," when referring to acts of communication by humans, it must be remembered that humans act on information in at least two general ways: First, humans act on information in a kingdom-specific or animal fashion. Sebeok (1968, 1972, 1977) referred to this form of communication as zoosemiotic. Humans' use of zoosemiotic communication reflects the fact that as humans we share a common heritage or repertoire of communication behaviors with other animals. Zoosemiotic communication employs all *modes*, or the general means by which stimuli are made known to the senses (i.e., acoustic, visual, olfactory). Furthermore, human zoosemiotic communication relies on a *language*, or a system of organizing stimuli into information, that is exclusively sign based (Dance, 1982; Dance & Larson, 1972; Johnson 1983; Sebeok, 1968, 1972 1977). This sign-based language system is characterized by stimuli that have single, concrete, and fixed meanings regardless of context in which the stimuli are used (Dance, 1982; Johnson & Dance, 1980). Humans' use of zoosemiotic communication, like all forms of zoosemiotic communication, serves the biological functions of regulating behavior and socialization. For example, studies of human infant–caregiver interactions have found that infants are capable of coordinating and regulating the interactions they have with adults. Infants have been observed moving in synchrony with adult speech patterns as early as 20 minutes after birth (Condon, 1979).

The second way humans act on information is in a species (Homo sapien) specific fashion, or what Sebeok (1968, 1977) referred to as anthroposemiotically. Anthroposemiotic communication has two unique characteristics. First, it employs *speech*, or the production of phonated and articulated sound (Dance, 1982, p. 126), as the specific means of manifesting acoustic stimuli. Second, it relies on a *symbolic* language system characterized by stimuli that have contextually flexible, abstract, and arbitrary meanings (Dance, 1982). Developmentally, speech and symbolic language are said to live separate lives until when, at approximately 18-24 months, the two merge to form *spoken language*. Dance (1982) defined spoken language as: "The fusion of genetically determined speech with culturally determined [symbolic] language" (p. 126).

Ontogenetically, spoken language is the initial and principal means by which the majority of humans anthroposemiotically communicate. Spoken language is found in all known cultures, whereas visual forms of symbolic communication, such as writing, are restricted in application. The principal, natural way in which humans anthroposemiotically act on information is through spoken language (Dance, 1982; Ong, 1967, 1977).

Before defining intrapersonal spoken language, it would be helpful to examine the nature of its counterpart, extrapersonal.

Extrapersonal Spoken Language

The *extrapersonal* level can be defined as occurring when the producer and intended consumer of the spoken language are not one and the same person. Therefore extrapersonal spoken language must involve a minimum of two individuals and be intended for someone outside (extra) of one's self.

Extrapersonal spoken language serves as a means to express our symbolic thoughts to others. The expression of thought in turn serves the secondary functions of regulating behavior and linking or socializing the human to his or her environment.[1]

Extrapersonal spoken language manifests itself through modalities other than acoustic (speech and audition). These include vision (reading and writing) and tactile (braille). Extrapersonal spoken language is also extended through the use of technologies such as radio, film, video, television, telephone, and computers. All symbolic communication directed toward others, regardless of its form (reading, writing, television, etc.), shares the common attribute of being a derivative of extrapersonal spoken language.

Two of the most often studied sublevels of extrapersonal spoken language are commonly referred to as interpersonal and public. The debate as to the exact attributes of these two levels of spoken language has been going on for what seems eons and most certainly this chapter will not put this issue to rest.

I have chosen not to differentiate these two levels on the basis of psychological and sociological differences in the information exchanged or the absolute number of

---

[1]For a discussion of the functions see Dance and Larson (1972, 1975).

communicative participants. Instead, I prefer to understand the difference as resting on the basis of the potential for feedforward (stimuli or output sent forward) and feedback (stimuli sent back to the source, regarding the stimuli fed forward).

Interpersonal Spoken Language

Interpersonal spoken language is defined as a sublevel of extrapersonal spoken language in which there exists a potential for an equal or near-equal opportunity for all individuals involved to both extrapersonally speak and listen. Therefore, there are potentially high levels of spoken language feedforward and feedback among all communicative participants.

We witness interpersonal spoken language being used in a variety of ways and settings. Strangers talking about the weather, a married couple talking with each other about their relationship, family members discussing what they want to do over the weekend, or a manager talking with a subordinate about how to increase sales are all examples of interpersonal spoken language.

Public Spoken Language

Public spoken language is defined as a level of extrapersonal spoken language in which there *does not* exist a potential for equal or near-equal opportunity for all individuals involved to both extrapersonally speak and listen. Therefore, there are low levels of spoken language feedforward and feedback among all communicative participants.

We can witness public spoken language being used in a variety of ways and settings. Examples include the President of the United States addressing both houses of Congress, a salesperson giving a persuasive presentation to a group of potential buyers, a professor lecturing to a class, and students giving presentations in a public speaking class.

Regardless of whether it is public or interpersonal spoken language, both forms share the common attribute of being expressive speech acts designed to reveal our thoughts to someone other than self. As you will read in the final section of this essay, this attribute, combined with the variation in potential for equal or near-equal speaking and listening, significantly increases our understanding of the nature of extrapersonal spoken language competency.

Intrapersonal Spoken Language

Some readers may question the necessity of specifying mode (speech or spoken) and language when referring to symbolic forms of communication. Would it not be just as easy and accurate to refer to the phenomenon as intrapersonal communication? Although it might be easier, it would be a less accurate label. For example, do all forms of intrapersonal communication rely on speech and use a symbolic language system? Are there not sign-based or zoosemiotic forms of intrapersonal communication? Of course there are, and these intrapersonal forms of communication are used to maintain our body temperature, heart rate, respiration, reproductive cycles, and so forth. This chapter, although acknowledging the existence of intrapersonal communication, as manifested through modes other than speech- and sign-based language systems, is concerned exclusively with intrapersonal communication expressed through spoken language.

Intrapersonal spoken language, like extrapersonal spoken language, is defined on the basis of who the producer and intended consumer of the spoken language is. With this in mind, *intrapersonal* spoken language is defined as taking place when the producer and intended consumer of spoken language are one and the same person. Therefore, intrapersonal spoken language is intended for one's self (intra).

Intrapersonal spoken language, like extrapersonal, also serves as a means to express our symbolic thoughts. However, the expression is intended to be limited only to oneself. Intrapersonal spoken language also acts as a means to create or generate symbolic thought.[2] The former is referred to as *expressive intrapersonal spoken language* (encoding) and latter as *generative intrapersonal spoken language* (decoding). Expressive and generative forms of intrapersonal spoken language are central to all other levels and forms of symbolic communication. In one sense, the process of humans symbolically communicating can be described as beginning and ending as an intrapersonal process. Furthermore, expressive and generative intrapersonal spoken language are critical to the various functions of human communication including what Vocate (Chapter 1, this volume) refers to as the cognitive adaptation of self to others and Dance and Larson's (1976) three functions of linking of individuals to their social environments, developing higher mental processes, and regulating behaviors of others and self. Luria (1982) in conceptualizing the process of symbolic communication argued that the process ought to be investigated from the perspective of speech as a receptive or decoding act (generative) and speech as a expressive or encoding act. Luria described symbolic communication as a process bound to these two speech acts. The expressive speech act begins with

> a certain formation of a general idea (or plan) to be
> converted into speech, it then passes through the very
> important (and still inadequately studied) stage of 'internal
> speech' in which the initial plan begins to assume the form
> of a verbal [symbolic] expression, and it ends with the
> expanded verbal communication. During the understanding
> (decoding) or verbal expression the process is reversed.
> (Luria, 1982, p. 486)

---

[2]Symbolic thought, or conceptual thought, is defined as the generation of associations or thoughts between or among nonsensory or nonperceptually based stimuli. Symbolic thought may be further described in terms of Pavlov's (1960) second signal system or Dance and Larson's mentation function. Symbolic thought is a higher mental process involving such activities as displacement, conceptual memory, planning, and foresight. Adler (1967) further clarified the concept by differentiating it from perceptual thought. Adler's thesis is that animals other than humans can and do think but their thinking is limited to stimuli that are perceptually present, in the here and now. Conceptual thought, through the use of symbols, transcends the here and now to include associations with events in the distant past and future, as well as with objects or ideas which have no perceptual reality.

The expressive forms of intrapersonal spoken language manifest themselves in various ways. For example, there are audible and subvocalized *expressive* forms of intrapersonal spoken language. A good percentage of our daily activities are spent talking aloud and silently to ourselves. In fact these self-directed monologues are often among our most entertaining and delightful conversations. Seldom do we find ourselves boring speakers and our comprehension rates are near 100%. These expressive forms of intrapersonal spoken language vary on several dimensions, including the level of audible speech (ranging from silent to out loud), the actual content of what is said (i.e., you say things silently that you would not say aloud for fear of being overheard), and the degree to which the semantics (word meanings) and syntax (word arrangements) are elaborated (i.e., rehearsal of future extrapersonal statements using grammatically complete sentences or the utterance of brief elliptical statements to self). It should be no surprise that we express our thoughts to ourselves, either silently or aloud, differently than we express them to others.

Generative forms of intrapersonal spoken language are used to make sense out of what we hear by making associations between or among concepts. One of the principal generative forms of intrapersonal spoken language is *inner speech*. Owing to its central role across all levels of symbolic communication, I will examine its structure and function in great detail.

Inner Speech

The term *inner speech* refers to subvocalized or silent intrapersonal spoken language used to *generate* symbolic or conceptual thought while in the process of creating word meanings.

Inner speech operates in many ways like making extremely abbreviated statements to yourself. While using inner speech, we silently produce a few key words to help us make associations with much larger ideas or concepts. For example, when reminding ourselves of things we need to do, we might silently say to ourselves, "car, dinner, kids." This abbreviated statement is a quick and efficient way to jog our memory when we set off to accomplish the tasks. Our list does not need to elaborate the exact nature of each task because we know what each concept means. To ourselves, "car" obviously means to fill up the gas tank, "dinner" refers to getting one gallon of 2% milk and a loaf of whole wheat bread, and "kids" means to pick up John and Kate from daycare before coming home.

Vygotsky (1987), in his classic text *Thinking and Speaking*,[3] was among the first scholars of this century to argue that inner speech and symbolic thought, although related and interdependent, are not one and the same thing. Vygotsky disputed the idea that inner speech was solely thinking silently to yourself. Instead, he understood inner speech and symbolic thought to coexist, with each dependent on the other for the generation of word meaning. Symbolic thought is used to make associations between or among words/concepts, thus creating word meanings. In-

---

[3]The first translation of *Thinking and speech* was incorrectly titled *Thought and Language*.

ner speech, on the other hand, dramatically influences symbolic thought by significantly increasing the speed and efficiency at which these associations and word meanings can be made. Although it is possible to symbolically think without inner speech, the use of inner speech significantly reduces the time and effort necessary to make associations between or among words or concepts. For example, instead of using the highly efficient "car, dinner, kids," we would have to say to ourselves, "Make sure to fill up the car's gas tank, stop by the store and pick up a gallon of 2% milk and a loaf of whole wheat bread, and be certain to pick up John and Kate from daycare before coming home".

Inner speech, as a result of its unique method of processing information, radically shapes how we generate conceptual thought. To help you better understand how inner speech operates in relation to conceptual thought, let me present its structural and functional characteristics as outlined in the writings of Dance (1979), Johnson (1982, 1984), Korba (1986, 1989), Luria (1966, 1982), Sokolov (1972), and Vygotsky (1986, 1987).

Structure of Inner Speech.   Inner speech has four interdependent characteristics. It is important to note that these four characteristics are not unique to inner speech. They are found, in varying degrees, in all forms of intrapersonal and extrapersonal spoken language. What is unique about the structure of inner speech is that all four characteristics are always present to a very large degree. As you will read later, the reason for this rests on the fact that inner speech is a *generative* form of intrapersonal spoken language, designed to produce conceptual thoughts while serving self rather than others.

The first structural characteristic of inner speech is that it is *always silent*. When we use expressive forms of intrapersonal spoken language we will often do so by talking silently to ourselves. However, when we use inner speech we *always* do so without producing audible speech. Although we are unaware of the speech movements of inner speech, previous research has shown the physiological and articulatory activities of the auditory–speech mechanisms are used to produce inner speech (Korba, 1986; McGuigan, 1978; Sokolov, 1972). Sokolov (1972), in referring to the presence of speech production during inner speech, stated, "The usual characterization of inner speech as 'soundless' is justified only from the point of view of the outsider; for the thinker himself, however, inner speech remains linked to the auditory speech stimuli even in the case of maximal inhibition of speech movements" (p. 55).

Inner speech's second structural characteristic, *syntactical ellipsis*, concerns how words are arranged. Inner speech's syntax (or arrangement of words) and grammar has been referred to as predicated (Sokolov, 1972; Vygotsky, 1986, 1987), elliptical (Leontiev, 1969), crushed, or condensed (Johnson, 1984). These various descriptions refer to the compressed form of inner speech's syntax and grammar. Inner speech uses extremely high levels of syntactic ellipsis.

Vygotsky considered this characteristic to be inner speech's central distinguishing quality (1986, 1987). This syntactic ellipsis allows for the omission of the subject of the sentence and all other parts excluding the predicate. The syntax of inner speech is, therefore, incomplete or elliptic. The statement, "I am going to the store" in inner speech might be syntactically reduced to "going store."

Vygotsky, in explaining this structural characteristic, mentioned that *expressive* forms of spoken language often exhibit syntactic ellipsis or predication. Predication occurs in expressive spoken language in two cases: (a) as an answer to a question, or (b) when the subject of the sentence is known beforehand to all concerned. The answer to, "Would you like to go for a ride in the car?" is never, "No, I would not like to go for a ride in the car." Instead we usually reply, "No," or, "No thank you." The compressed syntax of our reply is possible only because the subject of the request is understood by all parties involved. Now imagine that several people are waiting in a checkout line for a cashier. When the cashier approached the cash register no one in line would say, "The cashier, for whom we having been waiting, is finally coming." The syntax of the utterance would more likely be an abbreviated, "Finally!" The reason the speaker can compress the syntax of his or her utterance is that everyone hearing the utterance understands the subject of the statement based on the situation or context.

Although extrapersonal spoken language often involves compressed syntax, it's level of compression does not compare to the high levels of syntactical compression found in inner speech. Because the sender and receiver of inner speech are one and the same, there is never a situation in which the person using inner speech does not understand the subject of the statement. Therefore, there is no need to have an elaborate syntactical structure to achieve understanding.

Inner speech's third structural characteristic is referred to as *semantic* (word meaning) *embeddedness*. When using inner speech, a single word typically has an extremely elaborate or complex meaning. The semantic embeddedness of the words used in inner speech is very high. Therefore, the number and diversity of words used in inner speech is typically very limited. In the previous example, the "things to do" list included a reference to "car." When the semantics of "car" are elaborated it can be understood to mean, "Fill up the car with regular unleaded gasoline." The single word "car" therefore has very rich or dense semantics or word meaning.

In contrasting the semantics of inner speech with that found in extrapersonal, or even expressive intrapersonal, spoken language, we note that the subject of inner speech is always known to the user of inner speech and requires no semantic elaboration. However, someone communicating at the extrapersonal level, such as a public speaker, has the arduous task of elaborating his or her symbolic thoughts and meanings for the audience. The degree to which we have to elaborate the meanings of our expressive spoken language varies based on the extent to which our audience shares the same meanings for the words we use.

Inner speech's fourth structural characteristic is that it is *egocentric*. By egocentric, I am referring to the fact that when we use inner speech we do not bother to cognitively assume the perspective or viewpoint of other people.

Most explanations of communicative egocentrism (e.g., Chandler, Greenspan, & Barenboim, 1974; Flavell, 1968; Greenspan & Barenboim, 1975; Piaget, 1955, 1973) have identified it as an expressive speech act, meaning that a speaker produces an egocentric statement. However, these expressive forms of egocentrism are outward manifestations of the egocentrism that occurs during the generative phase of symbolic communication (Johnson, 1982, 1984, 1993). Therefore, it is not only possible for a speaker to produce an egocentric statement, but also for a listener, while generating meaning or conceptual thoughts regarding the message, to egocentrically interpret a message. Egocentrism, as associated with the process of symbolic communication, is present whenever a speaker or listener fails to cognitively assume the perspective of the other when producing or listening to expressive spoken language. Egocentrism should not be confused with being greedy, thoughtless, self-indulgent, narcissistic, or selfish. Furthermore, a speaker's frequent use of "I" or "me" statements is not evidence of egocentrism (Johnson, 1982).

Because inner speech is a form of intrapersonal spoken language designed exclusively for one's own generation of meaning or conceptual thought, the producer and receiver of inner speech does *not* have to cognitively assume a perspective other than his or her own. Inner speech, by its very nature and function, is therefore highly egocentric.

The fact that inner speech is both a silent and generative form of spoken language makes it impossible to provide a sample of "real" inner speech. However, the structural characteristics of inner speech often manifest themselves in expressive forms of spoken language. For the sake of helping you understand the concept, let us assume that you need to go to the grocery store. You would use inner speech to generate your grocery list, which might include "lettuce, mayonnaise, oranges, beer, and so on." Notice that although you are using inner speech to generate the list of items that you do not identify why you are going out, where you are going to get the items, or the quantity or quality of the items. The syntactical ellipsis and semantic embeddedness of your inner speech are possible because you know the purpose of your trip, the name and location of the store you are going to, and the exact nature of what you want to buy. Consequently, the inner speech used to generate the list is also highly egocentric. Right before you are about to leave you decide you better mentally check your grocery items. You do so by expressing either silently or our loud to yourself the list and reflecting on each of the items.

Your expressive intrapersonal spoken language might be, "Let's see . . . lettuce, mayo, make that low fat, some oranges. Better make em big. Hmm . . . maybe I need some lemons." What we see in this expressive intrapersonal spoken language is a slight, but significant, expansion of the syntax and semantics of your earlier inner speech, which is necessary for the reflective process to occur. As luck would have it, right before you are about to leave, you remember that you have to stay home and wait for a very important phone call. You ask your spouse to go instead and she or he agrees. To help you spouse understand what you want from the store you expand your earlier expressive intrapersonal statement. You might say, "You'll need to get two large heads of lettuce, some milk, a jar of mayonnaise, a dozen large navel oranges." Notice that your message to your spouse expresses in greater detail the items to be purchased. However, some details were omitted such as the type of mayonnaise and milk because you assume that your spouse understands this. A few minutes later your luck again falls short when your spouse says he or she can't go to the store after all. You still need the groceries so you ask your house guest to go to the store for you. Because you house guest is not at all familiar with your buying habits you need to elaborate your message even more than you did to your spouse. You might say something like, "Hey, Jim, mind going up to Pick and Save? You know, we passed it yesterday when we went into Grafton. Hey thanks, you're great. What I need is two large heads of lettuce, make them romaine; a quart of Cedarburg Dairy skim milk, one quart of Zippy low fat mayonnaise, make sure its *low* fat, Kathryn nearly gags on the regular stuff; one dozen, large, firm navel Florida oranges; and so on. . . . Are you sure you know how to get there? Here's some money and the car keys. Thanks a million Jim."

Inner speech, as a result of its four structural characteristics, is an extremely fast and efficient method of facilitating symbolic thought or making associations between or among concepts (Johnson, 1984, 1993; Korba, 1986). Although inner speech and symbolic thought are not one and the same process, inner speech's unique structural characteristics shape symbolic thought and meaning. To more fully understand how this process operates, we need to examine the role inner speech plays in facilitating symbolic thought and word meaning. As Vygotsky (1986) asserted, "The relation of thought and word cannot be understood in all its complexity without a clear understanding of the psychological nature of inner speech" (p. 224).

Functions of Inner Speech.   Investigating the function(s) of inner speech allows us to know its natural (without intent) and inevitable consequences (Dance & Larson, 1972, 1976). This, in turn, provides us with an idea as to how inner speech interfaces with extrapersonal forms of spoken language.

Korba (1986) offered a comprehensive analysis of the functions of inner speech. He argued, using the work of others (e.g., Dance, 1967, 1979; Feldman, 1976; Galperin, 1969; Johnson, 1982, 1984; Kuczaj, 1986; Kuczaj & Bean, 1982; Luria, 1966, 1982; Luria & Yudovich 1959; Sokolov, 1972; Vygotsky, 1986, 1987), that the functions of inner speech are similar to those of other forms of spoken language and therefore can be classified using the functional schema of Dance (1967) and Dance and Larson (1972, 1976). The three functions proposed in this schema are: (a) linking or helping humans associate with and relate to their physical, psychological, and sociological environments; (b) regulating or controlling human behavior; and (c) developing and maintaining higher mental processes or symbolic thought. However, inner speech, although serving the first two of these functions, does so as a consequence of its central role in the third function, developing or generating symbolic thought or word meaning.

Inner speech is designed to serve self rather than others. It is an exceptionally fast and efficient method of transforming expressive spoken language into symbolic thought and meaning. Inner speech is used to facilitate symbolic or conceptual thought while in the process of creating word meanings. It is the principal means through which we make sense and bring symbolic meaning to the expressive spoken language we hear.

Extrapersonal and expressive intrapersonal spoken language serve to express our symbolic thoughts and meanings to others and self. The expression of our symbolic meanings in turn serves the secondary functions of regulating self and others' behavior and linking or socializing self and others to the environment.

Expressive spoken language, which is used to reveal symbolic thoughts and meanings, must expand the syntax and semantics of our inner speech to a level we think is necessary to be understood by others or even ourselves. Furthermore, if we are engaged as extrapersonal spoken language we must make this process audible to someone other than ourselves. Even when we are engaged in expressive intrapersonal spoken language we often find ourselves expressing aloud our symbolic thoughts and meanings.

The structure and function of inner speech makes it central to the various forms of extrapersonal spoken language. Korba (1986), in referring to the centrality of inner speech, stated: "All verbal interaction (and a great deal of nonverbal interaction) requires the use of inner speech, either in the preparation (encoding) of spoken language for others, or in the understanding (decoding) of spoken language of others" (p. 33).

Vygotsky and Sokolov, like Korba, underscored the belief that inner speech is central not only to the generation of symbolic thought but that it also affects how we express thought. If inner speech is such a central player in the process of symbolic communication then why don't models of human communication address its role in the process?

A MODEL OF INTRAPERSONAL
AND EXTRAPERSONAL SPOKEN LANGUAGE

Since the 1949 publication of Shannon and Weaver's classic text, *The Mathematical Theory of Communication*, there has been a substantial growth in the development of models of communication. Although many of these models cannibalized much of Shannon and Weaver's original model, there has been a dedicated effort at generating original models and theories of symbolic communication. Collectively, these models and theories have served to elevate our understanding of symbolic communication. However, these models also have shown a decided preference toward describing and explaining the phenomenon in a reductionistic and phenotypic manner.[4] By this I mean that our models and theories have tended to reduce the study of symbolic communication to those variables that are directly observable and/or quantifiable. It is as though we decided to restrict symbolic communication to an "Out of Head" phenomenon. We have, by relying so one-sidedly on this type of analysis, ignored that fact that symbolic communication begins and ends as an internal state that by itself has no outward manifestations directly comprehensible to phenotypic analyses.

This trend has led to a large and problematic void in our understanding of the internal, as well as external, processes of symbolic communication. In particular,

---

[4]For a discussion of phenotypic and genotypic analyses see Lewin (1935) and Vygotsky (1978).

the generative forms of intrapersonal spoken language have received very little attention. An excellent example of this limitation can be found in communication competency research.

Whereas researchers have described communication as involving "decoding" and "encoding" processes, little effort has been paid to how these two processes work in concert with each other. For the most part, researchers have failed to integrate both expressive (encoding) and generative (decoding) forms of intrapersonal spoken language into discussions of communicative competence (see for example, Allen & Brown, 1976; Cooley & Roach, 1984; Hymes, 1971, 1979; Rubin, 1982, 1985; Spitzberg & Cupach, 1984, 1989). Communication researchers, by insisting that symbolic communication is strictly a socially observable phenomenon, have ignored the issue of what role, if any, spoken language plays in the internal generative and expressive forms of symbolic communication. As Marx (cited in Vygotsky, 1978) so eloquently pointed out, "If the essence of objects coincided with the form of their outer manifestations then every science would be superfluous" (p. 63).

There have been, of course, several attempts at modeling and explaining the role of intrapersonal in extrapersonal forms of symbolic communication. Notable are the Wiseman-Barker (1974) and Barnlund (1970) models. These two models attempt to interface intrapersonal with extrapersonal communication but do not offer elaborate or well-developed explanations as to how spoken language operates at these two levels. Flavell's (1968) models of egocentric and nonegocentric communication, although more elaborate than most, do not specify the nature of how spoken language is transformed from the intrapersonal to the extrapersonal level. All of us, intuitively, are aware that intrapersonal spoken language undergoes major changes during the generation and expression of our thoughts. It is this often-ignored, yet important, process that is the concern of this next part of this chapter.

The direct communication of symbolic meaning between humans, as often represented in standard sender–receiver models, is both physiologically and psychologically impossible (Vygotsky, 1986, 1987). Quite simply, we cannot read each other's minds. Instead, symbolic communication occurs in a very indirect manner, with inner speech playing an important role in the process. The process can be understood to occur when our symbolic thoughts are elaborated and converted into expressive spoken language. While listening to spoken language, the process is reversed, and extrapersonal spoken language is transformed into inner speech, which is used to generate symbolic thoughts (Johnson, 1993). The expressive forms of intrapersonal and extrapersonal spoken language as well as the generative forms of intrapersonal are integral parts of this dynamic process. When we listen to our own or others' spoken language we use inner speech to efficiently transform the words we hear into symbolic thoughts. When we use expressive intrapersonal or extrapersonal spoken language we are transforming symbolic thoughts into words.

Although our understanding of the process spoken language undergoes while being transformed from inner speech to extrapersonal language and vice-versa, is fairly limited we can say that it is not linear but helical. Because of this, both generative and expressive forms of spoken language exist in a symbiotic relationship. Sokolov, in commenting about this interrelationship, stated: "Let us also note

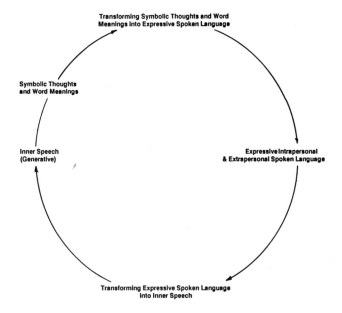

FIG. 8.2. A generative and expressive model of symbolic communication.

that under certain conditions all of these specific features of inner speech cannot be separated from external and regarded as an independent phenomenon. It is also quite evident, however, that external speech is functionally dependent on inner speech" (Sokolov, 1972, p. 65).

In previous writings, I outlined a series of models that illustrate the transformational process of intrapersonal and extrapersonal spoken language (Johnson, 1984, 1993). Figure 8.2 visually describes how the generative and expressive forms of spoken language interface or work together.

Figure 8.2 represents the relationship between expressive spoken language and symbolic thoughts as being a process in which expressive spoken language is transformed into inner speech, which is used to make symbolic thoughts, which is then transformed back into expressive spoken language.

During this transformation, expressive spoken language (either at the intrapersonal or extrapersonal level) undergoes an implosive process wherein inner speech significantly reduces or collapses the syntactical and semantic structures of the expressive spoken language. This implosive transformation into inner speech is done in silence and renders the former expressive spoken language highly egocentric.

Inner speech—which is the product of this implosive transformation, results in spoken language characterized by highly embedded semantics, elliptical syntax, and egocentricity—is then used by symbolic thought to make associations between and among concepts and in turn creates symbolic meaning.

Expressing our symbolic thoughts and meanings to ourselves and others requires a process best described as explosive. Here the syntactical ellipsis and semantic embeddedness of our symbolic thoughts are expanded in an attempt to assist others in understanding our expressive spoken language.

The process of imploding expressive spoken language into symbolic thought and exploding symbolic thought back into expressive spoken language is extremely dynamic. There is no absolute beginning or end to the expression and generation of symbolic thought. In this respect, the interface between the expressive and generative forms of spoken language is similar to what Dance (1967) described in his helical model of human communication.

As previously mentioned, inner speech's four structural characteristics make it an exceptionally fast and efficient method of transforming expressive spoken language into symbolic thought. When we listen to expressive spoken language and then implode it into inner speech, we significantly reduce the syntax of these messages. Research by Feldman (1976), Gough (1972), and Landauer (1962) estimated the rate of word recognition and message comprehension of spoken language to be somewhere between 275 and 400 words per minute. Korba (1986), noted that, although these rates may indicate a maximum number of words used in inner speech, they do not take into account the semantic embeddedness of inner speech. Korba argued: "It clearly stands to reason that if one word, conjured through inner speech, requires 100 words to adequately express its meaning in fully prepared, syntactical external speech, then each internal word carries a tremendous amount of idiosyncratic meaning for the individual" (p. 84).

To estimate the richness of the meanings of the words used in inner speech, Korba (1986) asked participants to list the key words they used while completing a simple problem and to expand these words into extrapersonal spoken language. The participants' list of key words and narratives was triangulated against the results of a spectral analysis of electromyography frequencies of the participants' speech to verify that the participants had subvocalized. Results revealed that it would take an equivalent of 4,000 words to extrapersonally express 1 minute of inner speech.

The fact that inner speech uses high levels of syntactical ellipsis and semantic embeddedness is useful in explaining why our rate of listening is so much faster than our speaking rate (e.g., Nichols, 1955, 1957; Wolvin & Coakley, 1988). It also explains why the difference between expressive speaking and listening rates could encourage listeners' inattention (Nichols, 1957).

The meanings of the words we use in inner speech are extremely complex. As Korba's (1986) research indicated, a single word used in inner speech has a diversity of meanings far more complex than those found in expressive spoken language. Furthermore, as a consequence of inner speech being inherently and structurally egocentric, the meanings we give to the words we speak and listen to are extremely idiosyncratic.

EXTRAPERSONAL SPOKEN LANGUAGE COMPETENCE

There is no doubt that research regarding communication competence has resulted in an endless series of academic debates. Arguments over the distinction between performance and competence, the role of context, and the criteria of appropriateness have occupied large amounts of text and journal space. However, there does seem to be a consensus that communicative competence involves the appropriate adaptation of spoken language based on the context of the extrapersonal interaction (see Spitzberg & Cupach, 1984, 1989). For example, one of the major tasks in competently using expressive spoken language is producing a message that listeners can understand.

Our symbolic thought and word meaning, as consequence of being created through inner speech, is highly egocentric, semantically embedded, and syntactically elliptical. When speaking with others we have to overcome the natural egocentricity of our symbolic thought. To do this we must explode the word arrangements (syntactics) and word meanings (semantics) of our symbolic thought to a level sufficient for the listener(s) to comprehend our intended meaning. This requires a basic, yet extremely important, competence in transforming intrapersonal into extrapersonal spoken language. Similarly, when we listen to others we have to overcome the natural egocentricity inherent in the inner speech we use to implode expressive spoken language into conceptual thought. This process requires us to reduce the word arrangements (syntactics) and word meanings (semantics) of the expressive spoken language to a level sufficient to decode the meaning of the expressive spoken language. This too requires a basic, yet important, competence in transforming extrapersonal into intrapersonal spoken language.

A large percent of our *in*competence in using extrapersonal spoken language can be attributed to the inherent egocentrism of our inner speech (Johnson, 1983). That much of what we say to others results in misunderstanding should not be surprising given that the symbolic thoughts we express, because they are generated through inner speech, are highly egocentric and that as listeners we also use inner speech, which is inherently egocentric, to make sense out of what we hear. More often than we want to believe, our inability to achieve competent communication through mutual and shared meaning can be traced to the fact that our conversations are filled with egocentric expressive and generative spoken language. Take for example a conversation that my wife and I had recently. We were sitting at the kitchen table when all of sudden I said:

Jack:	I can't believe it!
Kathryn:	Yeh, I know what you mean.
Jack:	How do these things happen?
Kathryn:	Hard to say.
Jack:	We need to do something about it.
Kathryn:	Why do we have to do something about it?
Jack:	You don't want to help?
Kathryn:	Look, it won't work. You can't argue with the Town of Cedarburg.
Jack:	Town of Cedarburg! Weren't you listening?
Kathryn:	Of course I was listening.
Jack:	Then, what does the Town of Cedarburg have to do with John writing on the walls with his crayons?
Kathryn:	What do you mean, writing on the walls? I thought you were talking about the tax bill . . . .
Jack:	What tax bill?

Conversations like this are really not that uncommon and reflect the fact that symbolic communication begins and ends as an internal and egocentric state. That we exhibit any competence in using extrapersonal spoken language and are able to make sense out of each other's utterances is a miracle and a consequence of our ability to cognitively assume the perspective of each other.

The skill we use to cognitively assume a perspective other than our own is referred to as *decentering*. This intrapersonal behavior involves the capacity to differentiate a single point of view from other points of view. Decentering, like empathy, involves perspective taking. However, when we decenter, we consciously assume more than one *cognitive* perspective. In empathy, we unconsciously assume more than one *emotional or physiological* perspective and feel as another feels (Johnson, Powell, & Reynolds, 1983). Although both forms of perspective taking are critical to communicative competence, decentering plays a central role in dealing with the egocentrism of expressive generative spoken language.

Piaget (1955, 1962, 1973) argued that decentering is a cognitive behavior that develops to counter the natural state of egocentrism. Along with numerous researchers, Piaget discovered that the ability to assume multiple perspectives was found across a wide variety of situations including physical, intellectual, spoken language (Elkind, 1972; Flavell, 1963; Piaget, 1955), perceptual (Bowd, 1974; Elkind, Larson, & Van Doorninck 1965), and spatial (Rubin, 1974; Shantz & Watson, 1971).

The expansion or explosion of the semantics and syntax of our symbolic thoughts is an elaborate process. Under ideal conditions, it is characterized by the speaker attempting, both prior to and during the conversation, to decenter to the listener's perspective, or, as Flavell (1968) said, "to discriminate those role attributes of L [listener] which appear to be pertinent to the L [listener's] ability to decide communicative input regarding X [message]" (p. 9).

As we assume the cognitive perspective of the listener(s) we make choices concerning what words, illustrations, narratives, and syntactical and organizational structures to use to help the listener(s) understand our expressive spoken language. Even if we are capable of assuming the listeners' perspective we face the natural tendency to regress and express our symbolic thoughts using words and syntax that make sense only to ourselves (Flavell, 1968).

Most research treats the process of communicative decentering, like that of communicative egocentrism, as an exclusively expressive phenomenon. The fact is that decentering can and does also occur in the receptive or generative forms of spoken language, such as listening (Johnson, 1993).

As we listen we are imploding expressive spoken language into inner speech. Usually this process of implosion requires the listener to assume the cognitive perspective of the speaker. Decentering occurs during listening when the listener assumes the cognitive perspective of the speaker in order to understand the speaker's intended meaning. The processes of decentering used in listening and in speaking are very similar. Typically, an aural message is heard and is then imploded into inner speech that is used to make associations or generalizations (symbolic thought). Listeners, in making these associations, are confronted with the ever-present need to suppress their own tendency to egocentrically interpret the words of the speaker. Decentering allows the listener to avoid the natural tendency to egocentrically interpret the spoken language of others.

The presence of egocentrism and decentering in both expressive and generative spoken language creates numerous opportunities for both understanding and misunderstanding to occur. Sometimes as speakers we use expressive spoken language that is highly egocentric but our listener(s) make sense of what we say because they decenter to our perspective to figure out our intended meaning. Similarly, sometimes we produce spoken language that is nonegocentric but our listener(s) egocentrically interpret our expressive spoken language. Of course, sometimes both speakers and listeners are highly egocentric in their expressive and generative spoken language, as you saw in the earlier example I gave of my wife and I talking. These are the times that our minds are like ships passing in the night. Competence in using extrapersonal spoken language is therefore dependent on decentering occurring at the intrapersonal level.

Competent speakers and listeners, therefore, are required to decenter to avoid their own, as well as others', levels of expressive and interpretive egocentrism. Of course there are numerous variables that affect the degree to which we have to decenter while using spoken language. The final section of this essay will examine some of these factors.

Levels of Spoken Language

Earlier in this essay I introduced the concepts of intrapersonal and extrapersonal and differentiated these two levels of spoken language on the basis of whether the producer and intended consumer of the spoken language were one and the same person. The degree to which a speaker or listener has to elaborate the semantics and syntactics of a message varies greatly between and across these two levels. If the expressive spoken language is taking place exclusively at the intrapersonal level there is little need to elaborate your expressive speech beyond that required for your own understanding. This is why your own "things to do" list can have extremely high levels of semantic embeddedness. Whereas "car, dinner, kids" makes complete sense to you, its meaning would be a mystery for most others. However, express this same spoken language at the extrapersonal level and undoubtedly you will have to expand the semantics and syntax of your expressive spoken language. As obvious as this may be, each and every one of us produces and consumes countless messages that, although extrapersonal, carry with them the high levels of egocentrism, semantic embeddedness, and syntactical ellipsis of symbolic thought and inner speech.

However, not all of our spoken language needs to be elaborated to the same degree. What determines the degree to which we need to elaborate the spoken language we use as speakers and listeners? In a previous article I outlined a series of rules that can be applied when answering this question (Johnson, 1984). In brief, the answer rests with the form of extrapersonal spoken language we are engaged in and the degree to which we and those with whom we are communicating share the same word meanings.

Forms of Extrapersonal Spoken Language

The principal difference between interpersonal and public spoken language is that with the former there exists a potential for an equal or near-equal opportunity for all individuals involved to both extrapersonally speak and listen. Therefore, with interpersonal spoken language there are potentially high levels of spoken-language feedforward and feedback among all communicative participants. In public forms of spoken language the potential does not exist and, therefore, there are not high levels of feedback from listeners.

During interactions where individuals can speak and listen equally, as in interpersonal forms of spoken language, there is less of a need for the speaker to elaborate the semantics and syntax because the conversation can be stopped and clarification given and/or asked for. On the other hand, in public forms of the spoken language the speaker must more thoroughly elaborate the semantics and syntax of his or her message because audience members are typically not permitted to stop the speaker and ask for clarification. If a speaker elaborates the semantics and syntactics of his or her symbolic thoughts there is less of a need for listeners to use feedback and elaborate for themselves the meaning of the speaker.

Shared Meaning

Mead (1922) introduced the concept of "significant symbolization" and referred to it as occurring when the symbols used to express our symbolic thoughts have the same meaning for all communicative participants. Generally, there is a greater chance for significant symbolization when you are familiar with the other person's word meanings. As we increase the level of significant symbolization in our extrapersonal spoken language we also decrease the need to use high levels of semantics and syntactical elaboration. A one word utterance, if a "truly" significant symbol, can produce mutual understanding without high levels of semantic and syntactical elaboration and feedback.

Typically, when we participate in public forms of extrapersonal spoken language we have low levels of immediacy of feedback from the audience and can have, at times, limited significant symbolization with the audience or speaker. This problem is further complicated by the fact that the words we speak and listen to have both connotative and denotative meanings. More often than not, as a speaker you will have to elaborate the connotative meanings of your message by using examples, illustrations, and so on. As a listener you will need to decenter to the speaker's perspective in order to figure out the implied or connotative meanings of the speaker's message.

When we use interpersonal spoken language we can engage in highly elliptical conversations. While at the dinner table, and without any direct visual cues, the simple utterance of "pass it" while fixing or dressing a hamburger will result in the catsup being passed. Although "pass it" is highly egocentric, semantically embedded, and syntactically elliptical, it is understandable to those at the table because

"It" is a significant symbol. Typically, the development of relationships results in a language of mutual significant symbols. This, in part, might explain why conversations between couples often become more elliptical with the length of the relationship (Honeycutt, Knapp, & Powers, 1983; Vygotsky, 1987).

Instructional interventions designed to increase communicative competency must develop students' decentering abilities. The intrapersonal skill of decentering has for the most part been ignored in communication education literature. Yet, it holds one of the keys to unlocking the human potential of creating mutual symbolic understanding. It is paramount that communication educators investigate the nature of decentering and determine what instructional interventions are best suited to develop it. Furthermore, we should ascertain at what age or developmental period, if any, is it most efficient and effective to teach the skill. Questions surrounding the development of decentering are many. However, it is time that we accept the fact that one of the prime obstacles to achieving competence in using extrapersonal spoken language rests firmly in the realm of the intrapersonal.

CONCLUSION

This chapter provides a taxonomy of terms and definitions useful in describing the various levels of human communication. It also describes how intrapersonal spoken language affects and is affected by extrapersonal spoken language. Particular attention was given to describing and explaining the function of inner speech in this process. I suggested that inner speech, as a form of generative intrapersonal spoken language, is an exceptionally fast and efficient method of transforming expressive spoken language into symbolic thought used to create word meaning. As a consequence of the use of inner speech in generation of symbolic thought, both speakers and listeners must concern themselves with elaborating the semantics and syntax of the symbolic thought expressed and received. The degree to which speakers and listeners must elaborate semantics and syntax is related to the level at which the spoken language occurs, the opportunity to both speak and listen during the interactions, and the amount of word meaning shared between or among the speaker(s) and listener(s).

Human communication is an extremely complicated phenomenon. Our ability to understand how we use it competently is, in part, based on our willingness to go beyond phenotypic analysis, which has long dominated our research efforts. When we speak of "communicative competence" we are by necessity forced to understand both the internal and external worlds of spoken language. Similarly, when we seek to increase a person's competence in using extrapersonal spoken language we are by necessity required to develop the individual's intrapersonal spoken language. Our efforts at understanding and developing extrapersonal forms of communicative competence must recognize the fact that the process of humans symbolically communicating with each other is most accurately described as beginning and ending in the form of an intrapersonal process.

REFERENCES

Adler, M. (1967). *The difference of man and the difference it makes*. New York, NY: Holt, Rinehart and Winston.

Allen, R., & Brown, K. (Eds.). (1976). *Developing communication competence in children*. Skokie, IL: National Textbook.

Altman, S. (Ed.). (1967). *Social communication among primates*. Chicago, IL: University of Chicago Press.

Barnlund, D. (1970). A transactional model of communication. In J. Akin, A. Goldberg, G. Meyers, & J. Stewart (Eds.), *Language behavior* (pp. 43–61). Hague, Netherlands: Mouton.

Bowd, A. (1974). Factorial independence of perceptual egocentrism. *Perceptual Motor Skills, 38*, 453–454.

Chandler, M., Greenspan, S., & Barenboim, C. (1974). Assessment and training of role-taking and referential communication skills in institutionalized emotionally disturbed children. *Development Psychology, 10*, 546–533.

Condon, W. S. (1979). Neonatal entrainment and enculturation. In M. Bullowa (Ed.), *Before speech: The beginnings of interpersonal communication* (pp. 131–148). New York: Cambridge University Press.

Cooley, R., & Roach, D. (1984). A conceptual approach: In R. Bostrom (Ed.), *Competence in communication: A multidisciplinary approach* (pp. 11–32). Beverly Hills, CA: Sage.

Dance, F. E. X. (1967). Towards a theory of human communication. In F. Dance (Ed.), *Human communication theory: Original essays* (pp. 288–309). New York, NY: Holt, Rinehart and Winston.

Dance, F. E. X. (1970). The concept of communication. *Journal of Communication 20*, 201–210.

Dance, F. E. X. (1979). Acoustic trigger to conceptualization. *Health Communication Informatics, 5*, 203–213.

Dance, F. E. X. (1980). Swift, slow, sweet, sour, adazzle, dim: What makes human communication human. *Western Journal of Speech Communication 44*, 60–63.

Dance, F. E. X. (1982). A speech theory of human communication. In F. Dance (Ed.), *Human communication theory: Comparative essay*, (pp. 120–146). New York, NY: Holt, Rinehart and Winston.

Dance, F. E. X., & Larson, C. (1972). *Speech communication concepts and behaviors*. New York, NY: Holt, Rinehart and Winston.

Dance, F. E. X., & Larson, C. (1976). *The functions of human communication*. New York, NY: Holt, Rinehart and Winston.

Delia, J. (1977). Constructivism and the study of human communication. *Quarterly Journal of Speech, 63*, 66–83.

Elkind, D. (1972). Egocentrism in young children. *Education Digest, 37*(6), 34–41.

Elkind, D., Larson, M., & Van Doorninck, W. (1965). Perceptual decentration learning and performance in slow and average readers. *Journal of Educational Psychology, 56*, 50–56.

Feldman, J. (1976). Why I move my lips when I read. *Claremont Reading Conference, 40*, 128–134.

Flavell, J. (1963). *The development psychology of Jean Piaget*. New York, NY: D. Van Nostrand.

Flavell, J. (1968). *The development of role-taking and communication skills in children*. New York, NY: Robert E. Krieger.

Galperin, P. (1969). Stages in the development of mental acts. In M. Cole & I. Maltzman (Eds.), *A handbook of contemporary soviet psychology* (pp. 249–273). New York, NY: Basic Books.

Gough, P. (1972). One second of reading. In J. Kavanagh & I. Mattingly (Eds.), *Language by ear and by eye: The relationship between speech and reading* (pp. 331–358). Cambridge, MA: MIT Press.

Greenspan, S., & Barenboim, C. (1975, June). *A matrix test of referential communication*. Paper presented at the Fifth Annual Symposium of the Jean Piaget Society, Philadelphia, PA.

Hinde, R. A. (Ed.). (1972). *Non-verbal communication*. Cambridge, England: Cambridge University Press.

Hinde, R. A. (1974). *Biological bases of human social behavior*. New York: McGraw-Hill.

Honeycutt, J., Knapp, M., & Powers, W. (1983). On knowing others and predicting what they say. *Western Journal of Speech Communication, 47*, 157–174.

Hymes, D. (1971). Competence and performance in linguistic theory. In R. Huxley & E. Ingram (Eds.), *Language acquisition: Models and methods* (pp. 3–26.). London, England: Academic.

Hymes, D. (1979). Sapir, competence, voices. In C. Filmore, D. Kempler, & W. Wang (Eds.), *Individual differences in language ability and language behavior* (pp. 35–45). New York, NY: Academic.

Johnson, J. R. (1982). Egocentric spoken language and reading achievement: An examination of relationship. *Communication Education, 31,* 115–123.

Johnson, J. R. (1983). Understanding misunderstanding: A key to effective communication. *Training and Development Journal, 37*(8), 62–68.

Johnson, J. R. (1984). The role of inner speech in human communication. *Communication Education, 33,* 211–222.

Johnson, J. R. (1993). Functions and processes of inner speech in listening. In A. Wolvin and C. Coakley (Eds.), *Perspectives on Listening* (pp. 170–184) New York, NY: Ablex Press.

Johnson, J. R., & Dance, F. E. X. (1980). Taxonomic models of communication, human communication, and spoken language. Unpublished manuscript, University of Wisconsin-Milwaukee, Department of Communication, Milwaukee, WI.

Johnson, J. R., Powell, R., & Reynolds, E. (1983, November). *Empathy: An analysis of the lack of intersubjectivity.* Paper presented at the Speech Communication Association Convention, Washington, DC.

Korba, R. (1986). *The rate of inner speech.* Unpublished doctoral dissertation, University of Denver, Denver, CO.

Korba, R. (1989). The cognitive psychophysiology of inner speech. In C. V. Roberts & K. Watson (Eds.), *Intrapersonal communication processes: Original essays* (pp. 217–242). New Orleans, LA: Spectra.

Kuczaj, S. (1986). *Children's acquisition of word meaning.* Hillsdale, NJ: Lawrence Erlbaum Associates.

Kuczaj, S. & Bean, A. (1982). The development of noncommunicative speech systems. In S. Kuczaj (Ed.), *Language development, Volume 2: Language thought and culture* (pp. 279–300). Hillsdale, NJ: Lawrence Erlbaum Associates.

Landauer, T. (1962) Rate of implicit speech. *Perceptual and Motor Skills, 15,* 646.

Leontiev, A. (1969). Inner speech and the processes of grammatical generation of utterances. *Soviet Psychology, 7*(3), 11–16.

Lewin, K. (1935). *A dynamic theory of personality.* New York, NY: McGraw-Hill.

Luria, A. (1966). *Higher cortical functions in man.* New York, NY: Basic Books.

Luria, A. (1982). *Language and cognition.* New York, NY: Wiley.

Luria A., & Yudovich, F. (1959). *Speech and the development of mental processes in the child* (J. Simon, Trans.). London: Staples Press.

McGuigan, F. (1978). *Cognitive psychophysiological measurement of covert behavior.* Hillsdale, NJ: Lawrence Erlbaum Associates.

Mead, G. (1922). A behavioristic account of the significant symbol. *The Journal of Philosophy, 14,* 157–163.

Nichols, R. (1955). Ten components of effective listening. *Education, 75,* 292–302.

Nichols, R. (1957). Listening is a 10-part skill. *Nation's Business, 45,* 4.

Ong, W. (1967). *The presence of the word.* New Haven, CT: Yale University Press.

Ong, W. (1977). *Interfaces of the word.* Ithaca, NY: Cornell University Press.

Pavlov, I. P. (1960). *Conditioned reflexes: An investigation of the physiological activity of the cerebral cortex* (C. V. Amrep, Trans.). New York, NY: Dover.

Piaget, J. (1955). *The language and thought of a child.* New York, NY: New American Library.

Piaget, J. (1962). *Comments.* (E. Hanfmann & G. Vakar, Ed. and Trans.). Cambridge, MA: MIT Press.

Piaget, J. (1973). *The psychology of intelligence.* Totowa, NJ: Littlefield, Adams and Company.

Rubin, K. (1974). The relationship between spatial and communicative egocentrism in children and young and old adults. *The Journal of Genetic Psychology, 125,* 295–301.

Rubin, R. (1982). Assessing speaking and listening competence at the college level: The Communication Competency Assessment Instrument. *Communication Education, 31,* 19–32.

Rubin, R. (1985). The validity of the Communication Competency Assessment Instrument. *Communication Monographs, 52*, 173–185.

Sebeok, T. (Ed.). (1968). *Animal communication.* Bloomington, IN: Indiana University Press.

Sebeok, T. (Ed.). (1972). *Perspectives in Zoosemiotics.* The Hague, Netherlands: Mouton.

Sebeok, T. (Ed.). (1977). *How animals communicate.* Bloomington, IN: Indiana University Press.

Shannon, C. & Weaver, W. (1963). *The mathematical theory of communication.* Urbana, IL: University of Illinois Press.

Shantz. C., & Watson, J. (1971). Spatial abilities and spatial egocentrism in the young child. *Child Development, 42*, 171–181.

Smith, W. J. (1977). *The behavior of communicating.* Cambridge MA: Harvard University Press.

Sokolov, A. (1972). *Inner speech and thought* (G. T. Onischenko, Trans.). New York, NY: Plenum.

Spitzberg, B., & Cupach, W. (1984). *Interpersonal communication competence* Beverly Hills, CA: Sage.

Spitzberg, B., & Cupach, W. (1989). *Handbook of interpersonal competence research.* New York: Springer-Verlag.

Vygotsky, L. (1978). *Mind in society* In M. Cole, V. John-Steiner, S. Scribner, & E. Souberman (Eds.). Cambridge, MA: Harvard University Press.

Vygotsky, L. (1986). *Thought and Language* (A. Kozulin, Trans.). Cambridge, MA: MIT Press.

Vygotsky, L. (1987). *Thinking and speaking.* In R. Rieber & A Carton (Eds.), *The collected works of L. S. Vygotsky: Volume 1. Problems of general psychology* (pp. 39–285). New York, NY: Plenum

Wiseman, G., & Barker, L. (1974). *Speech/interpersonal communication.* New York, NY: Chandler.

Wolvin, A., & Coakley, C. (1988). *Listening.* Dubuque, IA: Brown.

III CAPSTONE: FORMING THE FUTURE

A potentially rich future for intrapersonal communication theory may lie in its dependence on speech and the applied research that dependence can engender. The on-going cyclical transformation of human talk from external to internal and back again creates a means whereby theorists can access and influence internal competence and its various manifestations in external performance.

In the final chapter, Dance presents a taxonomy of forms of spoken language and notes the symbiotic relationship of speech and thought that comes into existence at approximately 18 months for each of us. He then explains how one can influence the internal competencies of internal spoken language and thought by observing, assessing, and modifying the performance of external spoken language. Dance suggests that intrapersonal communication study requires further theorizing and research before intrapersonal theorists can move ahead to Whitehead's stage of generalization from the developing state of precision.

9 Hearing Voices

Frank E. X. Dance
University of Denver

The voices are as distinct now as then. It was, as I recall, in the fall of 1960. The new semester had just begun and I, a young assistant professor freshly equipped with a doctoral degree (ME), was walking across the sunny, tree-lined campus with a senior professor (SP) from my department.

(SP)	"Well, what are you working on?"
(ME)	"Drawing from my interest in Pavlovian psycho-physiology I'm trying to craft a position paper on the levels of speech."
(SP)	"What?"
(ME)	"The levels of speech."
(SP)	"What levels?"
(ME)	"The three levels of human speech."
(SP)	[Silence]
(ME)	[Feeling a pressure to say something.] "What I am proposing is that human speech manifests itself on three distinct but interrelated levels."
(SP)	[Silence]
(ME)	"The three levels I am thinking about are the Intrapersonal level, the Interpersonal level, and the Person to persons level."
(SP)	"I get what you mean by interpersonal and I guess you mean public speaking by person-to-persons, but what in heaven's name do you mean by the intrapersonal level?"
(ME)	"You know, when a person is talking to himself."
(SP)	"That's weird. It's not any of our concern. It's outside of our field."
(ME)	[Silence]
(SP)	"Do you play poker?"

Those remembered voices of more than three decades past still echo. Hearing voices is something all of us do. Doesn't seem to me to be a bad thing either. Whether the voices speak of the past, or of the present, or of the future, the voices arouse memory and passion and perhaps anticipation—all humane aspects of our being. In this book's collection of different voices sharing their different minds' views of intrapersonal communication there are areas of harmony as well as of dissonance. The word "intrapersonal" when joined with speech, speech communication, or communication can still arouse querulous reactions. Although some believe that intrapersonal speech communication or intrapersonal communication is a real behavior and a legitimate interest area, others seem convinced that there is a logical inconsistency between joining the term and concept *intrapersonal* with any form of the term and concept *communication*. For them, "intrapersonal speech communication," or "intrapersonal communication," or intrapersonal spoken language" are each and all oxymoronic.

If one believes that communication can only take place between/among two or more *distinct* organisms, then "intrapersonal" must seem an inappropriate focus of concern. On the other hand, if one believes that communication, in its broadest interactive manifestation, takes place between and among cells, between and among organs, within an individual when, for example, the individual is engaged in internal dispute ("Should I do this or not?"), rationalization ("I know I shouldn't buy a new car for the following reasons—but then again there are these other reasons why I should!", or is invested in careful reasoning—then terms such as *intraorganismic*, for instances such as occur intracellularly, or *intrapersonal communication/speech communication"* makes sense. Some organisms, such as cells, never exhibit personhood and other organisms grow into personhood so there seems to be room for considering both intraorganismic and intrapersonal communication.

Although there are some resonances in this chapter of themes introduced in prior segments of this work I hope that the variations serve to extend appreciation of the underlying tone of intrapersonal communication. My own research proclivity has segmented out from the overall concept of intrapersonal communication the specific area of internal spoken language as a form of spoken language.

In this chapter I first discuss the two forms of spoken language, then relate the forms to higher mental processes and critical thinking, give an example of the practical utility of that relationship, and, finally, reflect on the future of research in intrapersonal communication.

DEFINITIONS AND DEVELOPMENT

One early insight into intrapersonal communication may be found in the Pavlovian schema of human cognitive processes as situated in the interrelationship among the three signal systems; one subcortical, one cortical, and a second cortical signal system. The second cortical signal system (IISS) equates with spoken language. The Pavlovian position is that although all three signal systems within an individual are dynamically interrelated; the second cortical signal system (spoken language) enjoys hierarchial ascendancy and serves as a regulator of the other systems in the individual (Dance, 1967b). Oftentimes we find ourselves using the second signal

Behaviors
Vocalization->Speech->External Spoken Language->Internal SpLng*
Age
Birth----->3 to 6mos->12mos to 24mos; x = 18 mos---->5 to 7yrs

FIG. 9.1.   Developmental stages of spoken language behaviors.

*The term *Internal spoken language* affords a parallelism with the term *external spoken language* while freeing the term *speech* for the more specific usage given below.

system to govern our other signal systems, such as when we say to ourselves "calm down, take it easy, breathe slowly, relax," and our second signal system exhortations do indeed help to calm us physically.

Certainly a process such as "inner speech" or "internal spoken language" clearly implies a communicative or interactive element occurring within a single organism, within a single person, and is manifestly intrapersonal. If the constitution of internal spoken language (often termed *inner speech* and sometimes, with varying degrees of precision, referred to as "self-talk," "covert vocalization," or "private speech"[1]) moves developmentally from outside → inside, from external spoken language into internal spoken language, then there seems to be good reason for positing a communicative base for the behavior and for recognizing the behavior or internal spoken language as intrapersonal.

Internal spoken language is a transformation or metamorphosis of external spoken language (Vygotsky, original in Russian in stages during the late 1920s and the early 1930s; English translations in 1962, 1986, 1987). Human spoken language has two forms, the base form of external spoken language and the base's developmental transformation into that form labeled internal spoken language.

Life experience as well as research evidence suggests that the developmental progression of the acquisition of spoken language behaviors may be similar to the stages presented above: (Dance & Larson, 1972, pp. 62–92.)

The behaviors presented benefit from specification. First a definition of the behavior as the author understands that behavior (not to say that there is universal agreement as to the definition given) will be introduced and then a statement as to what function that behavior entails will be presented. The detailing of behavioral functions takes on importance when considering the role of behavioral and functional "passing through" or residue in developmentally ensuing behaviors in the individual and in society. The concept of residue is discussed later in this essay.

Function here refers to an "if this: then that" relationship and is free of the intentionality that is a characteristic of purpose rather than of function. A purpose is here considered to be a use to which a function may be intentionally directed. For

---

[1]"Inner speech," "covert vocalization," and "private speech," are each and all usually restricted to academic usage in a variety of fields such as psychology, linguistics, neurolinguistics, education, speech communication, and so on. "Private speech" with the meaning of child out-loud vocalizations either when alone or when with others but with no socially communicative intent is a well differentiated concept and has developed a respectable literature of its own. See, for example, the classic Kohlberg, Yaeger, and Hjertholm (1968), as well as some of the more recent studies on private speech such as Pellegrini (1980); Furrow (1984); and Berk and Garvin (1984). "Self talk" is frequently found in self-help usage.

example a hammer functions as a hammer when it pounds something but the pounding may have many purposes, such as to build or to destroy, to make or to mar (Dance, 1985). Vocalization is the first developmental behavior to be specified, the others follow sequentially.

Vocalization: the oral production of sounds by an organism.

The function of vocalization is *the expression of affect*.

The reflexive or involuntary utterance of sound carries with it an unintentional revelation of the affective or emotional state of the sounding organism. (A dog's bark or whine conveys a feeling for the dog's emotional state. A baby's vocalizations reveal to us that the baby is comfortable or uncomfortable. With experience an attending caretaker may even be able to identify the source of the comfort or discomfort such as hunger, contentment after being fed, etc. The baby doesn't, in its vocalization, discuss abstract topics such as the validation of geometrical theorems.) Of course, this revelation of affect, in humans after infancy, may consciously be controlled for the purposes of the organism. [This conscious control suggests an example of the manner in which purpose may relate to function. The angry speaker may consciously suppress or try to suppress the vocal indicators of anger when talking to someone else whom the speaker does not wish to know of the speaker's anger.]

Speech: the human, genetically determined, species-specific individual activity consisting of the voluntary production of phonated, articulated sound through the interaction and coordination of peripheral effector organs as a group as well as the speech-specific neural structures and pathways (Dance, 1989b).

The function of speech is *incipient mentation*.

The argument for this function of speech derives from speech's role in the human infant's earliest natural development of a sense of contrast upon which eventually is constructed complex cognition, ratiocination, or mentation (Dance 1982, 1985).

Spoken Language: the fusion of genetically determined speech with culturally determined language.

The function(s) of spoken language are *linking, mentation, and regulation*.

Although anticipatory echoes of linking and regulation may be found in animal communication other than human animal communication, the mentation function, unique to humans and resulting from speech, elevates linking and regulation to a human level (Dance, 1967a, 1967c, 1982, 1985; Dance & Larson, 1972, 1976.)

Form as in "the *forms* of spoken language "refers to the shape or structure of something as distinguished from that something's material. The form of a sonnet is something apart from, although integrated with, the subject matter of the poem. The content of an utterance is something other than, although blended with, the structure, the form, of the utterance. An exclamation is a form, that which is exclaimed is the content.

Spoken Language may take either or both of two forms, external spoken language or internal spoken language. One may be engaged in both forms simultaneously, as is commonly demonstrated when we are conversationally engaged as, simultaneously with our external conversation, we are glossing the on-going conversation and the conversation's course and planning our future conversational comments.

The developmental course of the two forms is launched when the neonate, born vocalizing, develops and refines speech, then joins genetically determined speech and culturally acquired language thus bringing into being the uniquely human behavior of spoken language, first in its external and finally in its internal form. (Dance, 1982; Vygotsky, 1962, 1986, 1987). In the combined maturational and developmental movement culminating in the development of internal spoken language there is an active "passing through" of the functions of the preceding behaviors resulting in an accrual of residue from the functions and forms of the newly absorbed preceding behaviors (Dance, 1989a). So when the infant vocalizes, the infant has an informational and communicative residue present in its vocalization; when a child speaks, the child's vocalization reveals something of the child's affective state even while the child is engaged in articulating and phonating vowels and consonants; spoken language has present in it an active residue of the functions of the communication, vocalization, and speech behaviors that developmentally precede spoken language in the child.

The preceding sentence is meant to address some of the same kinds of ideas as Walter Ong discussed when he differentiated between a primary and a secondary oral culture, noting that the secondary oral culture always contains some residue from the primary oral culture. Parallel ideas were intimated in Marshall McLuhan's discussion of new media serving as a "rear view mirror" for the content of past media so that, as McLuhan pointed out, for a long time the content of movies were books or plays and the content of early television was movies (Dance, 1989a; McLuhan, 1964; Ong, 1982.) Neither Ong's nor McLuhan's observations seem surprising given that the phenomenon of residue has its roots in the individual human being.

The import of this "passing through" of an earlier behavior and its functional residue has yet to be fully examined or explicated. However it seems that the vocalizing infant when acquiring speech adds a residue of vocal affect to the incipient mentative function of speech and then a residue of both of these functions (affect and incipient mentation) are projected into the three functions of spoken language (linking, mentation, and regulation). In both the external and internal forms of spoken language the appropriate residues of preceding behaviors will be in place.[2]

In its beginning stages spoken language is external. The child says aloud "mama" and "up." As the child matures and develops, external spoken language is gradually internalized. The child says "mama" aloud and at the same time says "mama" to herself or himself. This interior representation of "mama" elevates the child's capacity for abstraction and for flexibility in adaptation and control of herself or himself and the surrounding environment. Around the fifth year the child's external spoken

---

[2]S. Langer (1967, 1972) thoroughly investigated and discussed the emotional base of intellect from a philosophical perspective, and more recently the Grey and LaViolette (1982) model or theory of emotional/cognitive structures does the same from a neurophysiological/psychiatric perspective.

language begins to be sufficiently internalized so that the child is increasingly capable of solving complex cognitive problems with increasingly diminished reliance on external spoken language. This state of internal spoken language marks the completion of the formative development of spoken language in the child. Henceforth the task is not one of development but one of refinement, specialization, and sophistication.

The progression from (a) the vocalizing infant's initial perception and production of stimuli, to (b) its production of speech, to (c) its linking of genetically determined speech with culturally determined language resulting in the acquisition of external spoken language, to (d) its gradual internalization of spoken language may be considered as closely paralleling if not indeed the same as the development of the infant's higher mental processes (Dance & Larson, 1972; Vygotsky, 1962, 1986, 1987).

Level and form interaction: Both forms, external spoken language and internal spoken language, may be used on all three dynamically related and interacting levels on which spoken language occurs.

1. The Intrapersonal level upon which the individual serves as both the sender and the receiver of the message, internal Spoken Language is the customary Form on the first Level (Level 1), but one may, on occasion, speak aloud to oneself while simultaneously engaging in internal spoken language so that both forms of spoken language, external and internal, are in simultaneous operation. For example you could be rehearsing a speech aloud while accessing an answer to an audience question.

2. The Interpersonal level on which the sender and receiver(s) are separate from each other and are generally focused on distinctions between or among them, and

3. The Person-to-Persons level on which the sender and receiver(s) are separate from each other and are generally focused on similarities between or among them.

Once developed, the two forms of spoken language may be distinguished from one another on three dimensions. The dimension of sound/silence is self-explanatory. The dimension of grammatical or syntactic expansion/crushing has to do with the reality that when speaking aloud the grammatical usage of any natural language forces the speaker serially and relationally to develop a subject-predicate-object relationship, which in turn tests the logic of the utterance. This same syntactic expansion is absent in internal spoken language where a condensation resulting from pure predication is often the norm. The third dimension, that of semanticity, speaks to the fact that when speaking aloud a speaker who wishes to be maximally effective must make every effort to decenter to the audience and to recast any and all words or usages that may be idiosyncratic to the speaker so as to insure maximum audience understanding. When engaged in internal spoken language a speaker knows, in a rich and convoluted and overarching manner, both the meaning and the sense of his or her own utterances.

Silent spoken language is not the same as internal spoken language. Silent spoken language maintains all of the syntactic and semantic characteristics of exter-

TABLE 9.1
Characteristics of External/Internal Spoken Language

External Spoken Language	Internal Spoken Language
1. Sounded, exists in acoustic space	1. Silent
2. Grammatically, or syntactically expanded.	2. Grammatically, or syntactically condensed. [In Inner Spoken Language/ISL] "it is never necessary for us to name that about which we are speaking, i.e., the subject. We always limit ourselves only to what is being said about this subject, i.e. to the predicate. But this is precisely what leads to the dominance of pure predicativeness in" [ISL]. (Vygotsky cited in Sokolov, 1972, p. 47) "Because it is speech for oneself, serving above all to fix and regulate intellectual processes, and because it has a largely predicative character, inner speech necessarily ceases to be detailed and grammatical. It contracts, acquires a folded grammatical structure, always preserving, however, the possibility of developing into a complete, differentiated and complex utterance." (Luria, 1969, p. 143)
3. Semantically expanded.	3. Semantically condensed. This is what Vygotsky referred to as the quality of "synthesized" meaning wherein the word is flooded and permeated with all of one's past usages of it (Vygotsky, 1962, 1986, 1987).

nal spoken language but is spoken to oneself and lacks sufficient audibility so as to be heard outside of oneself. Examples of silent spoken language include the process one goes through in memorizing a part for a play, or memorizing a poem, anything where you find yourself silently reciting or rehearsing; in these situations all you would have to do is to increase the gain or the volume for others to hear and understand your utterance. If internal spoken language is audibly projected, its speed, grammatical condensation, and semantic condensation, make it incomprehensible to an external listener.

Even a quick consideration of the differences between the two forms of spoken language raises interesting questions and observations. Given the difference in speed between external spoken language (around 150 words per minute) and internal spoken language (somewhere between 400 and 4000 words per minute), processing time, ambiguity, difficulty of retrieval, richness of connotative meaning, all come into play (Korba, 1986). These same considerations are raised by the characteristics of syntactic and semantic crushing in internal spoken language. An understanding of the two forms of spoken language and the characteristics of the two forms also bears on any consideration of whether or not, and if so to what degree, one thinks in words. Einstein, when asked whether or not he thought in words replied to the effect that he didn't think in words as words are usually considered. There is a justifiable presumption that Einstein was unaware of the thinking and research on internal spoken language. Internal spoken language is quite different from words as usually considered. The saying "How do I know what I am thinking until I hear what I am saying" reflects an intuitive awareness of the relationship between external and internal spoken language.

One implication of the symbiotic relationship of the two forms is that a "revolution of intellects" could possibly result from integrating internal and external spoken language methodologies into educational objectives and classroom procedures. Expressing oneself does not simply serve the functions of linking and regulating but exposes that distinctive human function created by our unique capacity for spoken language: *mentation*.

The part played by the two forms of spoken language in our everyday lives, both as individuals and as social beings, is rich and is extraordinarily important. Certainly the relationship between internal spoken language and higher mental processes testifies to the importance and unique position of that form of spoken language in the everyday lives of the individual and of society. To those who believe little is gained by collapsing the concepts of internal spoken language and thought— they are right. The two terms "internal spoken language," and "thought" are not coterminous. (Vygotsky, 1987, throughout). There seem to be prespeech roots of conceptualization as well as preconceptual roots of external and internal spoken language. However mentation, higher mental processes, thought about thought, and ratiocination may well be exhausted by the concept of internal spoken language. The interleaved competencies of internal spoken language and of the higher mental processes with which it keeps company find their chosen exfoliation in the performance of external spoken language and its derivatives.

COMPETENCE AND PERFORMANCE

I believe that competence is that which underlies performance. This position is akin to Chomsky's suggestions relative to the surface transformation of underlying grammatical structures (Chomsky, 1972, and throughout his work). I believe that one does what one can do (Langer, 1972). I believe that what one is able to do echoes one's competence. Finally, I believe that doing what one is able to do *is* one's performance. Competence is not the same thing as performance. Performance is the manifestation of competence. One cannot perform unless one has the underlying competence to perform. When one says of someone else, "She is extremely competent," one is saying that the individual's performance manifests a highly developed underlying competence.

There has been a tendency to conflate the terms competence and performance so that when speaking of someone's competence one is talking about that individual's performative capacity. This terminological collapse leads to conceptual confusion so that instead of a competency being conceived of as an underlying ability to do something ("I believe he has the competency to do the job."), competency becomes the same as "adequate performance" ("He is a competent performer.").

In this essay competence is the covert ability underlying one's overt performance.

Probably only part of one's competence is revealed in any given instance of one's performance, but one cannot perform anything for which one lacks the competence. Performance is the primary and perhaps the sole means of accessing and assessing competence.

The fact that performance is the measure of competence should always be viewed in terms of the reality that performative assessment can easily vary in degree of accuracy. Competence is realized in performance. (But the performance should not be confused with the competence. They are two different but interactive processes—e.g., performative flaws such as vocal inadequacy or grandiose posturing on the part of a speaker who is either suffering from stage fright or from overconfidence and bravado ought not be taken as flaws of underlying conceptual competence. Nor should performative sheen on the part of a glib, overconfident, or show-off speaker be mistaken for conceptual splendor.)

Thought is covert, as here used, is not the same as the entirety of cognitive processes. Cognitive processes include perceptual and awareness components outside of this essay's specific focus. Here, I am discussing thought in its most elaborated form of *higher mental processes*.

Higher mental processes may be defined by contrasting them with lower mental functions. Lower mental processes are considered to be those neural activities that are apparently handled by portions of our nervous system other than the cerebral hemispheres and their cortical covering—activities such as unconditioned reflexes, vomiting, swallowing, postural reflexes, appetite regulation, arousal, and so on. The neuroanatomical location of control of the lower mental processes are also situated lower in the human organism and include such structures as the thalamus, hypothalamus, cerebellum, and medulla oblongata. Lower mental processes primarily are activities of what Pavlov, in his schema of the three signal systems, refers to as the subcortical signal system (Dance, 1967b).

The fact that the adequate functioning of higher mental processes is dependent on the adequate functioning of lower mental processes does not mean the higher mental processes are *caused* by lower mental processes. Many human behaviors are dependent on an adequately functioning nervous system but that fact does not lead to the inference that such activities are *caused* by the adequately functioning nervous system.

Higher mental processes, also referred to as ratiocination, conceptualization, or mentation, include intelligence, cognitive insight, thinking, judgement, reasoning, argument, and spoken language itself, as well as the derivatives of spoken language such as writing and reading or the expression of symbols in any of the other human modalities such as vision (Dance & Larson, 1976).

The competencies of the higher mental processes are, of themselves, covert. They are not directly available for assessment. Recent instrumentation such as tomography may assist in locating placement of cerebral activities but fails to demonstrate the quality or competence of such activities. The competencies of mentation are internal, interior, and not available through examination of surfaces by means of vision but are most directly accessible and assessable through sound, through spoken language.

Speech, when used in common parlance, is a term generally pointing to the behavior of spoken language. Most people not professionally involved in the topic use the word "Speech" to refer to spoken language.

Spoken language is overt. Spoken language as used here incorporates both speech and language but, as defined earlier in this essay, is more than the mere summation of these two processes.

Spoken language is the primary performative medium through which one accesses/assesses the competencies of both the prespoken language roots of thought and the competencies of the prethought roots of spoken language as well as the competencies arising from the interaction and continuing development of these two in the act of spoken language and its derivatives.

The competencies of spoken language are overtly manifested in behaviors accessible to self and others.

Some argue that thought may be accessed through vision. They suggest that you may gauge someone's intellect and intelligence by their facial appearance, by their body type, by their clothes, by their cleanliness, and so on. I think this position results from the pervasive confusion of verbal and vocal, of nonverbal and nonvocal and often, more significantly, of sign and symbol. Appearance, clothing, grooming, each and all may carry symbolic import. When we see someone dressed in a certain manner we say he or she is dressed "inappropriately," "sloppily," "inelegantly," "nicely," "in good taste," "like a hippie," and so on. We make judgments based on the meaning we attach to the clothing, grooming, bodily action, or muscle tone. We attach verbal or symbolic meaning to the nonvocal or visual stimulus. So I may choose to make a visual expression of my symbolic position by means of my dress or grooming, my gestures or my writing. All of these behaviors are verbal representations of a conceptually based judgment on my part.

Even truly reflexive and nonverbal behaviors on the part of a sender may be symbolically interpreted by the receiver of those behaviors. A skin rash, reflexive and nonverbal to the infant, is viewed and interpreted symbolically by the attending physician. The psychiatrist or psychotherapist gives a symbolic interpretation to the patient's bodily actions and odors. Thus all of these interpretive behaviors on the part of receivers may be considered to be derived from spoken language.

How are these two competencies of higher mental processes and of internal spoken language in the one performance of external spoken language related so as to account for their bond, for their symbiotic relationship? The focus here is on investigating the possible manner in which the bond between the competencies of higher mental processes and of spoken language emerges so as to better understand the phenomenon of two competencies–one performance.

One can try to answer that question either phylogenetically—"How, if at all, did spoken language and higher mental processes evolve and relate in the development of the human race?" or ontogenetically—"What is the relationship of spoken language and higher mental processes in individual development?"

Or one can focus on the question of assessment. "How best can we assess the quality of higher mental processes and of spoken language in the individual?"

Let us leave the phylogenetic question for another occasion and here briefly consider the ontogenesis and relationship of higher mental processes and of spoken language and then the possibility of assessing the quality of internal spoken language and higher mental processes in external spoken language performance.

In speculating on the possible relationships between thought and spoken language we may consider three cases.

Case one. May higher mental processes and spoken language be entirely separate, unrelated behaviors that accidentally find their expression in the same performance? In this case spoken language would reveal thought but not affect nor be affected by thought.

Number one is simply not the case as is evidenced by anyone who reflects on his or her thoughts prior to their utterance and finds changes taking place in either the thought, or the thought's utterance, or in both.

Case two. May higher mental processes and spoken language, like Janus, be two faces of the same being? May they be different names for the same thing?

Number two is more difficult to discuss. One reason being that spoken language, or its written derivative, must be used in the discussion. However, many can testify to having thoughts that slip and slide during utterance. In addition there is ample evidence of cognitive processes and even the organic stirrings of some higher mental processes in "prespoken language" infants as well as in very young children. There are also cases of spoken language seemingly devoid of any conceptual content, as in routinized swearing. Finding cases of higher mental processes existing without spoken language is more difficult due to the two competencies having a single performative bond.

Case three. May higher mental processes and spoken language be independent of one another in part and yet related in part?

The evidence for this third case seems to me to be the most compelling of the possibilities here discussed.

Although Langer's closely reasoned and appealing claim for the phylogenetic development of higher mental processes (thought) as the natural accompaniment of the phylogenetic development of spoken language (speech) would be worth presenting here if time and patience allowed, we have earlier committed to focusing on the ontogenetic argument (Langer, 1967, 1972, 1982).

Vygotsky presented evidence and argument for the proposition that in their ontogenetic development higher mental processes and spoken language (Vygotsky called them "thought and speech") have different roots. In their ontogenesis there is a preintellectual stage in the child's spoken language development as well as a prespoken language stage in the child's thought development (Vygotsky, 1987).

The preintellectual roots of a child's development of spoken language include activities such as vocalization, reflexive crying, affective gurglings, and speech (as defined above) that have nothing to do with higher mental processes. The sound-making behaviors of the subcortical signal system, and some of the behaviors of the first cortical signal system such as the sound making accompaniment of visual, proprioceptive, and kinesthetic activities, may also be in this grouping. Other likely candidates for inclusion may be the neuronal and motor organization of hearing, breathing, phonation, and articulation (Dance, 1979; Vygotsky, 1987, p. 81).

The prespoken language roots of a child's development of higher mental processes may include activities such as the completion of myelination, developing perceptual processes, the development and elaboration of the lower mental processes, and the development of neuronal organization and sophistication tied to the child's participation in relationships with responding others and the physical environment. Either an enriched or a deprived environment can affect the organic development of the child's brain and therefore the development of the child's emerging mind. In fact both for Vygotsky and for Langer, the communal, the social aspect surrounding the child's development of spoken language, is essential.

Up to a certain point the two operations of thought and speech follow differing lines and develop independently of each other. But at that "certain point," which occurs on the average around 18 months of age, these two formerly separate developmental lines meet, *whereupon thought becomes verbal, and speech rational* (Vygotsky, 1986, p. 82; Wilder, 1973).

It is exactly at this "certain point" that I would suggest that within the developing human individual the parallel structures of preconceptual speech and prespeech mental activities transform into the uniquely human behavior of *spoken language*, wherein genetically determined speech joins with culturally determined language.

Once this "certain point" has been reached there is, in the interaction of thought and spoken language, a continuing passing through of each to the other that makes their interrelationship—even though it is indeed the interrelationship of what, in their genesis and early development, are two separate activities—almost impossible to disengage.

External spoken language flowing from *internal spoken language* is the performative channel for accessing the competencies of both higher mental processes and of spoken language. I presume that those reading this chapter are proficient in the perception and analysis of spoken language performance and are comfortable in critiquing spoken language performance for the purposes of helping the speaker improve. Critiquing spoken language performance for the purpose of improving higher mental process competencies is a different challenge. What may be some techniques by which we can pass through the competency and performance of spoken language as spoken language and concentrate on listening to performative spoken language as the herald of the competencies of higher mental processes in the speaker?

When considering *conceptual competencies* most of us would include precision or accuracy of thought, flexibility, imagination or originality, intuition, breadth of information, breadth of understanding or sense-making, and critical or analytical abilities. Although these conceptual competencies overlap they are discrete enough for separate consideration and assessment. When engaged in "reasoning," the speaker uses the aforementioned competencies with the goal of drawing inferences or for supporting a proposal. Close reasoning, rigorous reasoning are earmarks of well-developed higher mental processes. Whatever the level of reasoning, whatever its complexity and sophistication, at the end of the performance the audience must have been able to follow and to understand the speaker's reasoning. Without such audience comprehension the absence of reasoning is as good as skilled reasoning.

When trying to construct Appendix A, where competencies of higher mental processes are matched against spoken language performative characteristics, I found myself making intrapersonal arguments justifying the attribution of certain spoken-language performative attributes to all kinds of higher mental processes competencies. *Inventio* (*Inventiveness* in *Appendix A*) for example, as the Cicero-nian canonical component of imagination and flexibility in selecting and approach-ing a topic, could attest to a conceptual competency of flexibility, of imagination and originality, or intuition, of breadth of information by suggesting that the con-ceptually inventive individual would find ideas and support where the less inventive might not even look. As a result of this richness of interpretation it was difficult to align specific conceptual competencies with specific spoken-language performative behaviors. My final decision was to opt in favor of rich interpretation and overlap-ping. A rigorous critic (or future research) will probably be more successful in producing a narrower match.

Rationality, a higher mental process, benefits from the assistance of spoken language to present itself both to oneself and to others. In fact the translation from internal spoken language to external spoken language helps test and secure ratio-nality for the speaker and the speaker's audience. A delivery elsewhere described as "transparent" (Dance & Zak-Dance, 1986) is designed to allow higher mental competencies and their content to be made as readily accessible as possible. As in many other pursuits, a "transparent" delivery—one that does not call any attention to the delivery itself—is difficult to develop, is planned, not accidental and is a prime example of art hiding art. Spoken-language performance helps the audience follow, comprehend, and understand the speaker's reasoning. One's rationality and reasoning could be flawless but if the audience were unable to access and under-stand that reasoning, flawless or not, the reasoning would also be worthless.

Even if the argument presented in this essay is found to be compelling, one may wonder to what practical end the argument is made. Theoretical value accepted and put aside, I would like to suggest the possibility of working with and through the bond of the single performance so as to heighten development and thus to enhance the underlying competencies.

Those specializing in the study, understanding, and improvement of internal and external spoken language may assist individuals and society in raising the presence and strength of higher mental processes as well as improving spoken-language competencies by consciously using spoken language performance as a means to that worthwhile end.

Since the inception of the core curriculum at the University of Denver in 1986, there has had a course entitled Speech and Thought. The avowed purpose of the course has been to examine the theoretical relationship between higher mental processes and spoken language and to assess the students' understanding of that relationship through public speaking performance. The course is organized around large audience lectures, laboratory sections (17 students to a laboratory section), and an individual assistance laboratory where students may view their public speaking performances together with an instructor other than their own—thus affording varying viewpoints and additional expert assistance.

The material presented earlier in this chapter comprises part of the course's content. Testimony from faculty in other departments suggests that Speech and Thought has had a beneficial effect on the quality of thoughtful presentations in other classes. Institutions such as the University of Colorado at Colorado Springs, that have positioned courses based on but not identical to Speech and Thought have had like results. Problems of making tight linkages between conceptual competency and performative competency continue but will, I trust, eventually yield to research and experience. Tightly focusing on the conceptual competence/performance dyad rather than on performance alone has also proved difficult for faculty and graduate assistants coming from a background of traditional public speaking teaching.

Shifting the basic human course paradigm from sole focus on performative delivery attributes to a new paradigm focusing on the critical thinking/spoken language duality addresses one of the critical attributes of spoken language while affording a curricular contribution absolutely central and essential to the individual and to society.

FUTURE VOICES

What of the future of intrapersonal communication research? Certainly today the senior professor [SP] of 1960 alluded to at the start of this chapter would be much more likely to at least recognize the term and concept of intrapersonal communication. Whether or not that professor would accept the concept as legitimate and appropriate to the discipline is another question. Since 1960 the consideration of intrapersonal communication has developed from an idea to a movement. The research, convention papers (e.g., Vocate, 1987), and the literature is growing. This volume's chapters bespeak a variety coming and derived, I believe, from uncertainty and novelty. In 1929, while discussing the rhythm of education, Alfred North Whitehead spoke of the stage of romance, the stage of precision, and the stage of generalization. The stage of romance is when we are totally enthralled by a topic or activity and we just cannot stop ourself from doing it. Someone gave us a guitar and we can't stop playing it. It's FUN! The stage of precision starts when we find out that there is a discipline to being a good musician, we have to gain some understanding of music theory and we have to practice long hours. In the stage of precision the structure and discipline of the activity begins to assert its role. The stage of generalization is when both the stages of romance and precision inform and shape each other. Those interested in intrapersonal communication seem to be vacillating between the stages of romance and of precision. We know that subject is fascinating and important, we can't really leave it alone, but we are still hazy as to its exact nature and dimensions. It will probably be a few years before we edge into the stage of generalization where romance and precision inform and augment each other (Whitehead, 1967.)

I can still hear the voices I heard in 1960. Not faint echoes either. Voices of doubt concerning the appropriate role of intrapersonal communication in human communication study can be heard at academic conventions as well as in collegial conversation. It was just a year or so ago that a friend send me a copy of a rejection letter received from the editor of a regional journal. The manuscript being rejected dealt with intrapersonal communication. The rejection letter was clear in its message that the editor wasn't even going to send the manuscript out for review, not because it was incompetently conceived or written but because it dealt with a topic that the editor did not feel belonged within the purview of an academic journal in human communication—namely, intrapersonal.

Intrapersonal communication will continue to gather research adherents and disciplinary recognition. As the field (of speech, speech communication, communication, spoken language, human communication) continues to redefine itself there will be increasing specification of exactly what parts of the phenomena of intraorganismic and intrapersonal communication fall within the disciplinary domain.

Theory is necessary for the move to the stage of generalization. Certainly theory and methodology are essential if we ever aspire to the culmination of Whitehead's stages of learning—the final stage of wisdom. There must be a continuing refinement of methodology—and this is important. How can we really measure what seems to be available only through inference? We need to find out how to do this with more precision. Research using triangulation strategy, such as Korba's (1986), technological advances such as tomography and magnetic resonance imagery, rediscovery and sharpening of old techniques such as the conditioned reflex as well as interdisciplinary efforts will all contribute to increased understanding of the role of intrapersonal communication and its importance to improving the human condition.

I trust that we are going to continue hearing voices—new voices, enriched voices, voices resonant with the competencies of higher mental processes and intrapersonal spoken language infusing thought into the spoken word.

REFERENCES

Berk, L. E., & Garvin, R. A. (1984). Development of private speech among low-income Appalachian children. *Developmental Psychology, 20*, 271–286.

Chomsky, N. (1972). *Language and mind* (Enlarged ed.). New York: Harcourt Brace Jovanovich.

Dance, F. E. X. (1967a). The functions of speech communication as an integrative concept in the field of speech communication. *Proceedings of the XVth International Congress of Communications.* Genoa, Italy: The International Institute of Communications.

Dance, F. E. X. (1967b). Speech communication theory and Pavlov's second signal system. *Journal of Communication, 17*(1), 13–24.

Dance, F. E. X. (1967c). Toward a theory of human communication. In F. E. X. Dance (Ed.), *Human communication theory: Original essays* (pp. 288–309). New York: Holt, Rinehart & Winston.

Dance, F. E. X. (1979). The acoustic trigger to conceptualization: a hypothesis concerning the role of the spoken word in the development of higher mental processes. *Health Communication and Informatics, 5*, 203–213.

Dance, F. E. X. (1982). A speech theory of human communication. In F. E. X. Dance (Ed.), *Human communication theory: Comparative essays* (pp. 61–74). New York: Harper and Row.

Dance, F. E. X. (1985). The functions of human communication: A review and some extensions. *Information and behavior, 1*(1), 62–75.

Dance, F. E. X. (1989a). Ong's voice: "I," the oral intellect, you, and we. *Text in performance quarterly 9*(3), 185–198.

Dance, F. E. X. (1989b). *The uniqueness of human speech*. Unpublished manuscript. University of Denver.

Dance, F. E. X., & Larson, C. E. (1972). *Speech communication: Concepts and behaviors*. New York: Holt, Rinehart and Winston.

Dance, F. E. X. & Larson, C. E. (1976). *The functions of human communication: a theoretical approach*. New York: Holt, Rinehart and Winston.

Dance, F. E. X., & Zak Dance, C. (1986). *Public speaking*. New York: Harper and Row.

Furrow, D. (1984). Social and private speech at two years. *Child Development, 55*, 355–362.

Gray, W., & LaViolette, P. (1982, March 8). *Brain/Mind Bulletin 7*(6).

Kohlberg, L., Yaeger, J., & Hjertholm, E. (1968). Private Speech: Tour studies and a review of theories. *Child Development, 39*(3), 691–736.

Korba, R. (1986). *The rate of inner speech*. Unpublished doctoral dissertation, University of Denver.

Langer, S. (1967). *Mind: An essay in human feeling. Vol. I*. Baltimore, MD: Johns Hopkins University Press.

Langer, S. (1972). *Mind: An essay in human feeling. Vol. II*. Baltimore, MD: Johns Hopkins University Press.

Langer, S. (1982). *Mind: An essay in human feeling. Vol. III*. Baltimore, MD: Johns Hopkins University Press.

Luria, A. R. (1969). Speech development and the formation of mental processes. In M. Cole & I. Maltzman (Eds.), *Handbook of contemporary Soviet psychology* (pp. 121–162). New York: Basic Books.

McLuhan, M. (1964). *Understanding media*. New York: McGraw-Hill.

Ong, W. J. (1982). *Orality and literacy*. London and New York: Metheun.

Pellegrini, A. D. (1980). A semantic analysis of preschoolers-self-regulating speech. *International Journal of Psycholinguistics, 20*, 59–74.

Sokolov, A. N. (1972). *Inner speech and thought*. New York: Plenum.

Vocate, D. R. (1987, December). *Inner speech and the domain of human communication theory*. Paper presented at the annual convention of the Speech Communication Association, Boston, MA.

Vygotsky, L. S. (1962). *Thought and language*. (E. Hanfman and G. Vakar Eds. and trans.). New York and London: The MIT Press and Wiley.

Vygotsky, L. S. (1986). *Though and language*. Translated, revised, and edited by Alex Kozulin. Cambridge, MA: MIT Press.

Vygotsky, L. S. (1987). "Thinking and speech," [Minick's much closer translation of Vygotsky's original title for the work under consideration]. In Vol. 1: *The collected works of L. S. Vygotsky: Problems of general psychology*. (R. W. Rieber & A. S. Carton, Eds., Tran. Norris Minick). New York: Plenum Press.

Whitehead, A. N. (1967). *The aims of education*. New York: The Free Press.

Wilder, L. (1073). Speech processes in the cognitive learning of young children. *Today's speech, 21*(1), 19–22.

APPENDIX

Spoken Language Performative Descriptions*	Higher Mental Process Competencies
Absence of fallacies[4]/audio-visual aids[1]/ grammatical correctness & precision[5]/ Outlines: their level of preparation/ organization/transitions: their appropriateness & sophistication/deduction & induction.	Analytical/critical
Inventiveness-topic indicates a wide acquaintainship with different choices/organization-arrangement of points indicates a range and understanding of available materials and their relationship.	Breadth of information
Exhibits evidence & examples[3] indicating prior consideration of audience expectations, occasion, topic, etc.	Decentering
Takes different spatial or temporal points of view. "Thinking about this from the point of view of a person living a century in the future . . ."	Displacement
Inventiveness/organization: when either or both of these qualities evidence the ability to make "on the moment" adjustments of materials or delivery.	Flexibility
Inventiveness/organization/vocabulary[7] examples[3]/delivery[2]	Imagination/originality
Inventiveness/audience adaptation	Intuition
Degree of note dependency/eye contact/ fluidity/illusion of spontaneity/handling of Q & A, et al.	Memory
Organization/vocabulary[7]	Precision/accuracy
Absence of fallacies/organization/appropriate use of supporting materials[6] the acceptance of the speaker's responsibility to make sure the audience tracks the argument and the supporting material.	Understanding/sense making

*Descriptors, which may serve as behavioral indicators of higher mental process competencies, may have varing levels such as "excellent" "satisfactory," and "unsatisfactory".

[1]Audio-visual aids. Suitability and level of preparation.

[2]Elocutio (choice and arrangement of words) & pronuntiatio (delivery): decentering, suiting each & both to audience expectations and demands of topic & occasion. Both behaviors support content. Cross modal support.

(continued)

---

[3]Examples: their suitability to the point being explained; to the audience, occasion, speaker, topic. Do they really "exemplify" the point to which they are applied?

[4]Fallacies: after this, therefore because of this (post hoc ergo propter hoc); appeals based on personal abuse, authoritative power, physical threat; bandwagon; begging the question; circularity; hasty generalization; it doesn't follow (non sequitur); red herring, et al.

[5]GRAMMAR: case agreement; indefinite referent, et al.

[6]Supporting materials: facts, references, quotations, testimony, authorities, analogies, examples, evidence, warrants (toulmin). Emotional appeals; appeal to one's own character; appeals based upon cultural standards and tradition.

[7]Vocabulary: accuracy, appropriateness to audience and occasion, breadth, focus, precision.

Author Index

Subject Index